IMAGES
of America

RINGGOLD COUNTY

ISBN 978-0-7385-8374-7

Published by Arcadia Publishing
Charleston, South Carolina

Printed in the United States of America

Library of Congress Control Number: 2010931805

For all general information, please contact Arcadia Publishing:
Telephone 843-853-2070
Fax 843-853-0044
E-mail sales@arcadiapublishing.com
For customer service and orders:
Toll-Free 1-888-313-2665

Visit us on the Internet at www.arcadiapublishing.com

This book is dedicated to the men and women who broke the prairie sod and braved untold hardships to establish our homeland, Ringgold County.

Contents

ACKNOWLEDGMENTS

We wish to express our appreciation and gratitude for the pioneer photographers, diarists, newspaper editors, reporters, and authors who recorded Ringgold County's history as it occurred. We are greatly appreciative of those who archived and preserved these records and photographs, making them available for our research when compiling this book.

We wish to thank many people who have opened their photograph albums and generously shared the contents with us. A special thank-you is extended to the Mount Ayr Depot Museum, the *Mount Ayr Record-News*, and the Mount Ayr Public Library for liberally allowing us to search through their archives. We wish to thank the Friends of Old Redding, Kellerton Friends, and the Bear family for their many valuable contributions.

Norma G. (Foland) Becker generously shared her photograph albums with us, many of the images taken by her mother Pearle V. (Bramon) Foland with her little Brownie camera between the years of 1919 and 1921.

Others who have generously shared photographs from their ancestral albums are Delbert Spencer, Julie Watts, Phillena Smelser, Sharon Lafferty, Andy and Joyce Johnston, Juanita Fields, Ken Baker, Mitzi Tann, Rod and Deb Bastow, Dallas Riedesel, Bill Adams, Max and Maxine Anderson, James Rueber, Liz Wiley, Gene Dolson, Jane E. Lyle, Bob and Kay Sickels, Jack W. Davis, Bill and Thelma Rusk, Rick and Lora Stull, Kathy Gregg, LaViece Barker, Ron Mackey, Arlene Sobotka, Eugene and Esther McAlexander, and Ron Abbott. These contributions show life in Ringgold County throughout the decades, and for this we thank you.

We wish to thank Betty Ruby and the Diagonal Printing Museum for sharing archival photographs that capture the spirit of Diagonal and the surrounding area.

The Delphos Museum and the Benton Museum have been very generous in sharing their archives with us. We are grateful and wish to thank these dedicated people.

We want to thank the people at Arcadia Publishing, Ted Gerstle, Joe Walker, and Winnie Rodgers, who have made helped to make this book a reality.

Introduction

At one time, Ringgold County's only inhabitants were bands of Sac and Fox Indians who migrated through the area on their annual hunting and gathering expeditions. Ringgold was one of the last of Iowa's counties to be settled. The first white settlers were Charles Schooler and his wife, followed by the James Tetherow family two years later in 1846. At the time, they believed that they were residing in the state of Missouri. This original settlement was located in what would become Lott's Creek Township of Ringgold County.

Charles K. Grimes, who would later found the town of Eugene, Iowa, arrived in May of 1858, settling in what would later become Tingley Township. The latchstring of the Grimes home was always out, as the family sheltered other settlers until they had built their own homes. Those of the Sac and Fox and Pottawattamie Nations were also welcome at the Grimes hearth when passing through the vicinity.

The exact location of Iowa Territory's southern border was hotly disputed by the state of Missouri. Perhaps the single worst contention of this dispute arose from whether Iowa Territory or Missouri could impose the taxation of trees harboring beehives, a valuable asset in the 1800s. It resulted in a bloodless confrontation known as the Honey War. The matter was resolved after the disputed territory was surveyed twice and consequently awarded to Iowa in 1850. The following year, commissioners were appointed to locate the county seat of the soon-to-be-organized county. The group placed a stake marking the location of Urbana, the new county seat, but the commissioners returned to Decatur County, and the stake could not be located again. It is believed now that the area marked was four miles south and one mile east of Mount Ayr, the current location of the Urbana schoolhouse. Consequently, Ringgold County was attached to neighboring Decatur County in 1851. In 1852, Judge John Lowe of Taylor County ordered that Ringgold County be made into an election precinct of Taylor County, dubbed Schooler Township of Taylor County.

Settlement into the area was somewhat sluggish. Then, in August 1854, the US General Land Office put Iowa land on the market out of the Chariton, Iowa, office. Luke Shay, the first Irish settler to Ringgold County, built a cabin near what would become Jefferson Township in 1855. Shay sold his land in 1864 and moved to a farmstead near present-day Maloy.

The site of Ringgold City, a ghost town today, became one of the oldest settlements in Ringgold County. The pioneers established a trading post for those passing through. Ringgold City was formerly known as Schooler's Grove and was established in 1855 by Sanford Harrow.

In January 1855, the Iowa State Legislature appointed commissioners to locate a site as close as reasonably possible to the geographical center for Ringgold County's seat. The commission's report, made to the Decatur County judge on April 18, 1855, selected a site and called it Mount Ayr—"Mount" because the site was located on the highest land in the southern tier of counties and "Ayr" to honor the poet Robert Burns who was born in Ayr, Scotland. John S. Sheller of Lucas County, who owned the land, promised to convey to Ringgold County one half of the quarter section and have it surveyed into town lots. This was the first deed recorded in Ringgold County.

Elections were held on May 14, 1855. County officers elected were Hiron Imus as sheriff, James C. Hagans as county judge, and Joseph Cofer as treasurer. Other officers were elected, and the county was officially open for business.

In 1855, nearly 100 families arrived in Ringgold County, with several villages being established over the countryside. Peter Walter established Caledonia, named for the Caledon of Sir Walter Scott's *Lady of the Lake*. James Drake built a cabin near the future site of Blackmore Corner, later known as Blackmore. Dr. John T. Merrill came to Ringgold County with his bride, and they moved to Mount Ayr around the year 1866. By 1880, the doctor had established a bank and a drugstore for the community. E.L. Soles and his son-in-law John Taylor set up a whipsaw and harvested the first lumber in Mount Ayr. A carpenter by trade, Soles was kept very busy. He made the first ballot boxes used in the county's elections. Soles also taught vocal music in his spare time.

One

Pioneers, Leaders, and the People of Ringgold County

Many of Ringgold County's early pioneers endured long and arduous treks over roads that were nothing more than trails through the prairie. The Imus family lost the father, Horatio, who drowned when they attempted to cross English Creek in Marion County. Encouraged by her older sons, Mary Dolbier Imus and the couple's 12 children proceeded on to the homestead that Horatio had earlier claimed for them.

The Jezek and Toman families came from Klasterec, Bohemia, in 1857. Other Bohemian settlers followed and established a flourishing little neighborhood near present-day Diagonal.

William Timby came from England, and after farming for 20 years he constructed many of the brick buildings on the Mount Ayr square. At least two of them are still standing today.

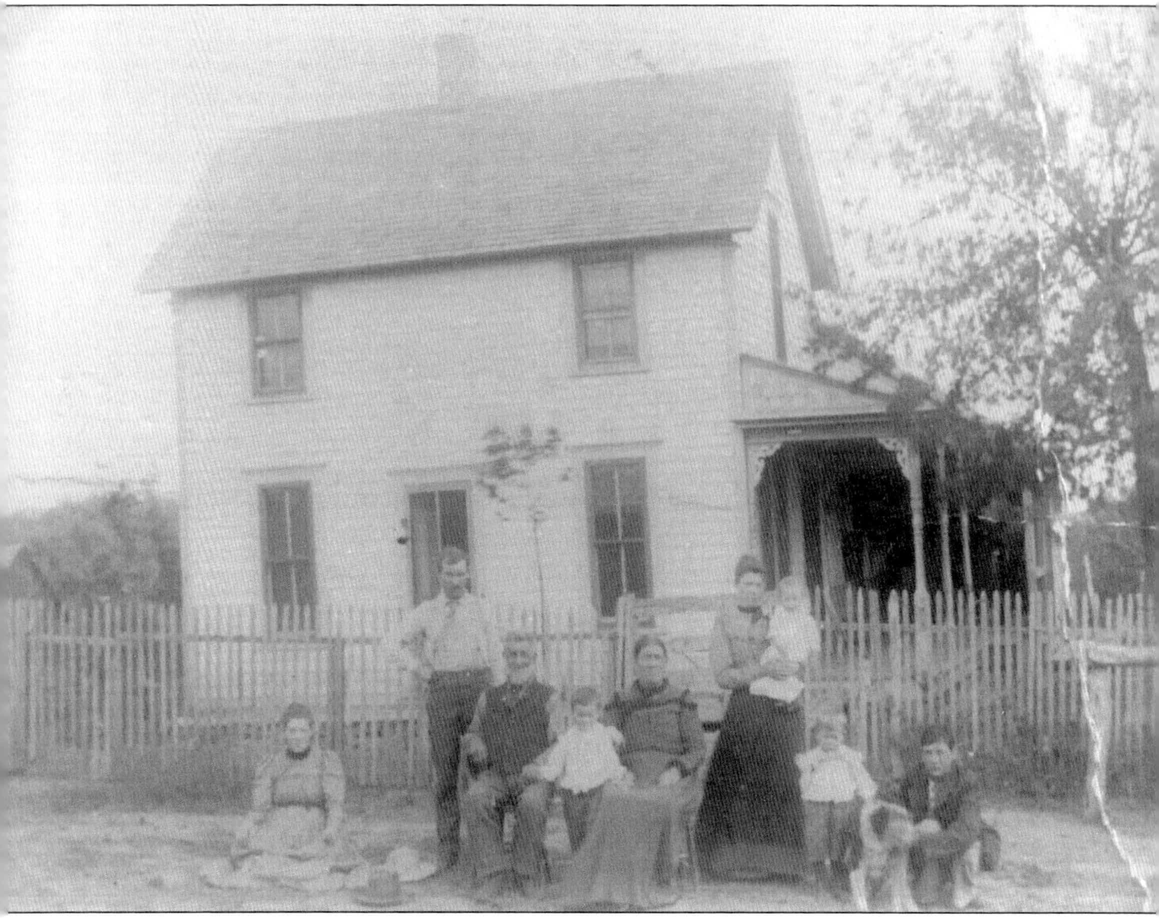

Solomon "Sol" Bear established his Ringgold County homestead on land located between Ellston and Kellerton. In 1864, Sol established the Bear Family Cemetery on his farm, located a short distance from the house and nestled in a stand of timber. The first burials were his year-old son, Lincoln, and his first wife, Sarah Walker Bear. Sol's brothers Adam and John, both Civil War Veterans, are also buried there. The Bear family erected Civil War gravestones for Adam's and John's grave sites in 2009, one hundred forty-four years after the close of the Civil War. Pictured in 1900, family members pose in front of the Bear residence. They are, from left to right, Mary Bear, Lance Maggard, Sol Bear, Norval Maggard, Amanda (Duly) Bear, Nellie (Bear) Maggard holding Lulu Maggard, Roy Maggard, and Frank Bear. (Courtesy of the Bear family.)

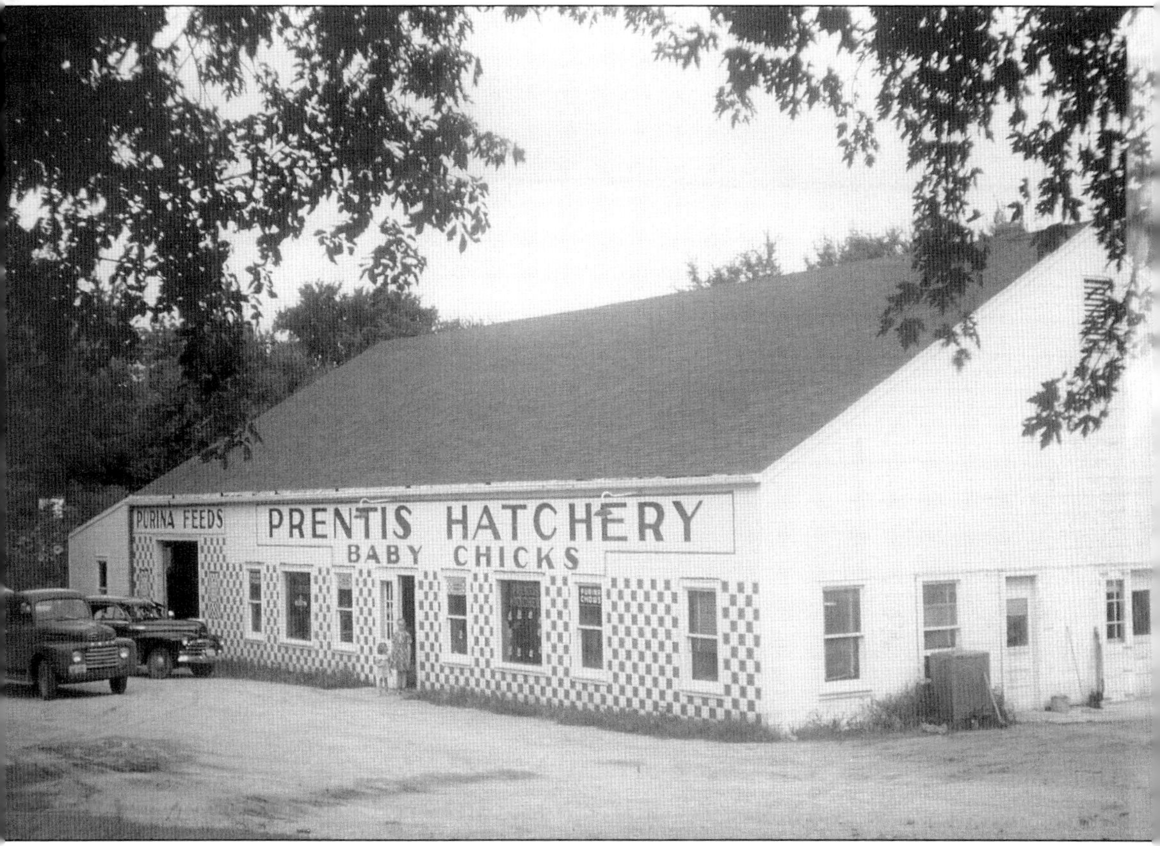

The Prentis Hatchery was located across the street north of the old high school in Mount Ayr. X.T. Prentis operated his business for about 50 years while serving the state of Iowa as a senator, representative, and state tax commissioner. He served his country in World War I, and he served his county as the Ringgold County Historical Society president. He labored many years for road improvements. Prentis may be best remembered, however, for the colored baby chicks his hatchery gave away at Easter time. (Courtesy of Julie Watts.)

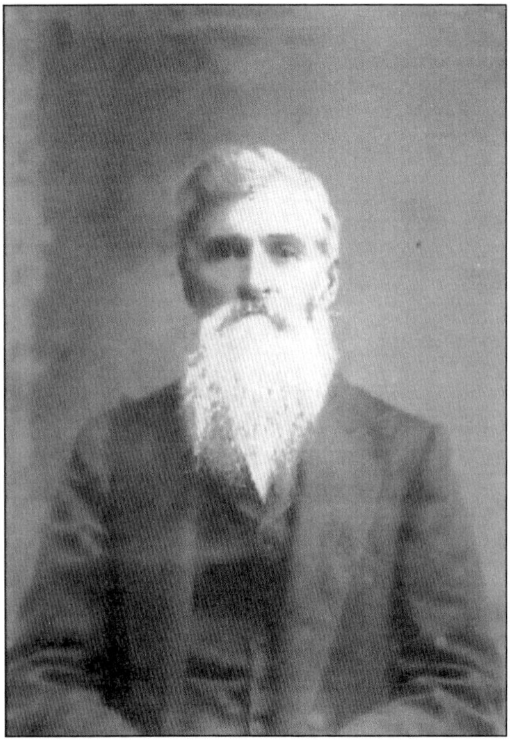

Rev. Jeremiah T. Hughes was one of the early Methodist circuit ministers and preached at churches in Mount Ayr, Diagonal, and other communities in surrounding counties. Reverend Hughes, too poor to own a horse, often commented that he wasn't a circuit rider—he was a circuit walker. (Courtesy of Juanita Fields.)

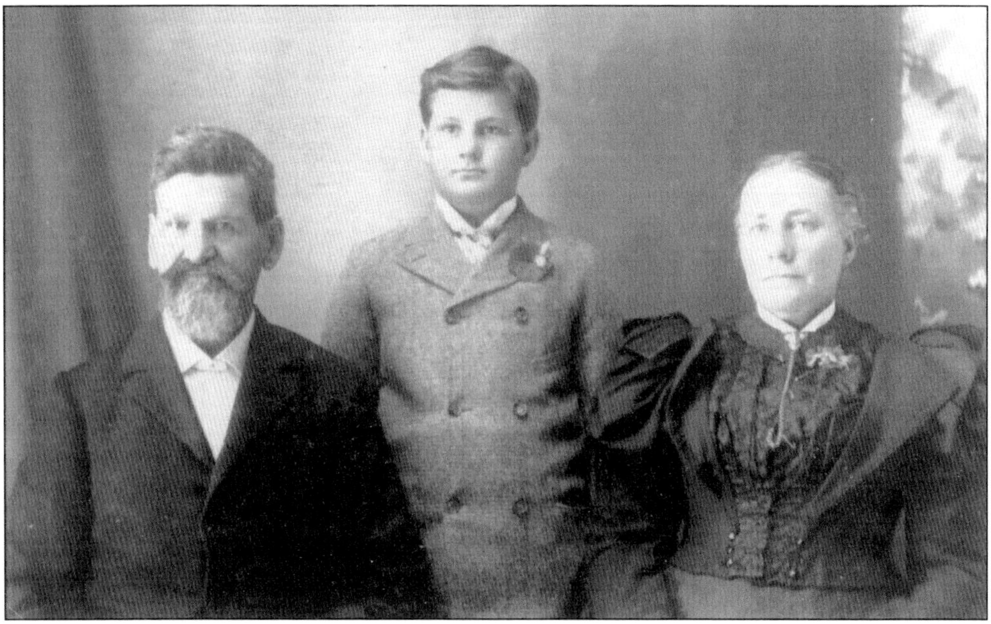

Dr. Franklin B. "Frank" Locke (1837–1909) resided at Blackmore Corner, where he enjoyed a splendid medical practice. Later, Dr. Locke had medical offices in Ringgold City and Wirt, present-day Ellston. Dr. Locke married Mary A. Bear (1850–1930), the sister of Solomon Bear. Dr. Locke, also an Evangelical minister, was instrumental in the establishment of the church at Ringgold City and at Wirt in the 1870s. He conducted many revival meetings throughout the county. (Courtesy of the Bear Family.)

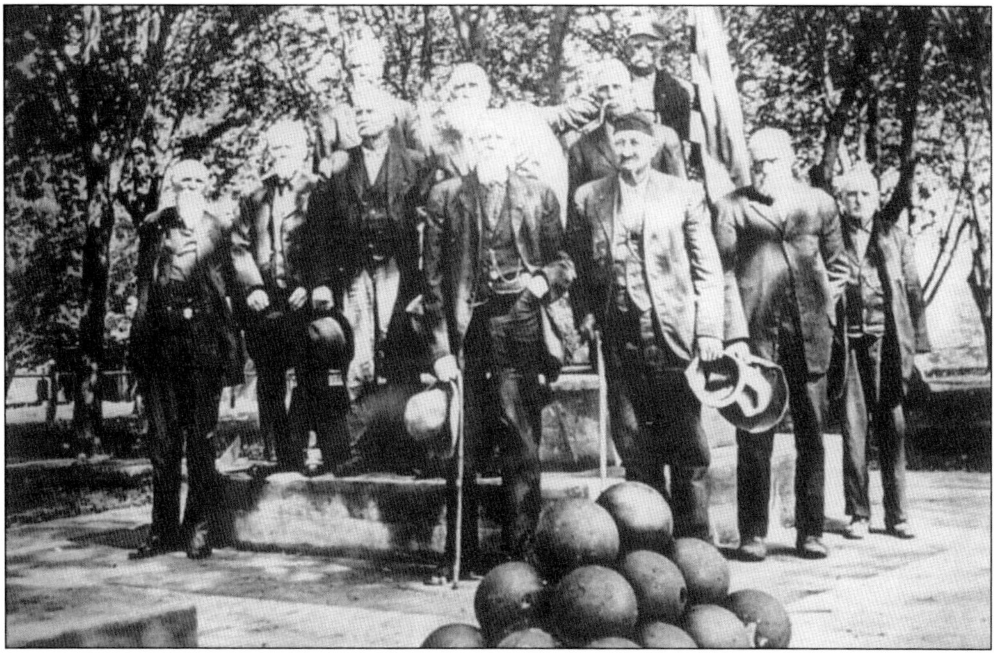

These Civil War veterans gathered in a Redding park are, from left to right, William B. McKemson, Wilsie Staton, Dwight Derickson, Ike Zook, T.A. Arneal, F.N. Oliver, Dan Hudson, Jim Edwards, John S. Hoffman, Harrison Norris, and Ora Benton Sr. All the men were members of the Grand Army of the Republic. (Courtesy of Friends of Old Redding.)

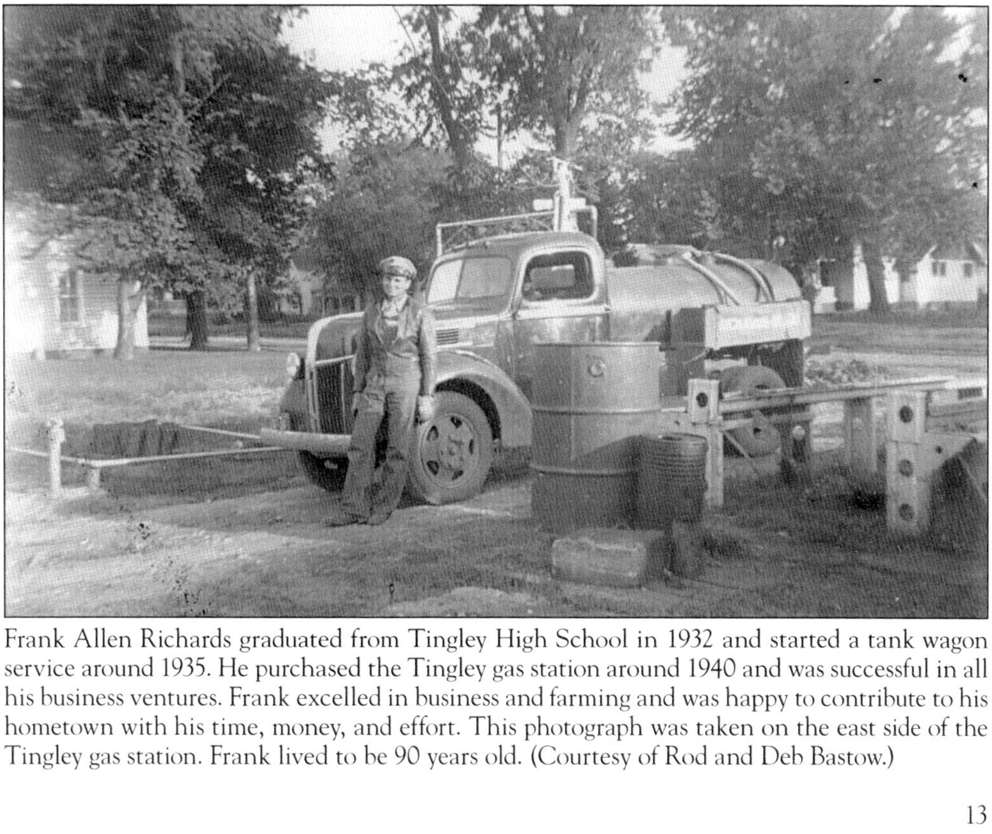

Frank Allen Richards graduated from Tingley High School in 1932 and started a tank wagon service around 1935. He purchased the Tingley gas station around 1940 and was successful in all his business ventures. Frank excelled in business and farming and was happy to contribute to his hometown with his time, money, and effort. This photograph was taken on the east side of the Tingley gas station. Frank lived to be 90 years old. (Courtesy of Rod and Deb Bastow.)

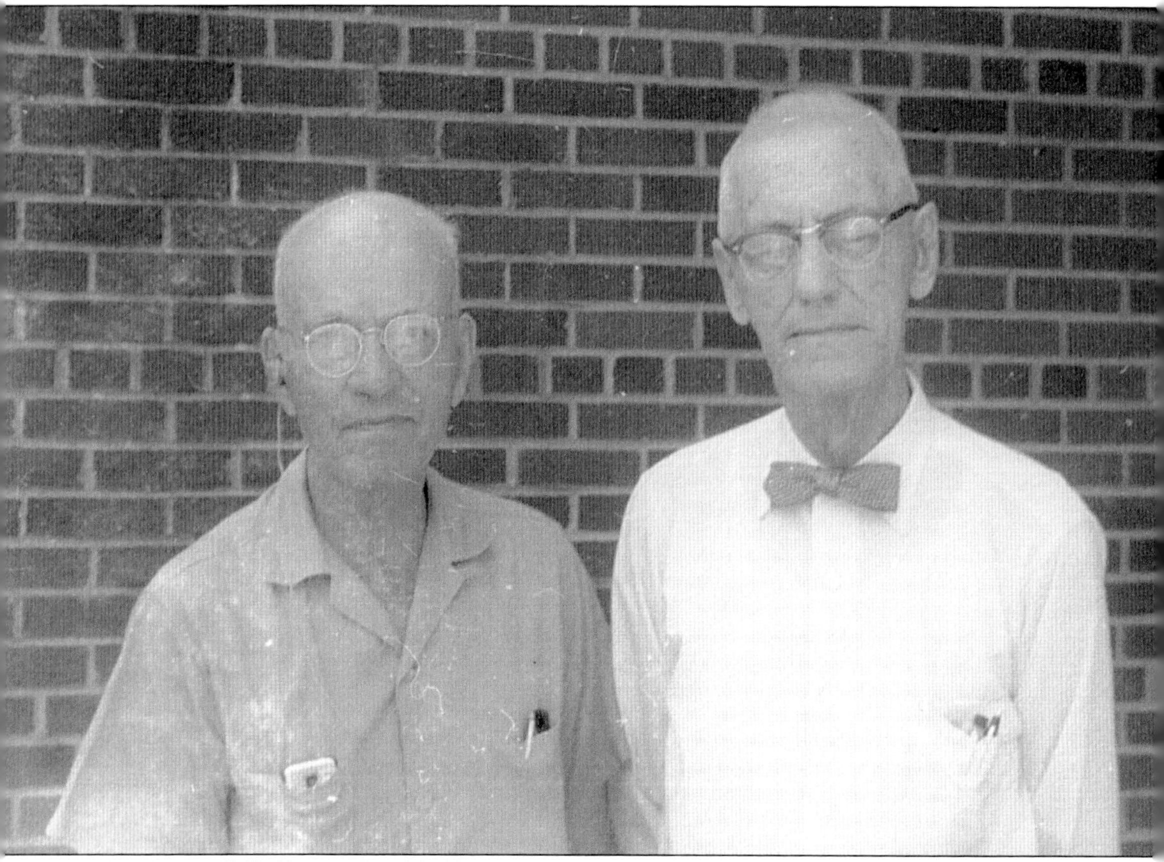

Dr. J.W. Hill (left) completed half a century of medical service to Ringgold County when he retired in 1957. He served on the Mount Ayr District Board of Education and was county coroner, city health commissioner, county chairman of the Heart Fund Drive, and chief of the Ringgold County Hospital staff. Dr. E.J. Watson (right) gave of his medical services to the towns of Diagonal and Knowlton, as well as surrounding areas. While at Knowlton, his office was located in the Independent Order of Odd Fellows (IOOF) building. In the early 1960s, Dr. Watson took over ownership of Diagonal's First National Bank and continued in this capacity until his death. (Courtesy of Mount Ayr Depot Museum.)

In the fall of 1856, Ithamar Spink "Ith" Beall taught at the first school in Mount Ayr. He taught winter-term classes, and Charlotte Swan taught spring and summer terms. Charlotte and Ith were married on June 17, 1858. Ith retired from teaching and served several terms in the county recorder's office. He established the *Ringgold Record* newspaper. (Courtesy of Sharon R. Becker and Mike Avitt.)

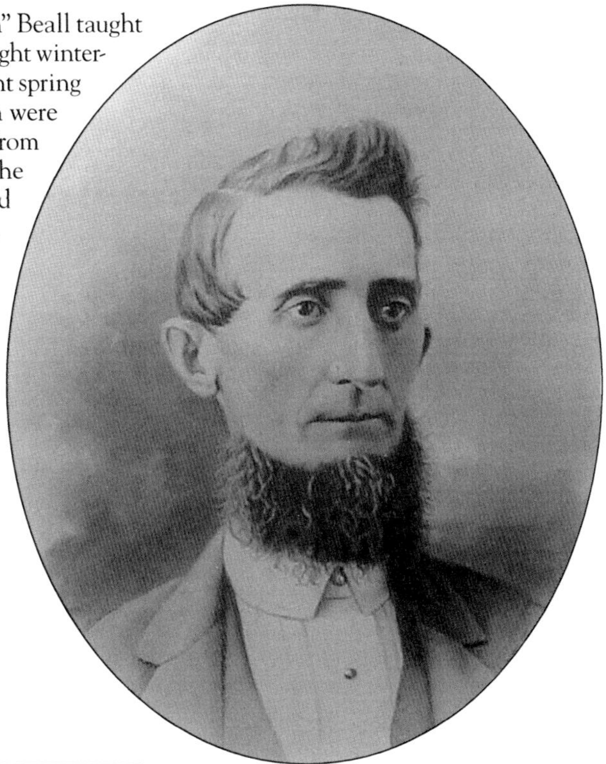

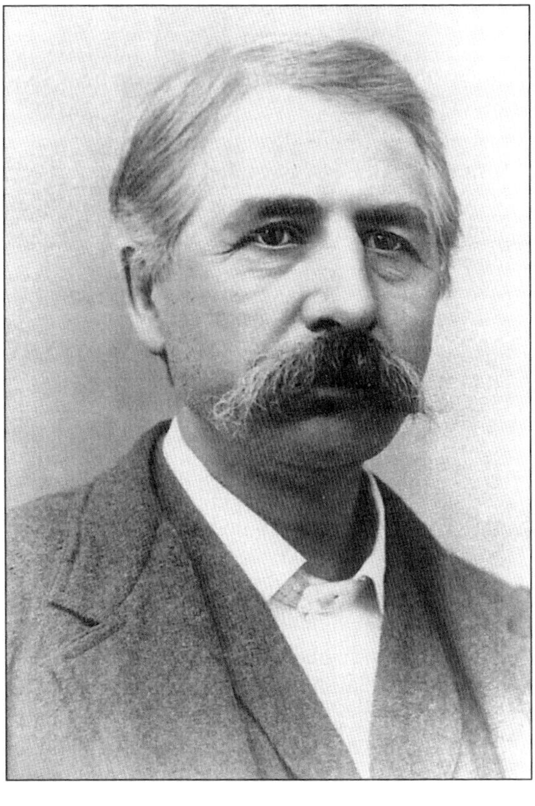

George B. Roby came to Mount Ayr and took over as editor and publisher of the *Ringgold Record* in 1866. He purchased a large Washington hand press on which the newspaper was printed. Roby also served Mount Ayr as postmaster from 1870 to 1872. (Courtesy of *Twice-A-Week News*.)

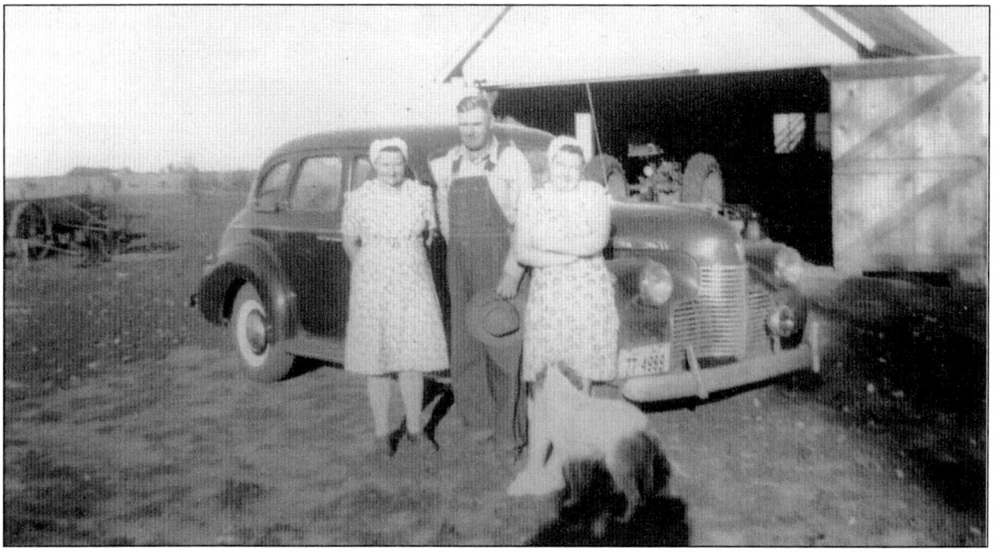

Pictured from left to right are Vesta, Harvey, and Georgia Lamb of rural Tingley. One of the most prized possessions of a rural farm family was the vehicle. Normally, a farm family went into town on Saturday selling cream and eggs and conducting their trade. Often, the family would enjoy evening entertainment at the movie theater or attended a dance with music provided by talented local musicians. (Courtesy of Bill Adams.)

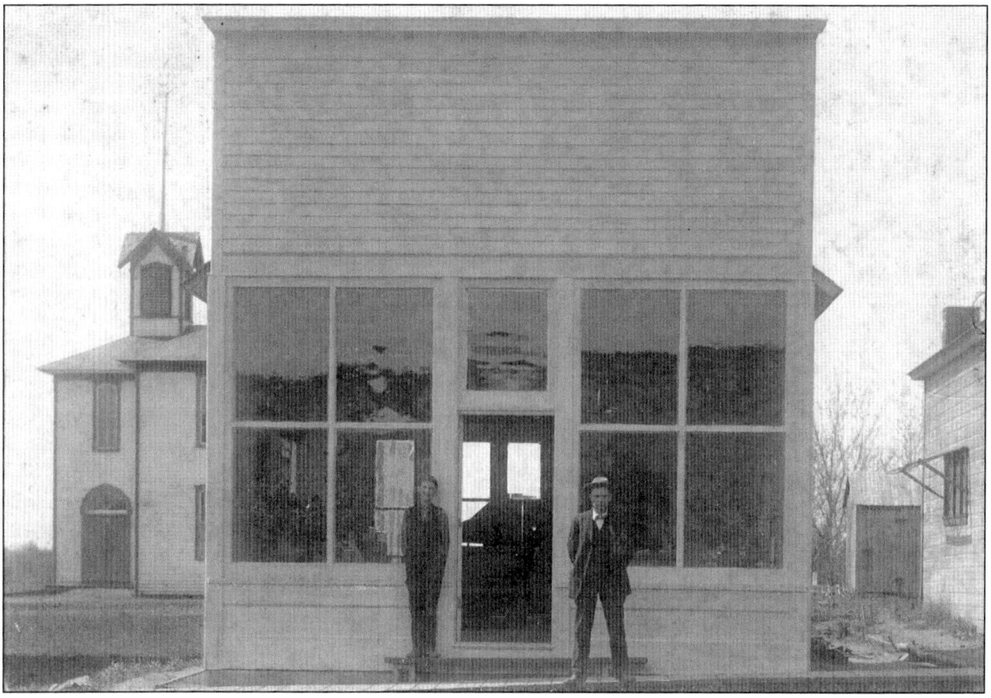

Jodie Norris is pictured at right in front of the Redding Print Shop. Norris was publisher and editor of the *Redding Register* newspaper. About 1915, Ralph Main bought the paper, changed the name to the *Redding Herald*, and published it from the same shop until 1957. Behind the shop, to the left, is the Redding School, built about 1889 and used until 1915. (Courtesy of Friends of Old Redding.)

Solomon "Sol" Bear walked from Cedar Rapids to Ringgold County in 1856 and selected land for his homestead. He made the trip three more times on foot before settling on his farm. After the death of his first wife, Sarah E. Walker, Sol married Amanda Elvina Duly. The couple raised five more children on their homestead, which was located between Ellston and Kellerton. Amanda was of Native American descent, although she never discussed her heritage, instead directing those who asked to read their Bible. Sol and Amanda are posing here for the camera in 1894. (Courtesy of the Bear Family.)

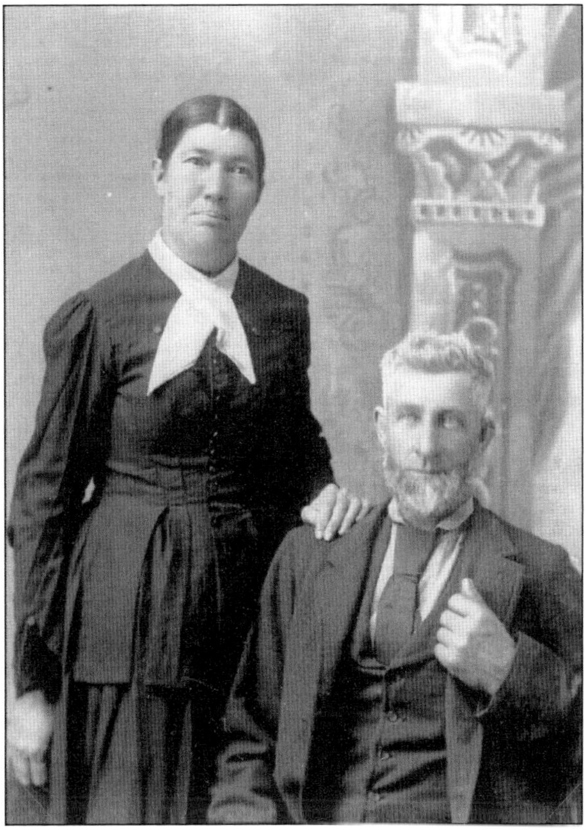

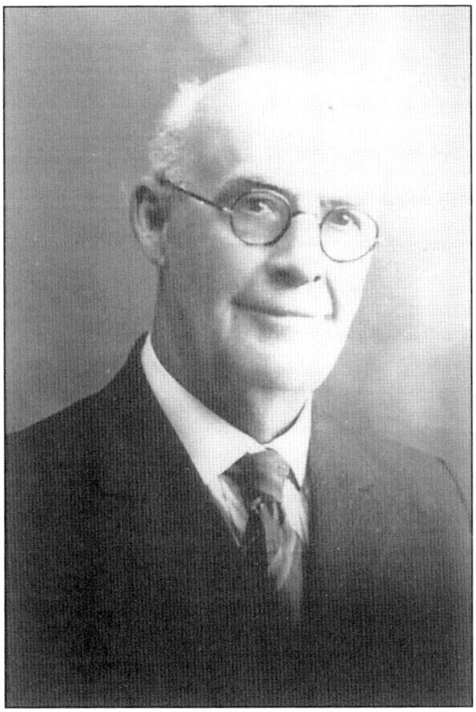

Dr. Allen Welch Reynolds, a graduate of Simms Medical College in St. Louis, Missouri, came to Caledonia, where he had a medical practice for nearly half of a century. His office was the last remaining building in Caledonia. (Courtesy of Cleola Geist.)

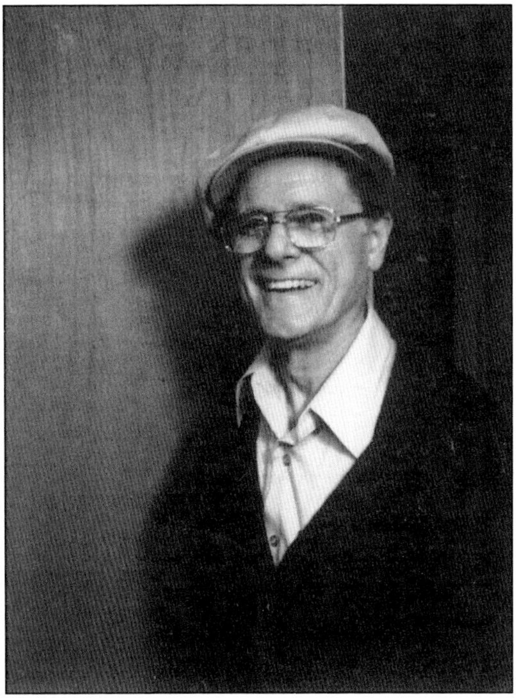

Holland Foster, the son of Homer A. and Beatrice (Holland) Foster, was born in Caledonia. He was an artist who studied under Grant Wood and John F. Carlson. Holland authored the book *The Ghost Town of Caledonia* and made the Caledonia diorama, now housed at the Cornwall Pioneer Museum in Ellston, Iowa. He is pictured here in 1975. (Courtesy of Mount Ayr Depot Museum.)

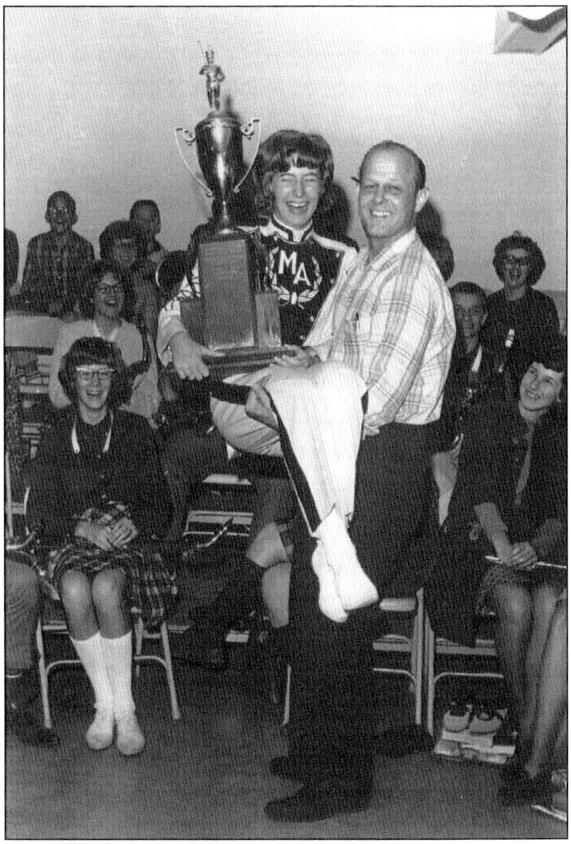

Mount Ayr High School drum majorette Leola Minnick celebrates a first-place finish in the 1965 Maryville, Missouri, homecoming parade marching-band contest. Supporting Leola is Mount Ayr band instructor Merrill Perry. Perry taught band at Mount Ayr for 23 years before retiring due to health reasons. Known as the Old Band Man, he was one of the first band directors in Iowa to start a jazz band. Merrill went into the insurance business and later became mayor of Mount Ayr. (Courtesy of Mount Ayr Depot Museum.)

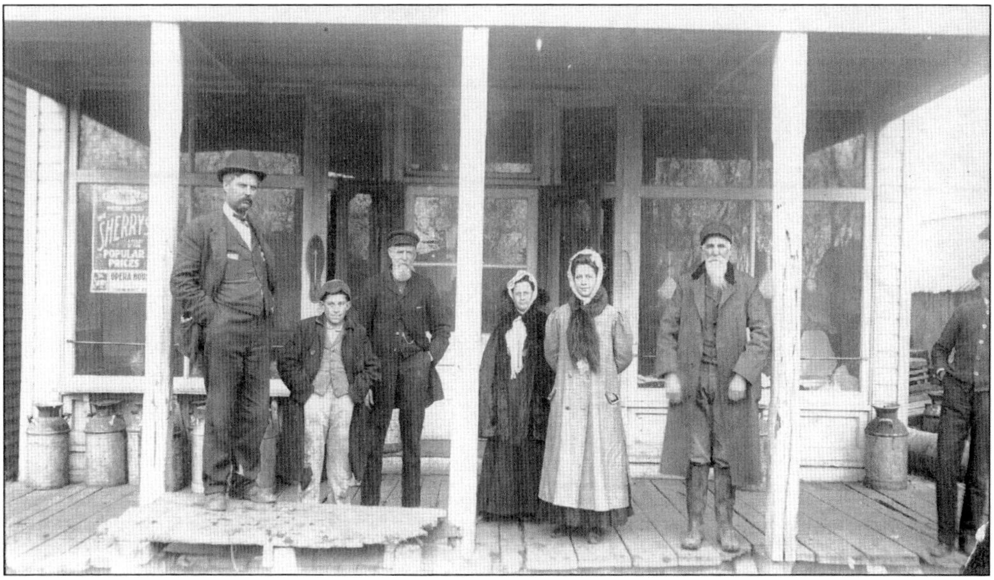

A group is posing for the camera in front of Nathan Miller's store in Redding. Pictured are, from left to right, Nathan Miller, a Herrington boy, Mr. Edwards, Ada Gray, Mrs. Earl Cochran, and Mr. Arneal. (Courtesy of Friends of Old Redding.)

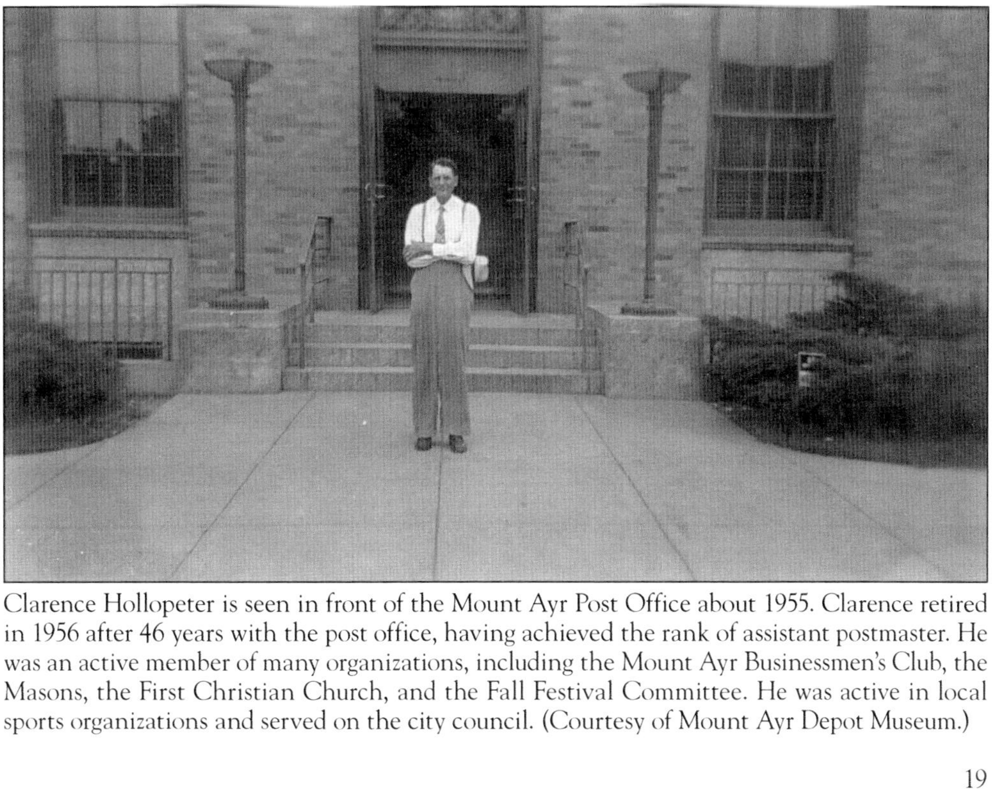

Clarence Hollopeter is seen in front of the Mount Ayr Post Office about 1955. Clarence retired in 1956 after 46 years with the post office, having achieved the rank of assistant postmaster. He was an active member of many organizations, including the Mount Ayr Businessmen's Club, the Masons, the First Christian Church, and the Fall Festival Committee. He was active in local sports organizations and served on the city council. (Courtesy of Mount Ayr Depot Museum.)

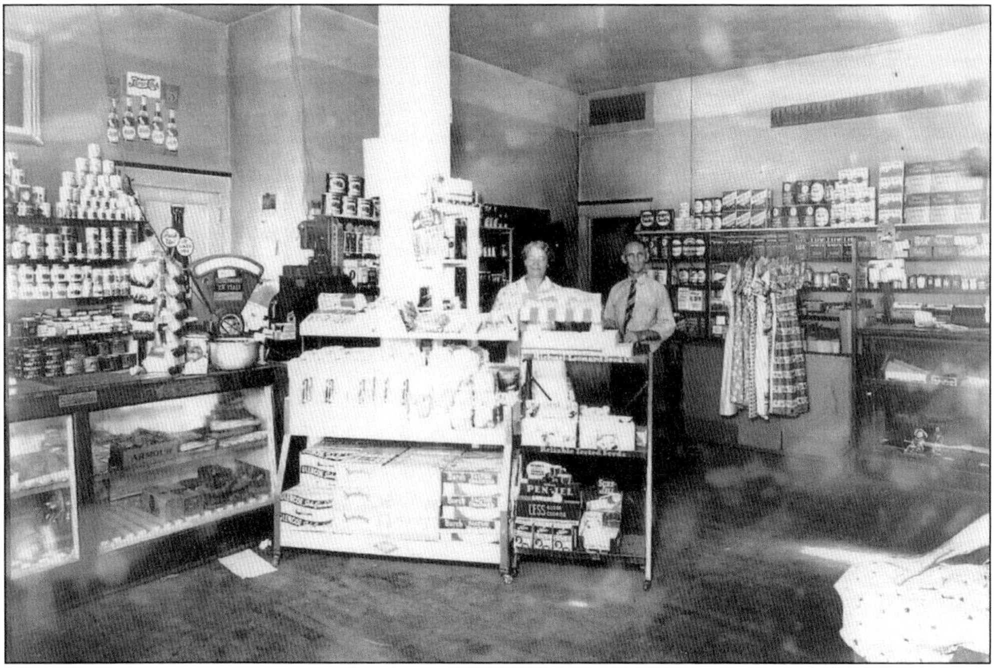

The Farmer's Store in Redding was owned by George (right) and Maude (Miller) Griffith (left). It is seen here in the 1920s. George was the son of Jethro J. Griffith, an early settler who came to Ringgold County in 1854. George and Maude's one daughter, Velma, married Delbert Sterner. (Courtesy of Friends of Old Redding.)

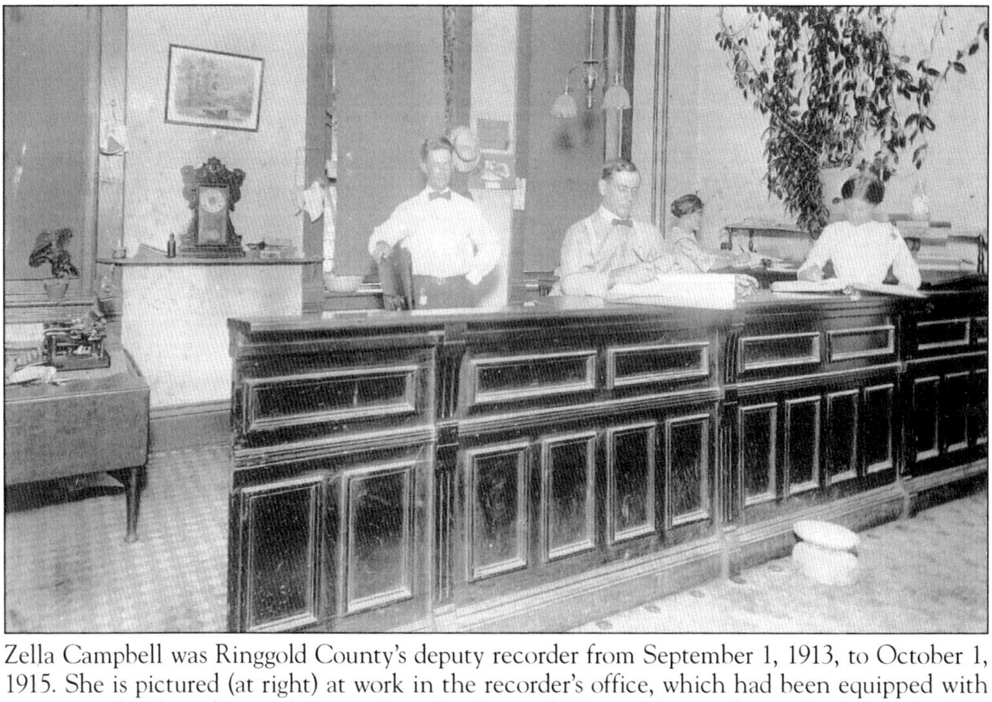

Zella Campbell was Ringgold County's deputy recorder from September 1, 1913, to October 1, 1915. She is pictured (at right) at work in the recorder's office, which had been equipped with a spittoon for the tobacco-chewing clientele. Ringgold County's recorder at this time was C.E. Thompson. (Courtesy of Mount Ayr Depot Museum.)

Jack Bonebrake operates one of the presses located at the Diagonal Printing Museum. He was a career newspaperman and enjoyed giving demonstrations at the museum. School groups and visitors watched as Jack operated the antique presses, which were modern equipment in his day. (Diagonal Printing Museum.)

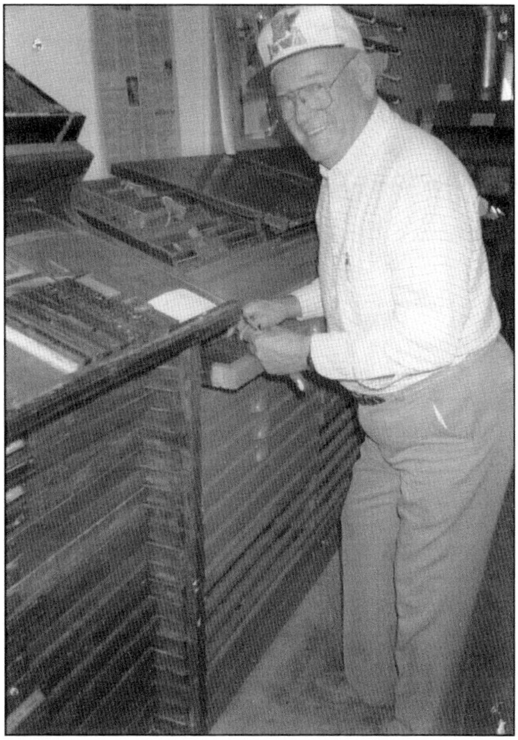

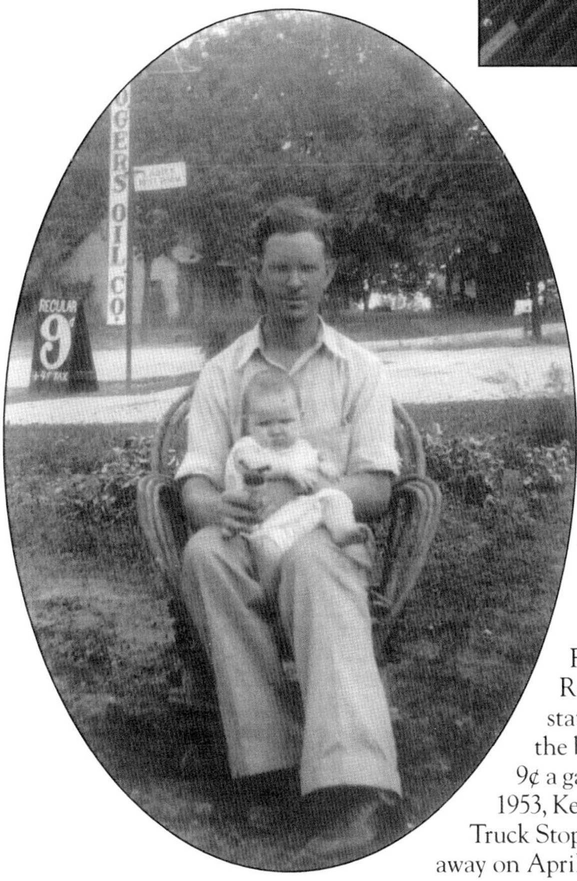

On June 7, 1941, Rogers Oil Company opened Gasoline Alley at 207 South Fillmore Street in Mount Ayr. Here, Keith Rogers sits near the driveway of his new station with one of his three daughters. In the background it can be seen that gas is only 9¢ a gallon, but the tax is 4¢. On December 19, 1953, Keith and his father, George, opened Rogers Truck Stop on Highway 2 East. Keith Rogers passed away on April 24, 1985. (Mount Ayr Depot Museum.)

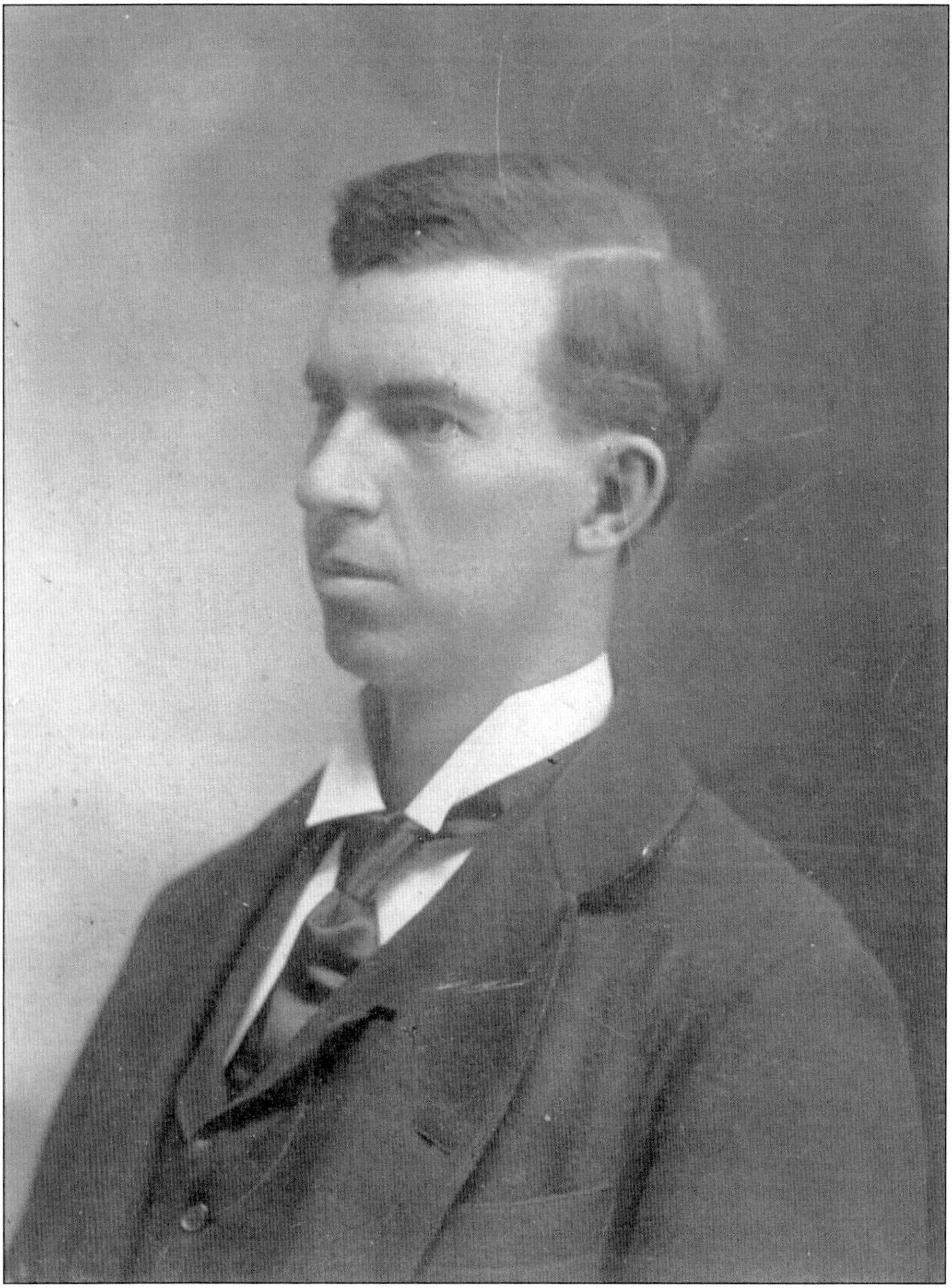

The sons of Ith and Charlotte (Swan) Beall, Randolph Sry and Walter Hamlin Beall, established a partnership and published the *Twice-A-Week News*. During this time, Randolph traveled the entire county by horse and buggy to compile the most comprehensive directory to date. It has stood the test of time and serves as a historical and genealogical resource well over 100 years after publication. A charter member of the Ringgold County Historical Society, Randolph published the *Ringgold County Old-Timer Bulletin*, later known as the *Bulletin* and finally the *Ringgold County Bulletin*. (Courtesy Mount Ayr Depot Museum.)

Two

Ringgold County Grows

Ringgold County's early pioneers and leaders were concerned about the spiritual and educational growth of their communities and rural neighborhoods. The first public building was usually a schoolhouse or a church. With the coming of the railroads, beginning in 1879, building materials such as mortar, steel, and glass hastened the erection of modern structures. Log cabins gave way to frame houses; brick buildings housed churches, schools, offices, and stores. Farmers improved their farms with income earned by shipping livestock and grain on the rails.

As the population grew, towns were incorporated, retail businesses increased, and roads and bridges were built to facilitate travel. Advancements in communication and transportation added to the county's growth. Industrious individuals, families, and corporations prospered, contributing to all aspects of life in Ringgold County.

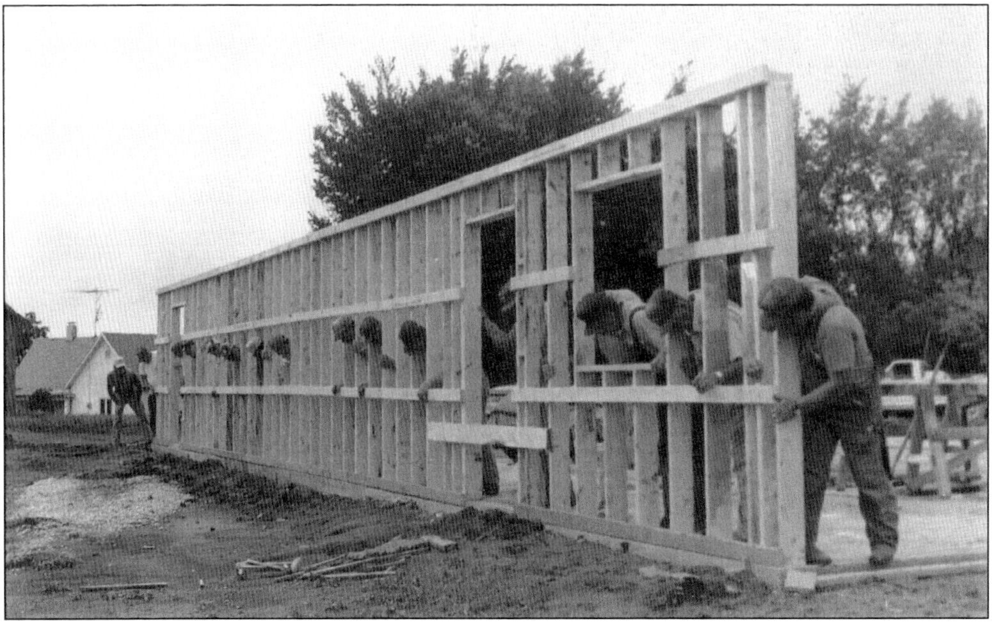

Pictured here, volunteers erect the Waubonsie Center's first wall in Benton on July 25, 1992. Land for the center was donated by Larry Bowen and Dick Motsinger. The center measured 30 feet by 60 feet. An addition, largely financed by J.R. Miller, was built in 2005 and serves as the town's museum. (Courtesy of *Mount Ayr Record-News*.)

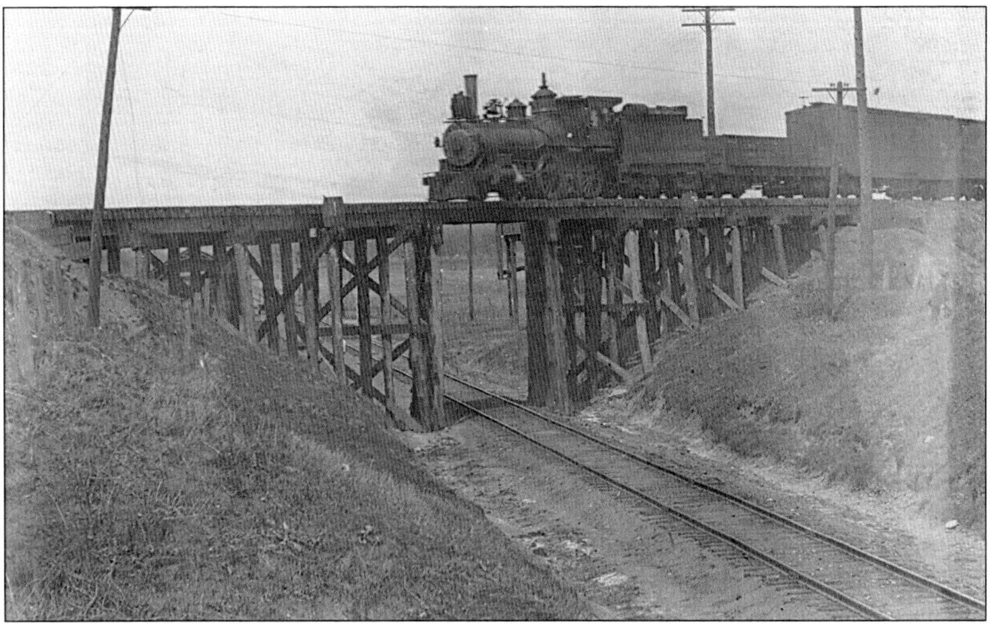

A westbound Chicago, Burlington & Quincy (CB&Q) train crosses the trestle at Diagonal. The Chicago Great Western Depot can barely be seen through the legs of the trestle on the left side. Diagonal was the only town in Ringgold County to have two railroads. This ended when the CB&Q abandoned its line in late December 1945. The Chicago Great Western was sold to the Chicago & Northwestern in 1968, and it abandoned the line in 1984. (Courtesy of Diagonal Printing Museum.)

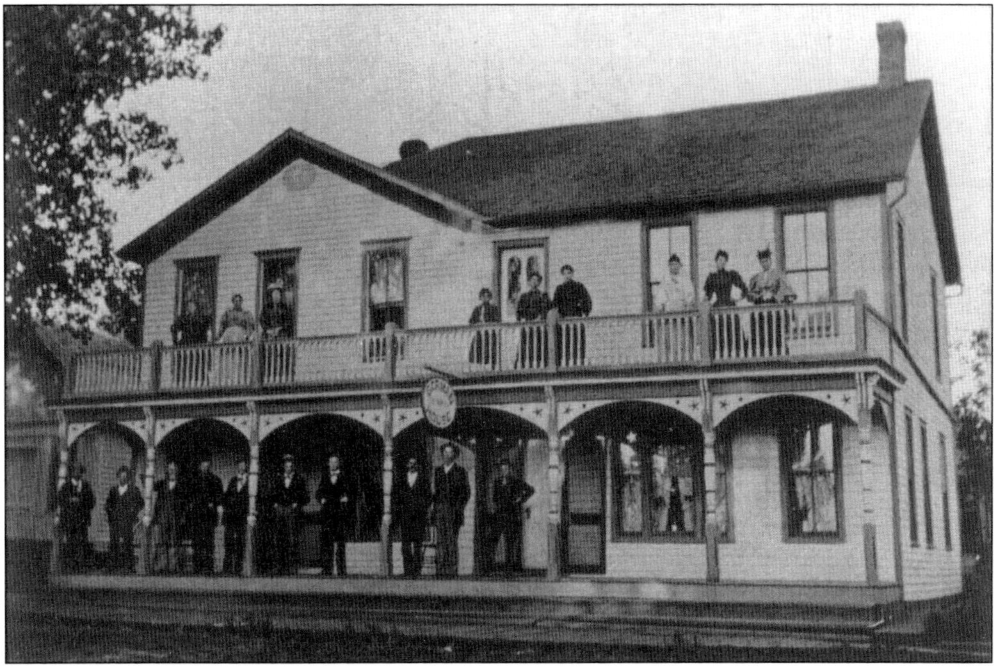

Rooming houses were common near railroad depots. The German House, pictured here in 1896, occupied the lot immediately north of the Neighborhood Center in Mount Ayr. It first appeared on a Sanborn map from 1893 and is referred to as the O'Neal House. It was later called Hart's Rooming House according to a 1919 Sanborn map. (Courtesy of Mount Ayr Depot Museum.)

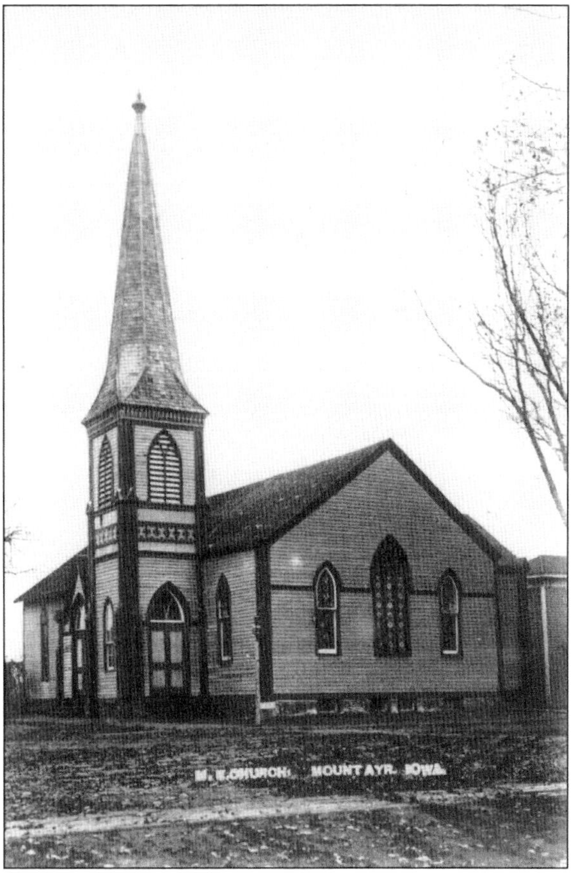

Pictured is the first church building erected in Mount Ayr. This Methodist church was built between 1870 and 1871. W.T. Smith was the pastor. It was located at the site of the current United Methodist Church. The building was torn down in 1911 to make way for a new brick and stone church. (Courtesy of Mount Ayr Depot Museum.)

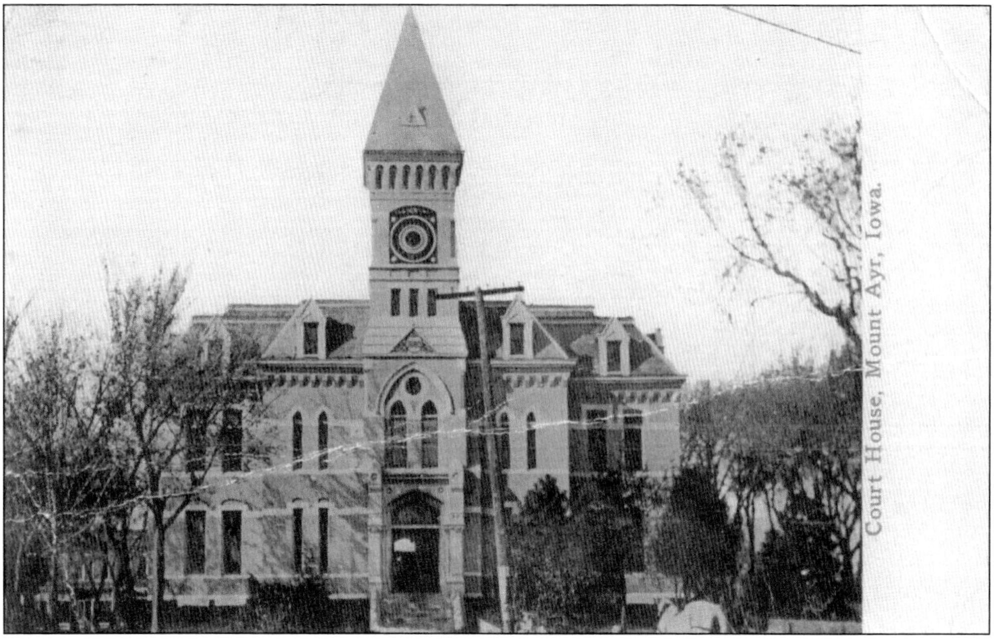

Ringgold County's first brick courthouse was built between 1883 and 1884. It had a 102-feet-high tower on the east side and measured 77 feet by 98 feet. The building served the county less than 40 years. Faulty material and construction caused it to be condemned in 1921. (Courtesy of Mount Ayr Depot Museum.)

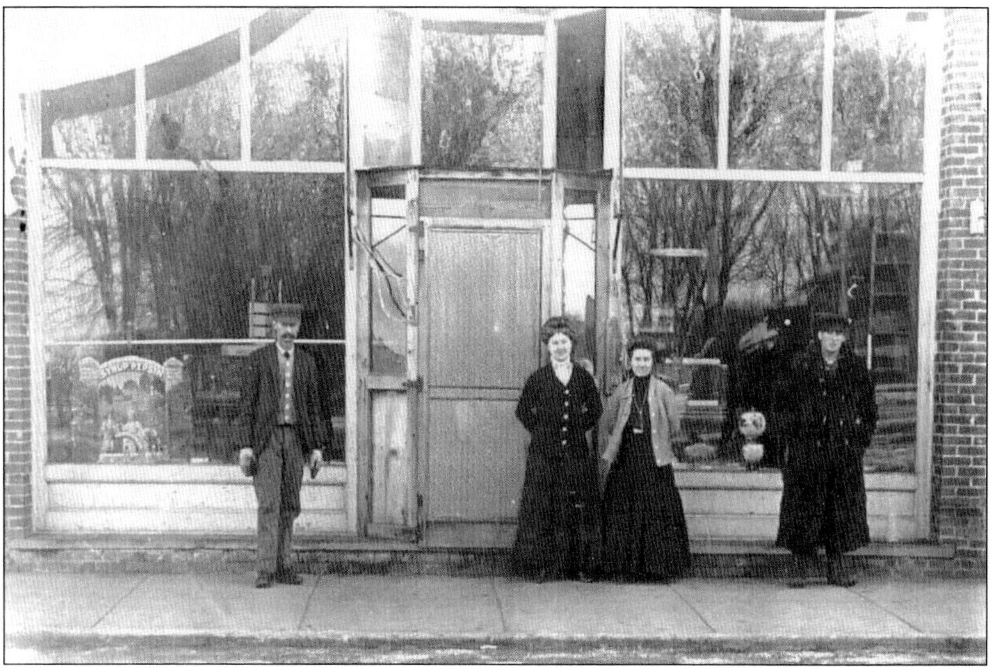

Abie and Frona Richardson operated the millinery shop, which made ladies' hats, located on the east side of the Redding square. The reflection on the shop window shows the trees from a Redding park. The store has a concrete sidewalk, which was very modern for this era. (Courtesy of Friends of Old Redding.)

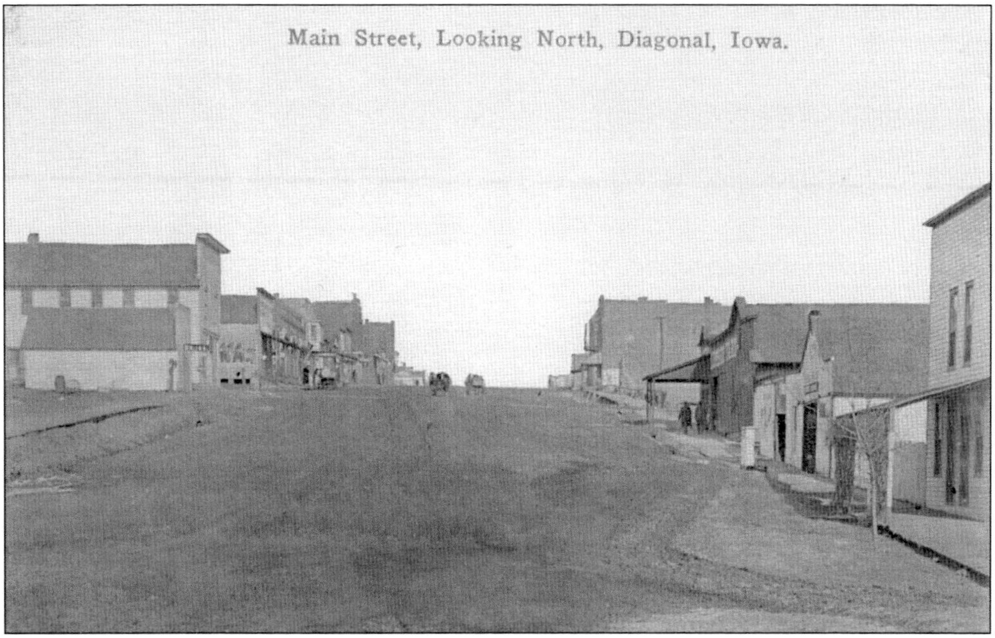

At one time, wooden sidewalks bordered Diagonal's main road. Retail stores, hotels, and offices go on for blocks, as Diagonal was one of the fastest growing towns in Ringgold County. (Courtesy of Diagonal Printing Museum.)

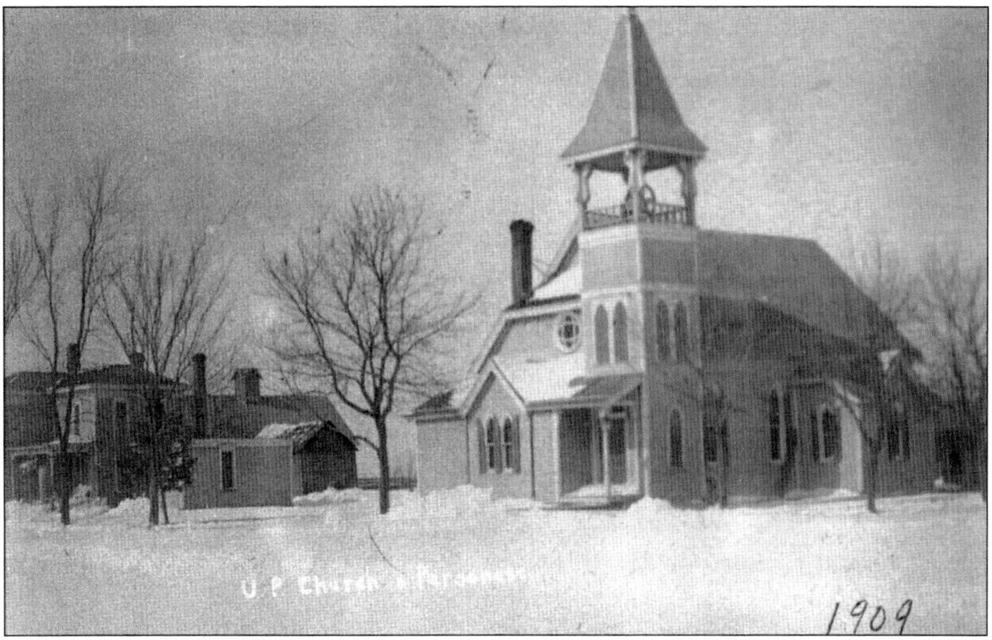

The Tingley United Presbyterian congregation was organized in 1883, and a church was built about 1888. By May 1896, the congregation numbered 250 members under the leadership of Rev. J.P. Gibson. The nine-room house to the left in the photograph is the parsonage. As the small towns lost residents, churches lost members. The last services held in this church were on December 27, 2009. (Courtesy of Mount Ayr Depot Museum.)

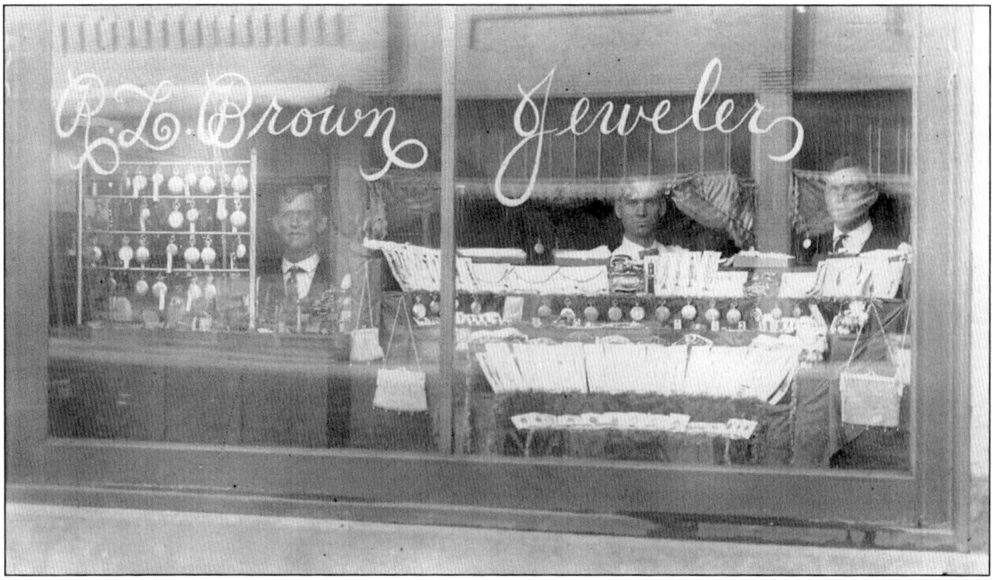

Pictured is the R.L. Brown Jewelry Store in Kellerton. Brown started his career in Mount Ayr before establishing this business. (Courtesy of Mount Ayr Depot Museum.)

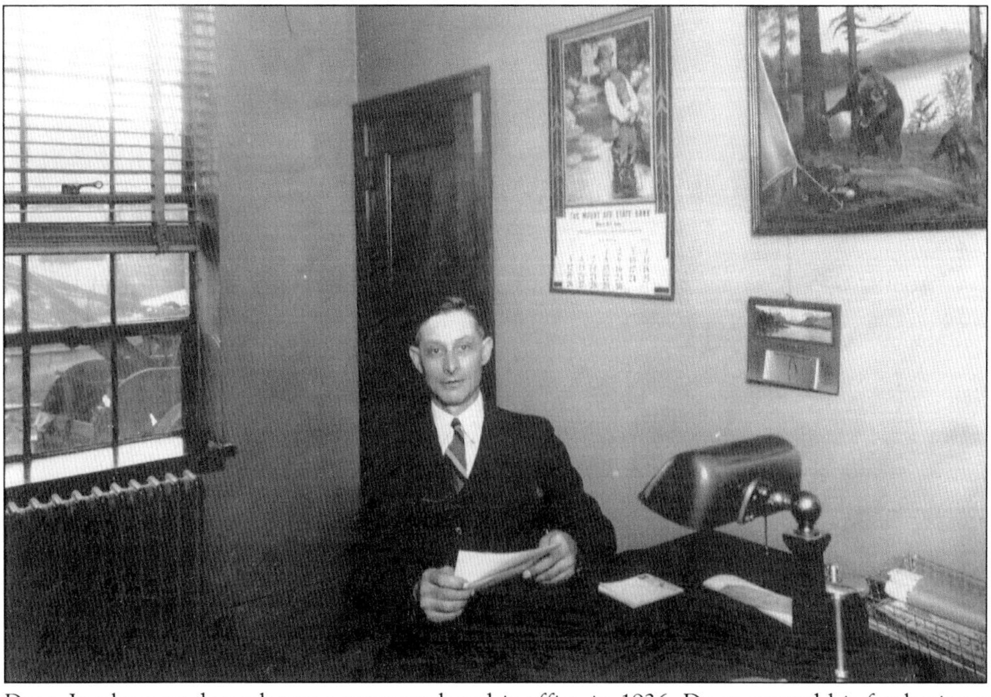

Dean Jacobs goes through some paperwork at his office in 1936. Dean started his fur business in 1906 at the family farm in Lotts Creek Township at the age of 16. He moved his business to Mount Ayr in 1921 and expanded his operation in 1933 after a fire damaged his old building. Jacobs eventually bought and sold fur internationally and had, perhaps, the most successful business enterprise in Ringgold County history. His Dean Jacobs Fur building still stands on the south side of the Mount Ayr square. (Courtesy of Lynnette Knight Hunt.)

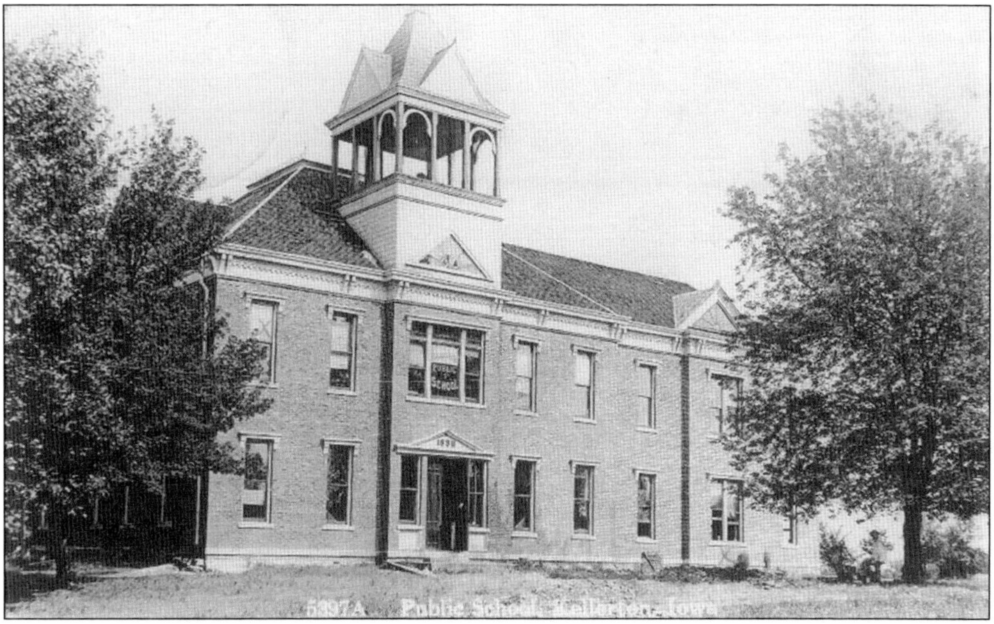

The railroad donated Block 20 in Kellerton as a school location. During the forenoon of February 5, 1895, one of the coldest days of the year, a fire broke out and soon spread through the two-story framed schoolhouse. Although the building was a complete loss, the teachers were able to get all of the students out without incident. A new two-story brick schoolhouse (pictured) was ready for classes in December 1895. (Courtesy of Ken Baker.)

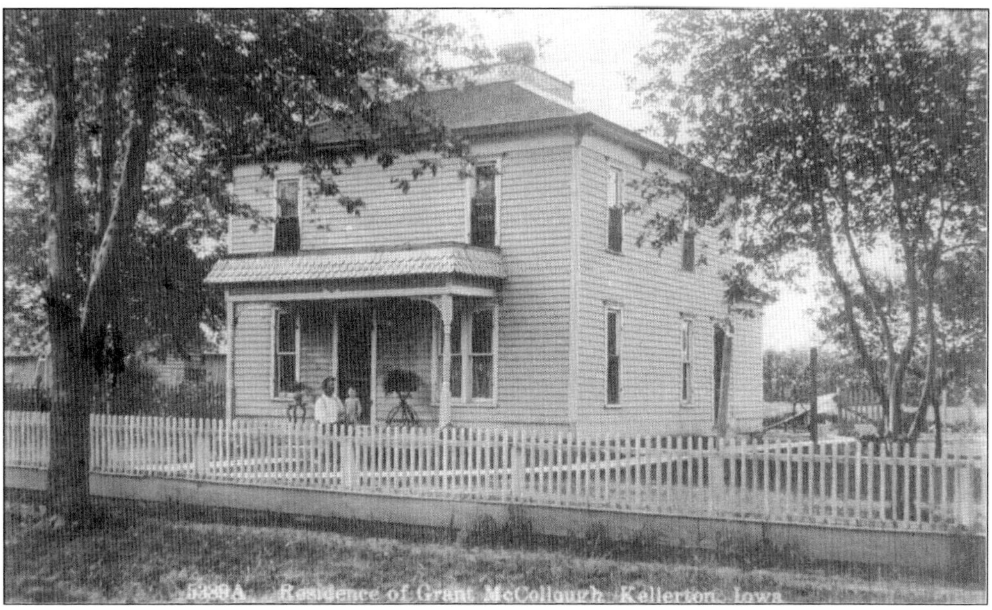

Businessman Grant McCullough served as a councilman for many years in Kellerton and lived in this stately home. Grant married Nora Benscoter and they had one son, Guy. After Nora's death, Grant married Eva Harrell, and they became parents of another son, Kenneth. (Courtesy of Mount Ayr Depot Museum.)

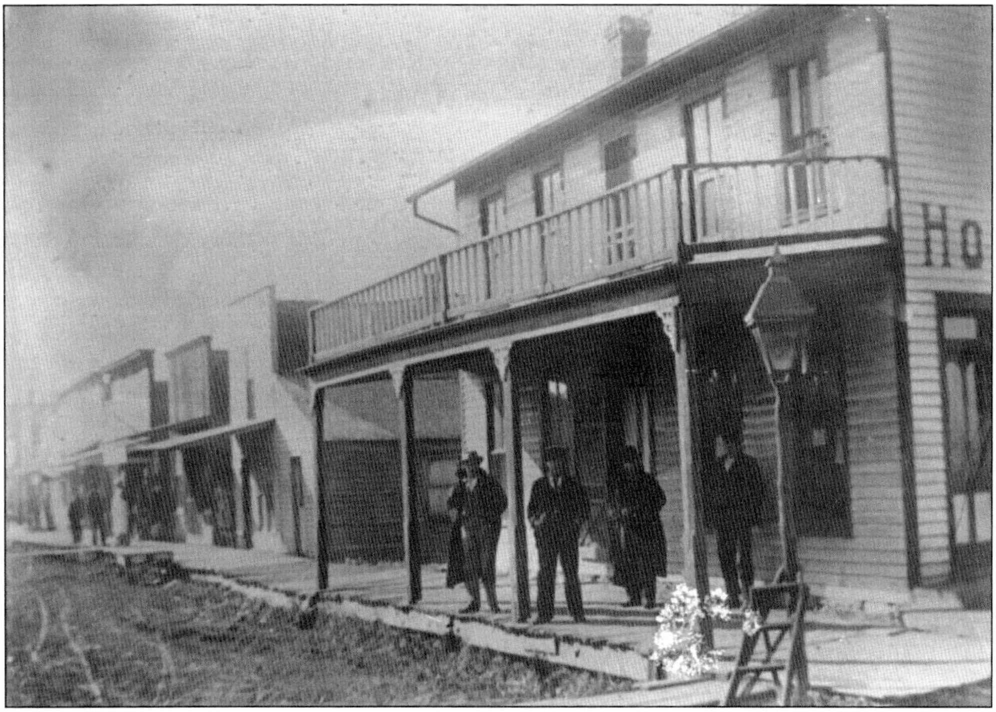

With the arrival of the railroad came many travelers. Hotels and boardinghouses were common near depots, and the Foley Hotel was established less than one block from Kellerton's depot. The McDonald family purchased the business and renamed it Hotel McDonald. The Kellerton Post Office is now located on this site. (Courtesy of Mount Ayr Depot Museum.)

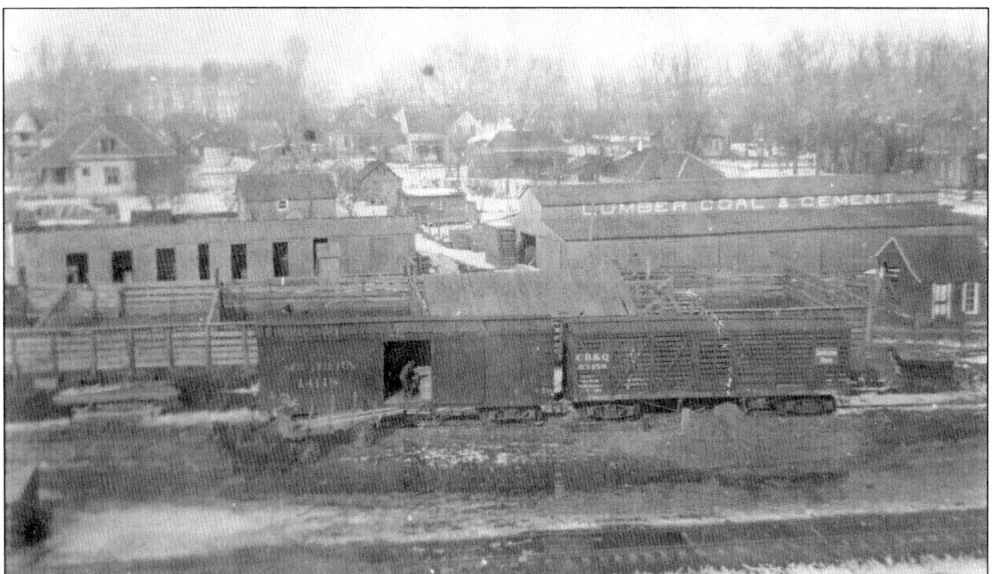

Crucial to any rural community was the railroad, which provided a means of bringing in goods and merchandise and shipping out produce and livestock. In this c. 1900 photograph, workers are unloading lumber from a boxcar at Kellerton. (Courtesy of Mount Ayr Depot Museum.)

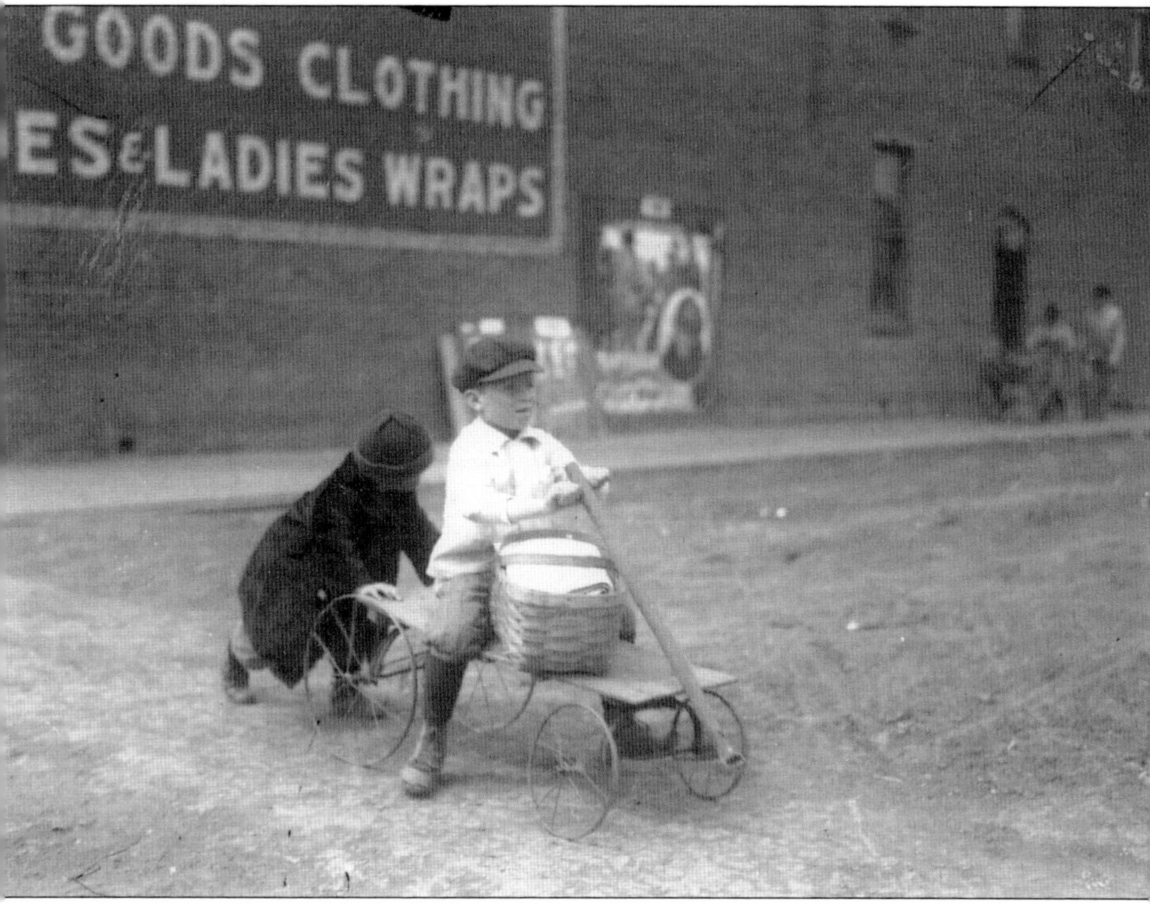

In the early 1900s, many young boys earned a few pennies running errands for the business establishments located around the Mount Ayr square. These two young boys, whose names have sadly been lost over time, are delivering a basket that perhaps contains lunch. (Courtesy of Mount Ayr Depot Museum.)

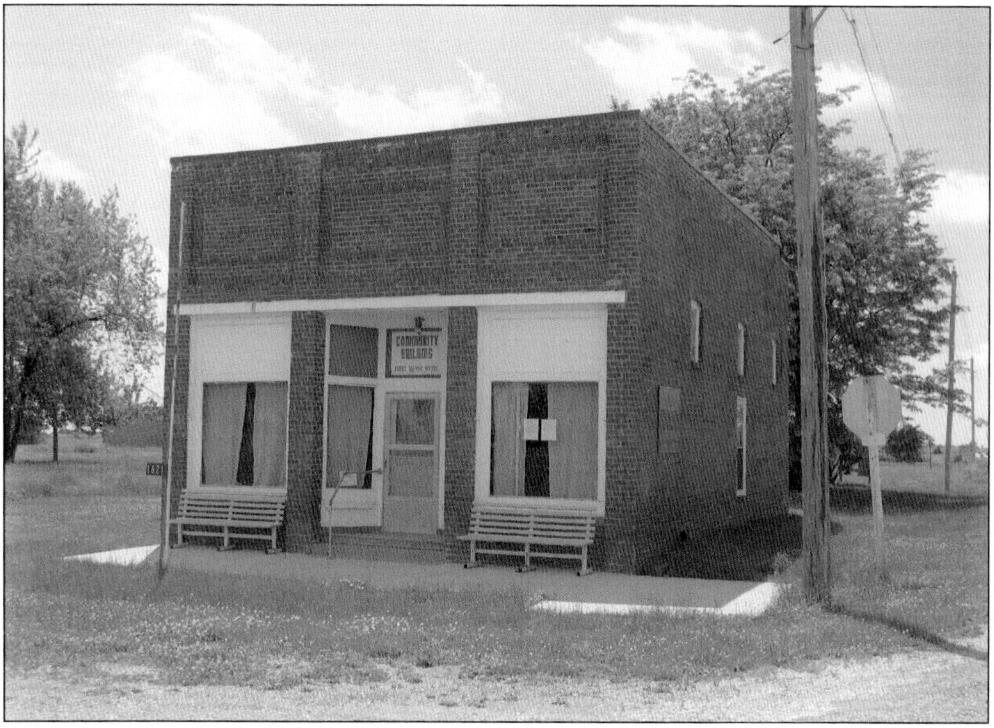

The Midwest grocery store chain known today as Hy-Vee, Inc. started in Beaconsfield in 1930. Charles Hyde and David Vredenburg went into business together with a general store and continued to establish stores in neighboring towns. They incorporated in 1938 and adopted the Hy-Vee name in 1952. The first Hy-Vee building is now the Beaconsfield Community Center and is the only business building left in town. (Courtesy of Sharon R. Becker.)

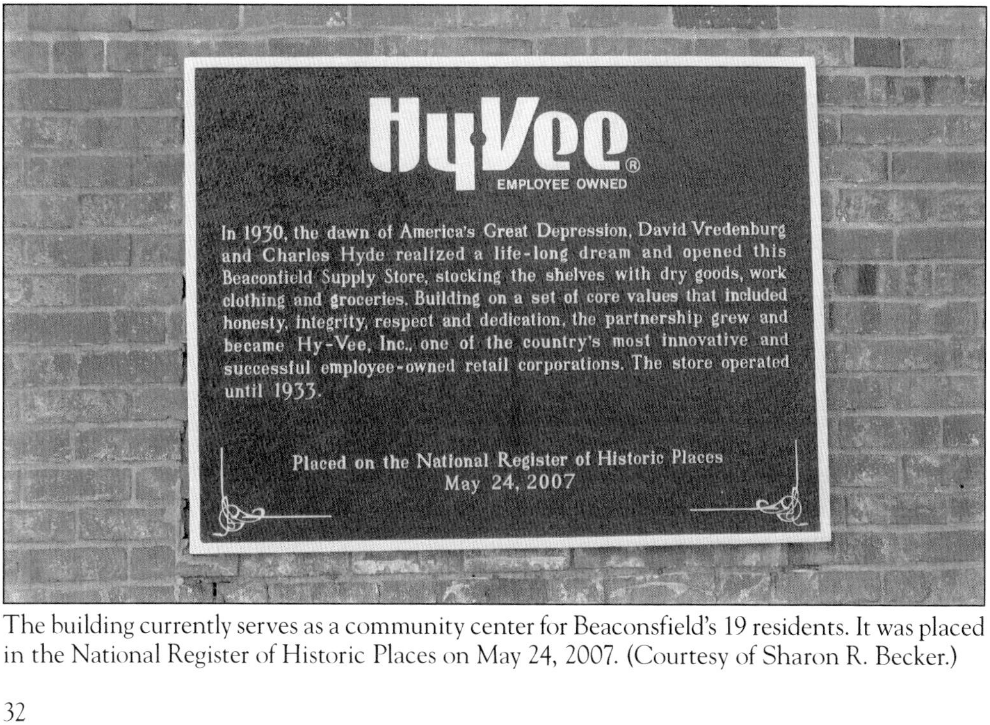

The building currently serves as a community center for Beaconsfield's 19 residents. It was placed in the National Register of Historic Places on May 24, 2007. (Courtesy of Sharon R. Becker.)

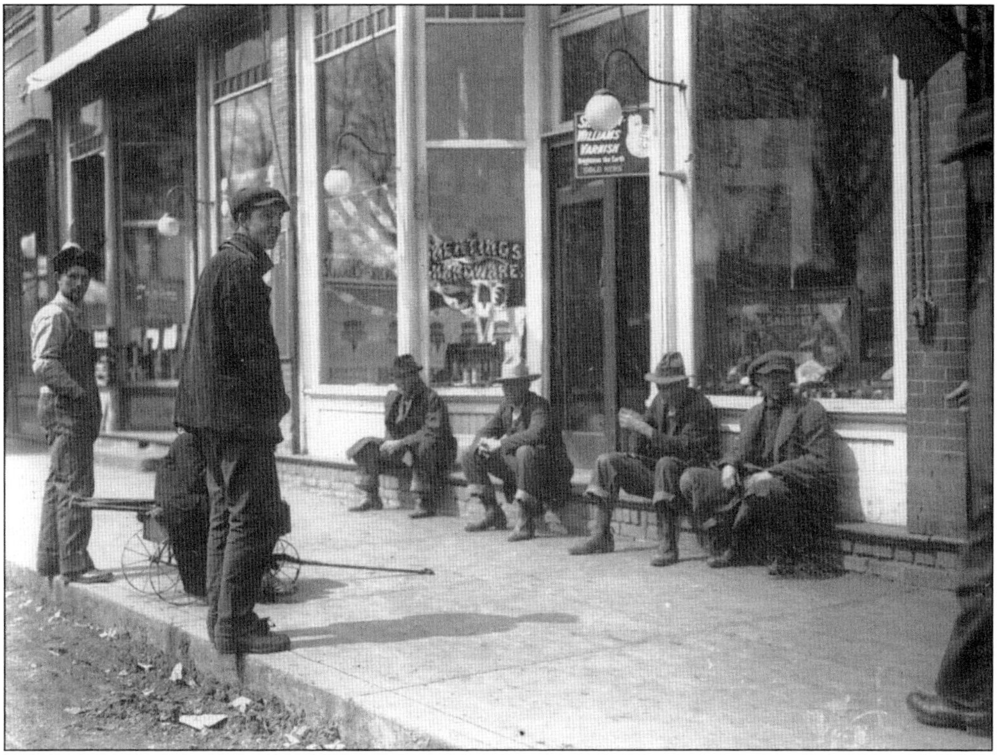

A jolly group gathers to discuss the price of a new lawn mower, or maybe the weather, in front of Keating's Hardware on the north side of the Mount Ayr square in 1913. Curtis R. Keating came to Mount Ayr in 1884 from Afton and was engaged in the hardware business until his retirement in 1928. (Courtesy of Mount Ayr Depot Museum.)

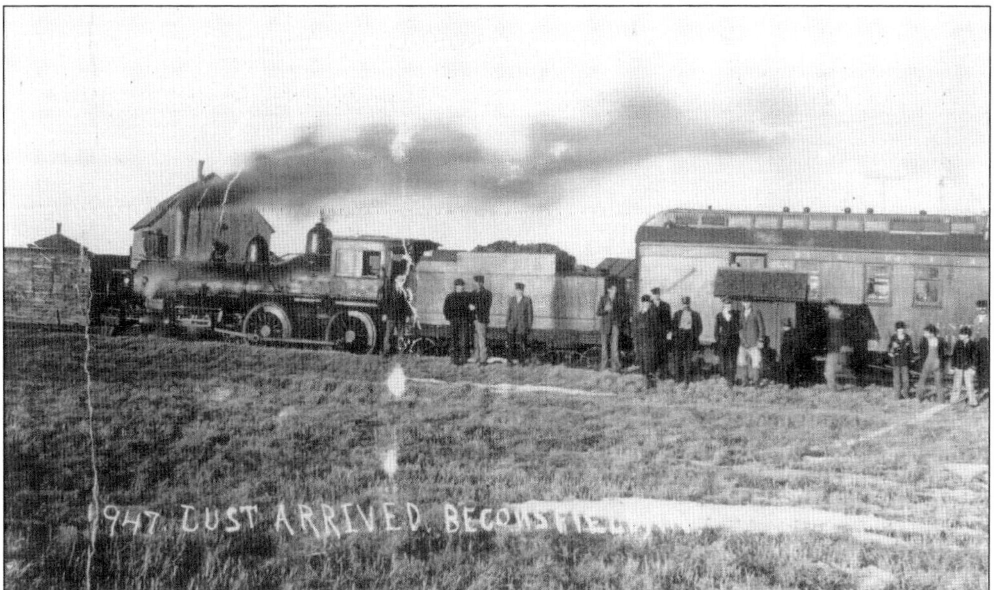

Pictured is a train that had just pulled into Beaconsfield in 1910. (Courtesy of Mount Ayr Depot Museum.)

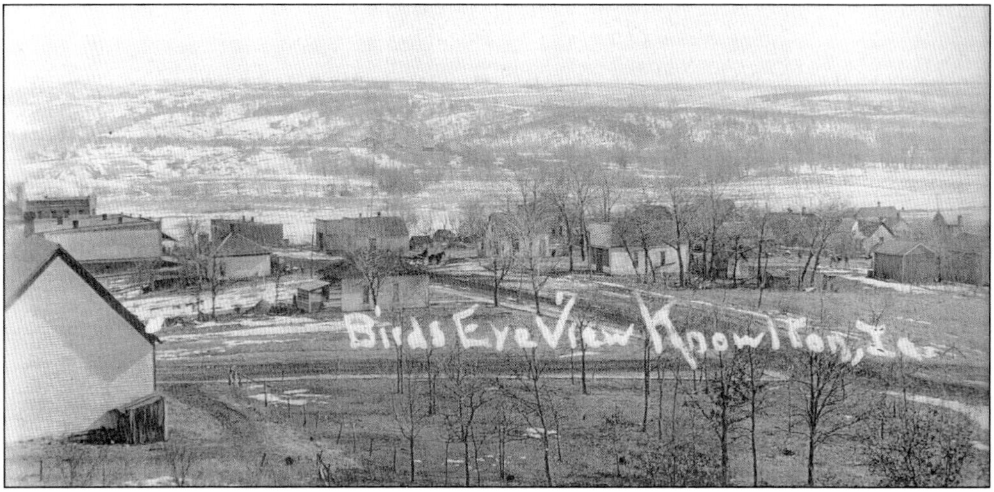

This photograph was taken from the schoolhouse and is looking east-southeast, giving a bird's-eye view of Knowlton High School. The business district is on the located on the left. (Courtesy of James Rueber.)

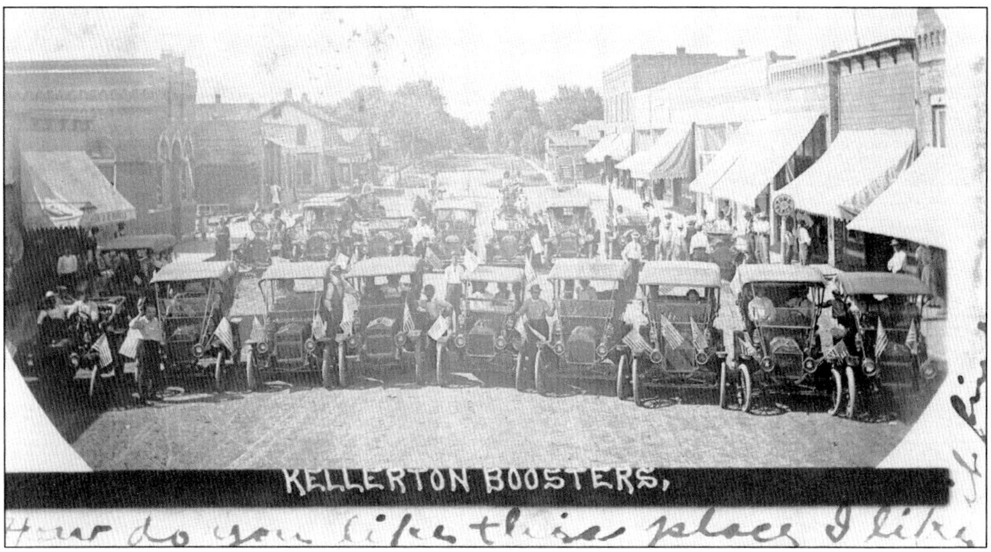

With the advent of automobiles, many towns started Booster Clubs. The motorists formed caravans, which included the town's band, and traveled to neighboring towns. Once there, they met with other motor enthusiasts to enjoy a meal and a concert. Pictured is the Kellerton Booster Club of 1911. (Courtesy of Ken Baker.)

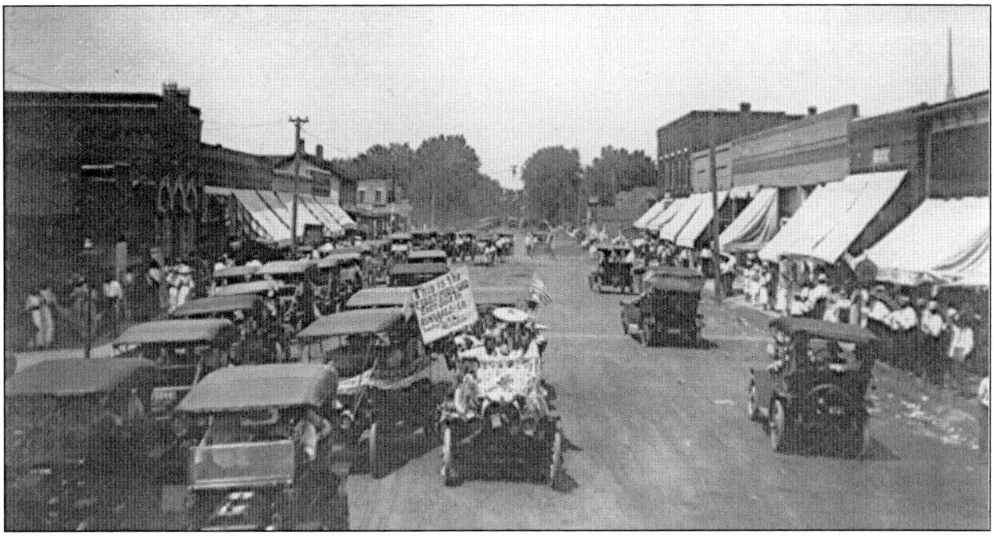

The sign reads, "This is the first Ford car ever sold in Ringgold Co., Seasholtz Motor Co." Road rallies, like this one in Kellerton around 1912, were often held. The Waubonsie Trail Association was formed in 1911 to promote road improvements and auto tourist travel. In 1942, the Waubonsie Trail became State Highway 2. (Mount Ayr Depot Museum.)

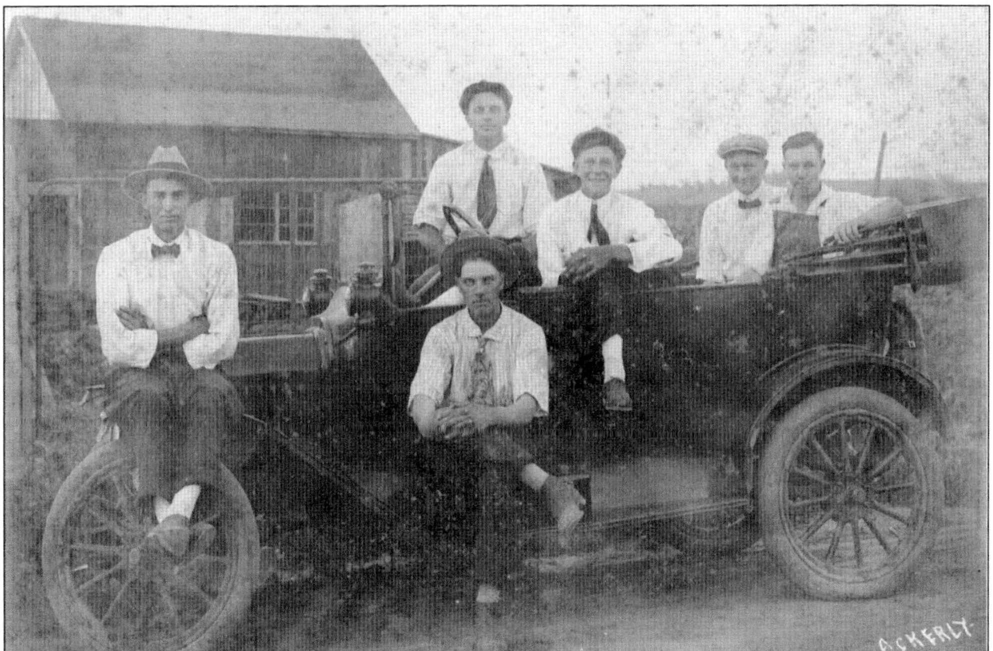

With the arrival of motorized vehicles, automobiles quickly became the mode of transportation, which the younger generation preferred over a team and buggy. Many people who were fortunate enough to own an automobile took a Sunday drive through the countryside, enjoying the sights and stopping to visit friends and relatives. Pictured in 1920, this group of young men setting out on such a sightseeing trip includes, from left to right, Jim Hopkins, Floyd Binning (on the fender), Lawrence Binning, Dewey West, Homer Foland, and Wilbur McKee. (Courtesy of Norma G. [Foland] Becker.)

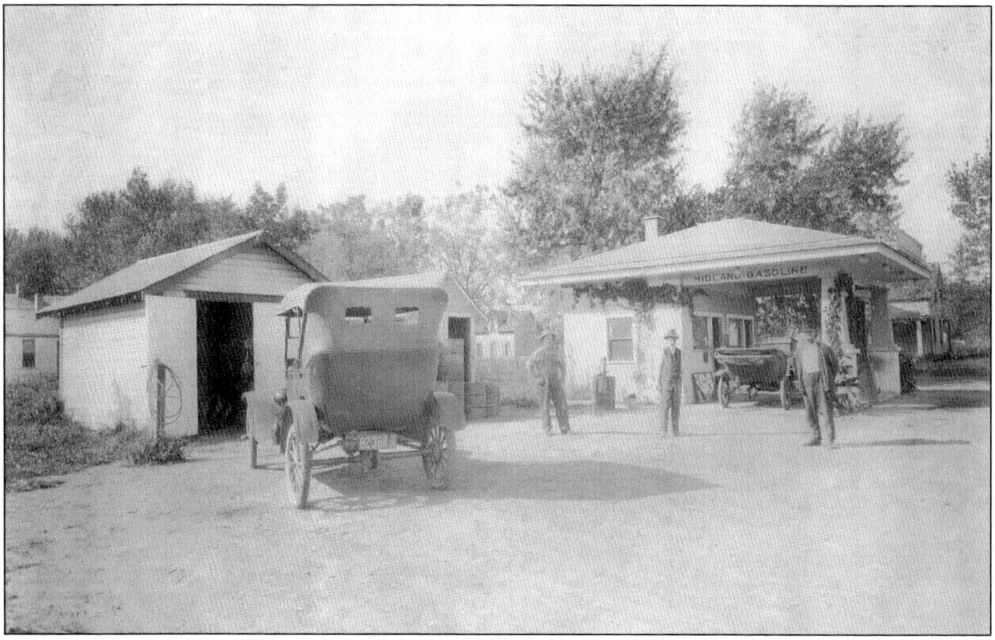

The Kellerton Oil Company was established in 1924. Harry and Ora Fugate bought the company in 1944 and built a cement-block addition to the east side in 1960. The addition housed a hoist and provided storage space for tires. (Courtesy of Mount Ayr Depot Museum.)

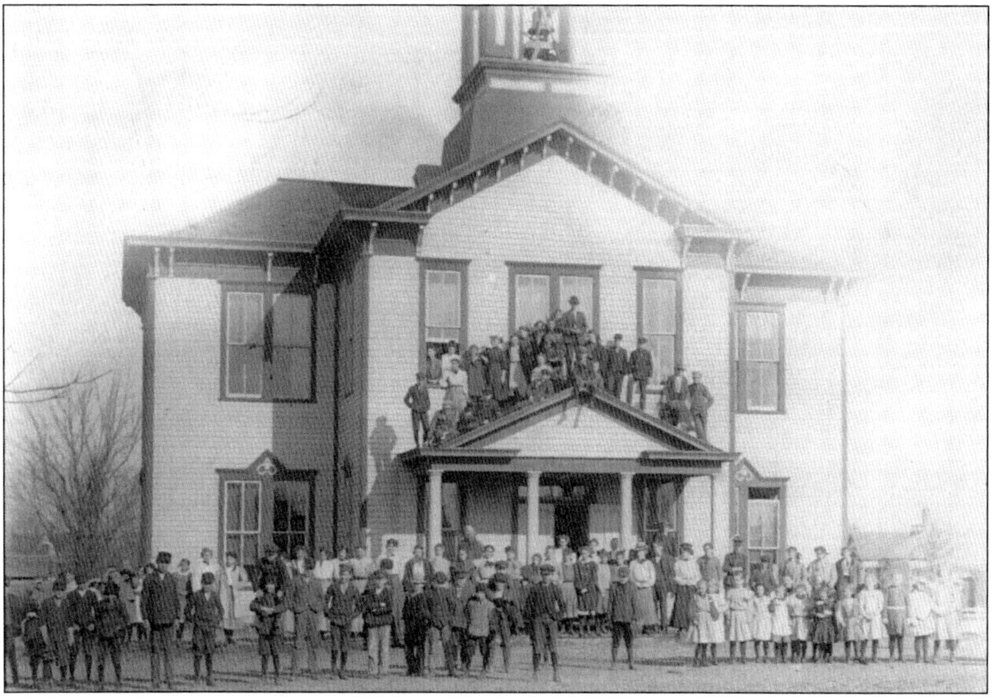

This postcard, with a 1908 postmark, shows the Tingley School with a large gathering of students. The Tingley school was built in 1885 at a cost of $3,300. Increased enrollment necessitated the construction of an addition in 1901. The building was used until 1918, when a new brick school was constructed. (Courtesy of Mount Ayr Depot Museum.)

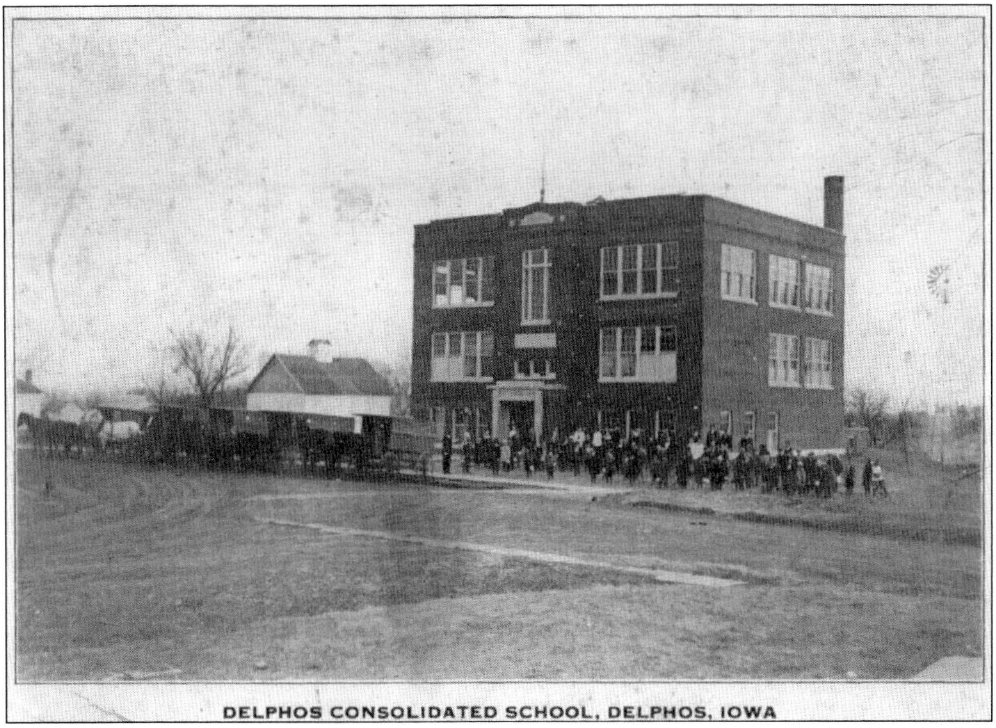

As school enrollments increased in Ringgold County's towns, former wood-framed schoolhouses were replaced with brick buildings. Delphos's schoolhouse, shown here, was built in 1916 at a cost of $25,000. By the 1950s, attendance at Delphos Consolidated School was declining. It was eventually closed and ultimately torn down, a fate awaiting many of the schools in Ringgold County's towns. (Courtesy of Norma G. [Foland] Becker.)

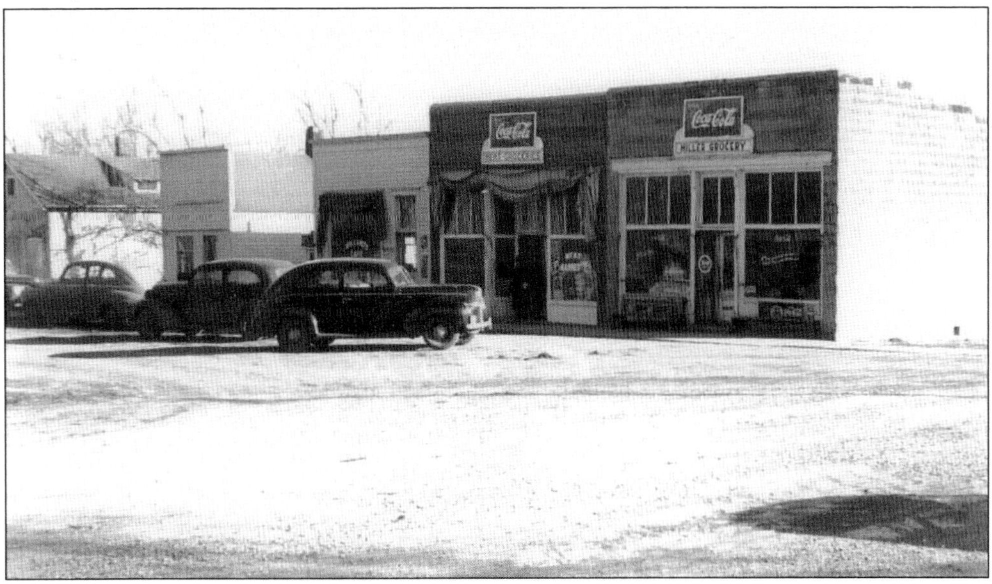

C.L. Herrington took this photograph of the east side of the Redding square in early December 1948. Miller Grocery and Reidlinger Grocery and Meat Market were successful businesses in Redding for many decades. (Courtesy of Friends of Old Redding.)

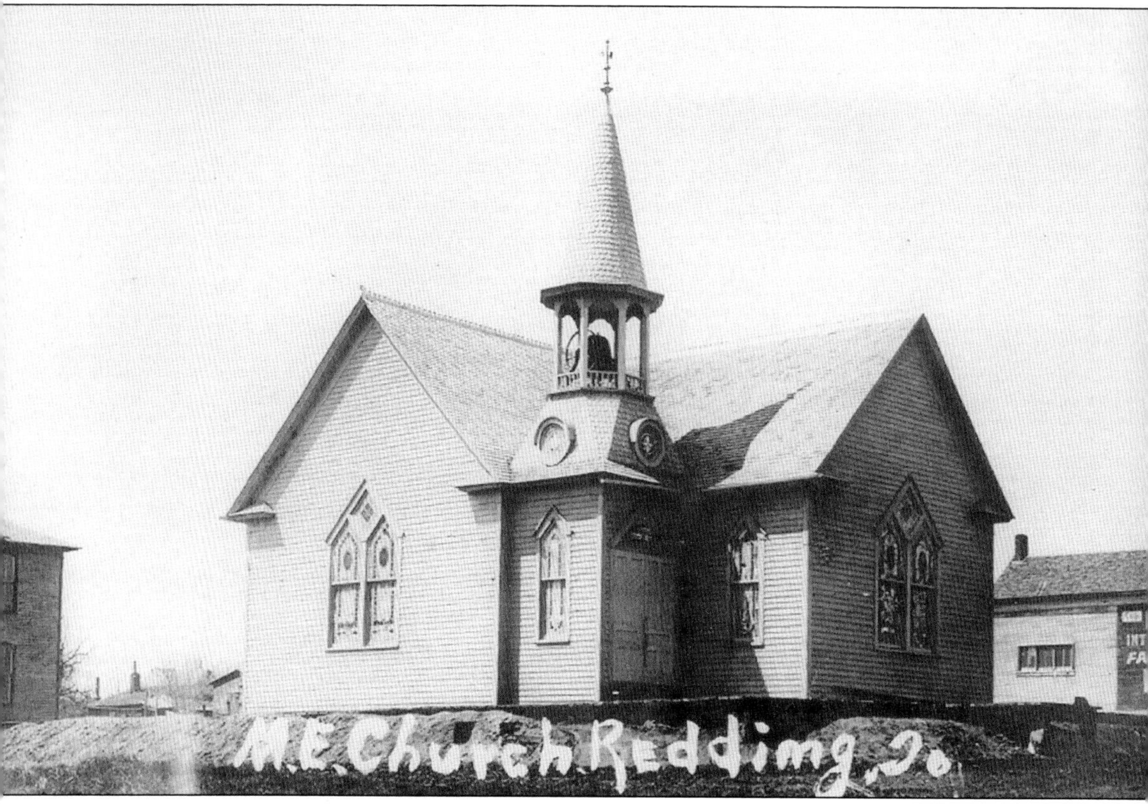

The Redding Methodist Episcopal Church was built in 1884 with a Reverend Johnson leading the way. Prior to the construction of the church, services were held in many locations, including rural schools. The church was rededicated on Christmas Eve in 1905 after a major remodeling. Another remodel in 1965 resulted in indoor toilets being installed in the basement. Today, the structure is the Redding United Methodist Church and is the oldest active church building in the county. (Courtesy of Mount Ayr Depot Museum.)

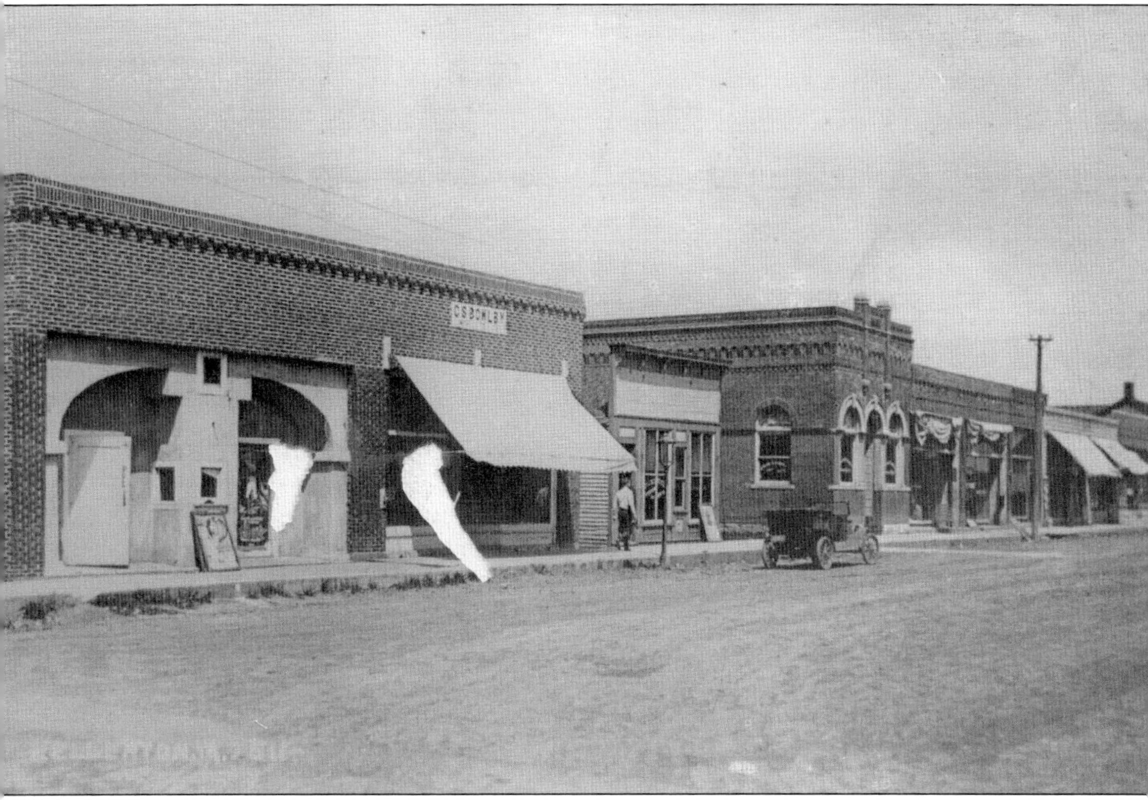

Pictured is the west side of Decatur Street in Kellerton. The near left building in the first structure, formerly the Avon Theater, was renamed the Tivoli Theater in the fall of 1946. Lillian Leuty purchased the theater and renamed it the Star Theater. A fire erupted in the projection room on September 9, 1950. The business reopened in May 1952 under the name Kellerton Theater. The second space in the left structure, with the "C.S. Bowlsby" sign, was the Jones Medicine Chest during the 1930s and later a feed store. The second structure from the left is currently a café. The Bank Building (arched windows) is now a residence. Hotel McDonald is to the far right, now the site of the Kellerton Post Office. (Courtesy of Mount Ayr Depot Museum.)

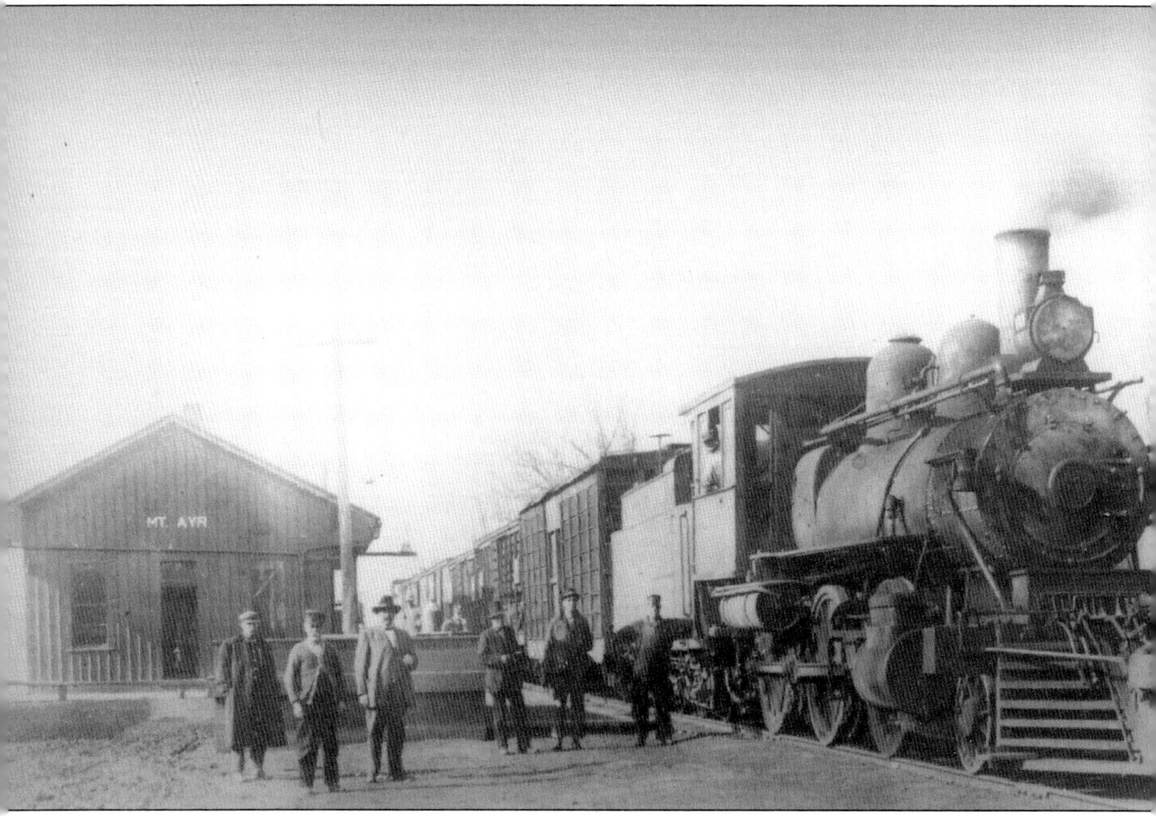

The Mount Ayr Depot was built in 1879, when the Leon, Mount Ayr, and Southwestern Railroad Company arrived. The CB&Q Railroad operated the line as the lessee. After being added to at least once, the depot underwent major reconstruction in 1916. Electricity, running water, and steam heat were added, as well as tile floors and a ladies' waiting room. A 20-foot addition was built on the east end, and the lobby was moved from the east end to the west end. A stucco finish was applied to the exterior, and paved walkways were added. The depot closed in 1968, but it became the Mount Ayr Depot Museum in 2000. This photograph is dated 1906. (Courtesy of Mount Ayr Depot Museum.)

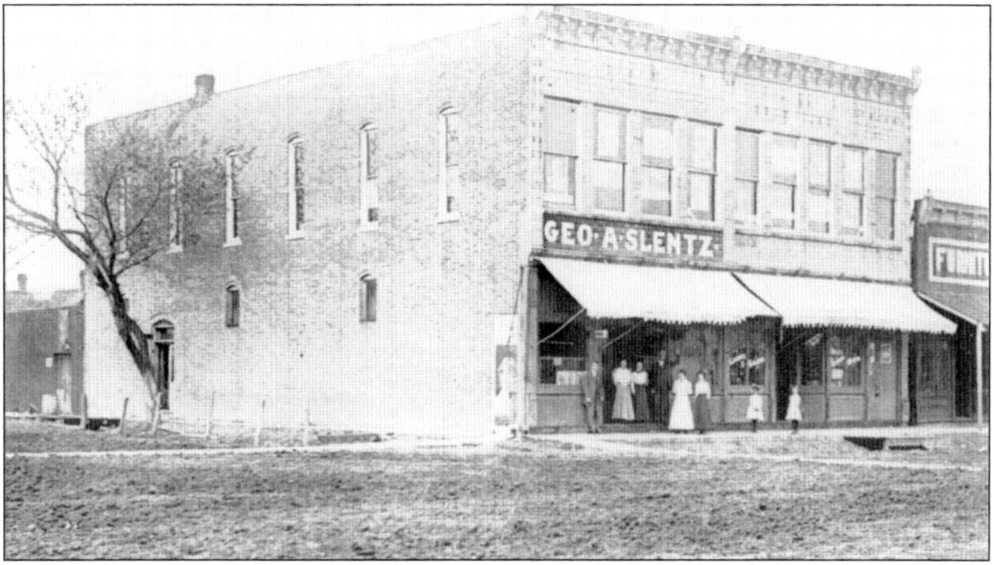

The streets were still mud, but George Slentz's store (pictured) is open for business on Tingley's Main Street. George's store was on the ground floor, with the Tingley Opera House on the second floor, where plays, basketball games, and other functions were held. Slentz had a store in Tingley for 18 years and was a model citizen and merchant. He was superintendent of the Mount Ayr United Presbyterian Church Sabbath School for 40 years. (Courtesy of Mount Ayr Depot Museum.)

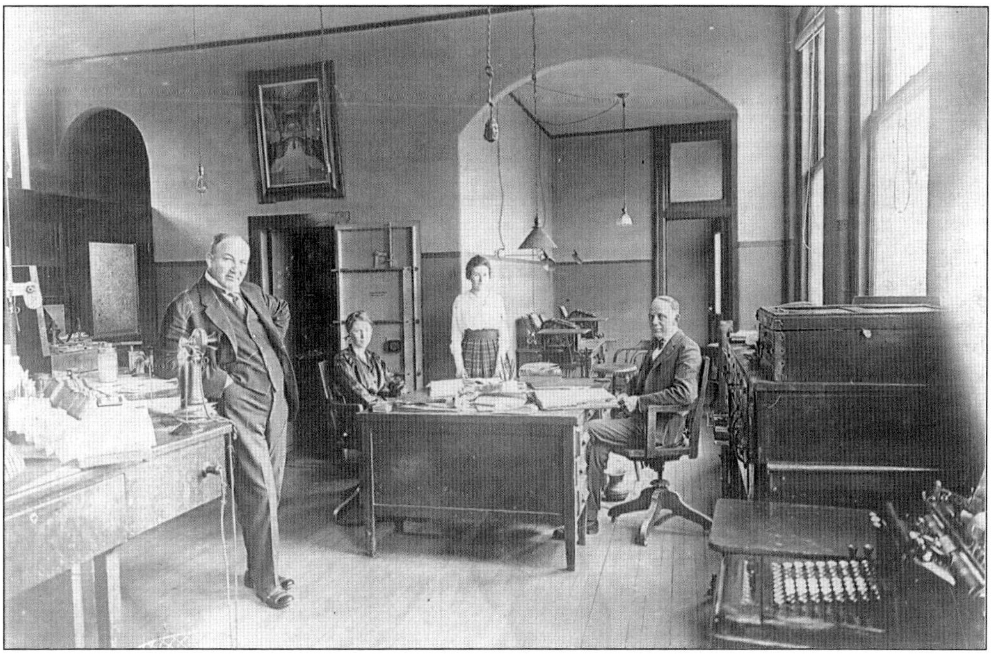
The Mount Ayr Bank building was erected in 1912. By the time this photograph was taken in the mid-1920s, the bank had reorganized as the Mount Ayr State Bank. In this photograph are, from left to right, Frank Sheldon, Zella Campbell, Bernice Moore, and Clare Allyn. Sheldon joined the bank in 1893 and became president in 1915. He was a politician and developer of Sheldon Heights, which became the location of Ringgold County's first hospital in 1951. (Courtesy of Mount Ayr Depot Museum.)

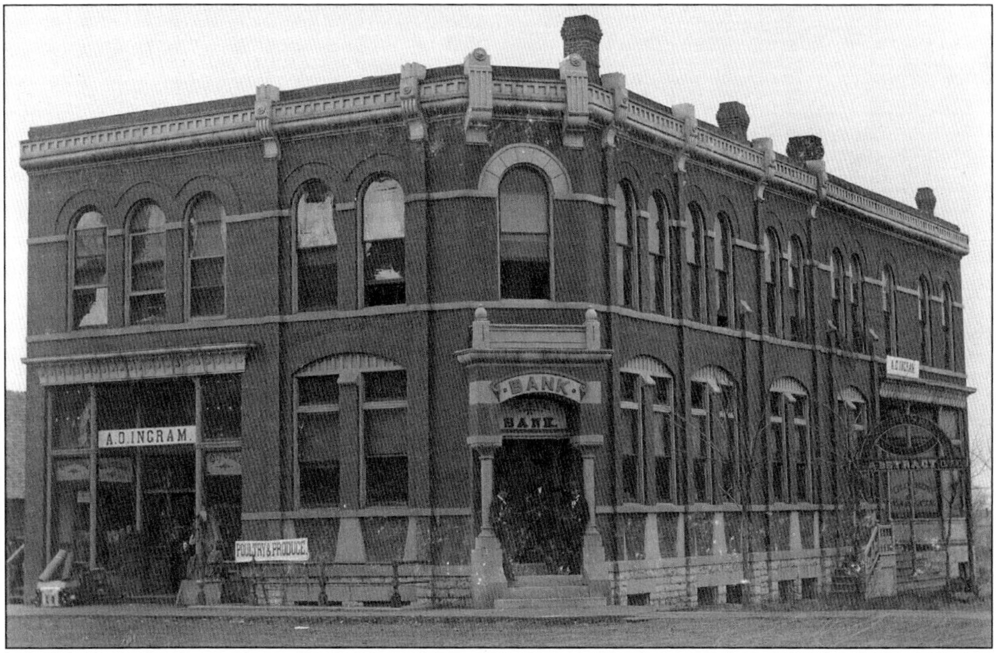

The Mount Ayr Bank, as seen here in 1895 on the southwest corner of the square, was owned by brothers George and John Allyn. A.O. Ingram, son of a Scottish immigrant, had possession of the dry goods store on the left. Judge R.C. Henry and future Ringgold County attorney Robert Spence had offices above the bank. A fire on November 14, 1900, destroyed this building and Lester's Shoe Shop to the east. There were no fatalities, and all except Ingram relocated and stayed in business. The Mount Ayr Public Library is located on this lot now. (Courtesy of Mount Ayr Depot Museum.)

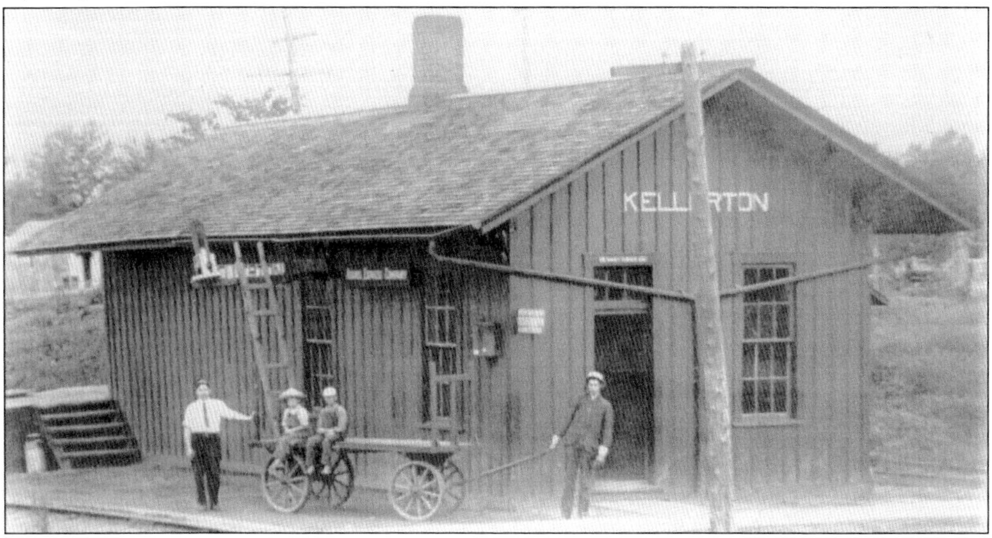

Kellerton was established with the arrival of the Leon, Mount Ayr and Southwestern Railroad late in 1879. It was the first town in Ringgold County that was platted by a railroad company. The depot was destroyed by a fire in 1934. The CB&Q Railroad replaced it with a coach car that was initially intended to serve only as a temporary depot. It remained in service until the railroad discontinued the operator position in 1954. (Courtesy of Mount Ayr Depot Museum.)

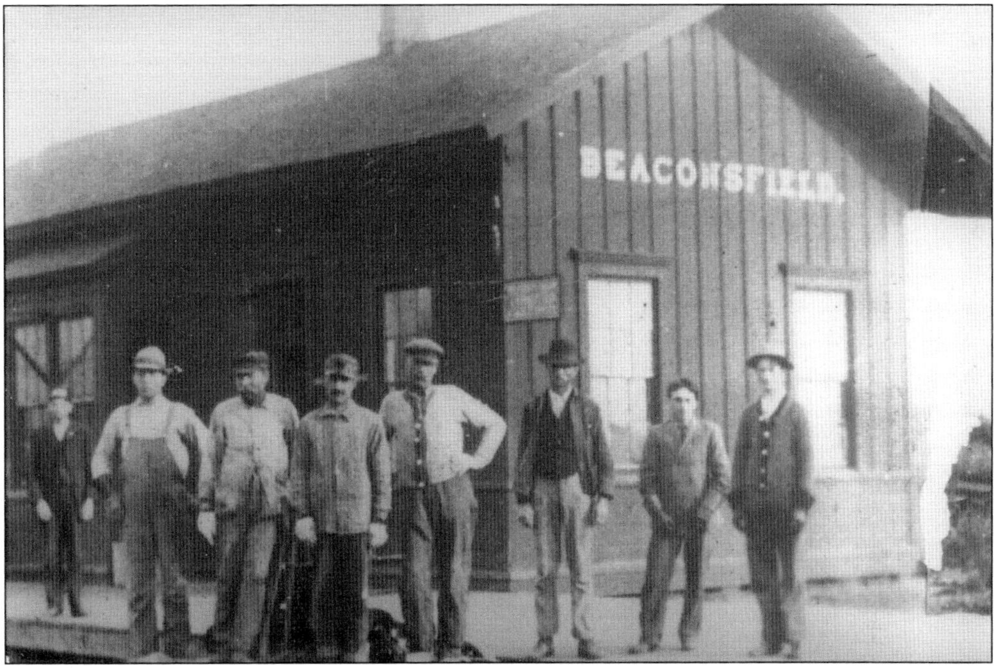

Surveyed in 1881, the Humeston & Shenandoah (H&S) branch of the Keokuk & Western (K&W) Railroad arrived in Beaconsfield in 1882. The H&S was later bought by the CB&Q. Although Beaconsfield never gained much in population, it produced high-quality people. The railroad abandoned the line on December 30, 1945. (Courtesy of Mount Ayr Depot Museum.)

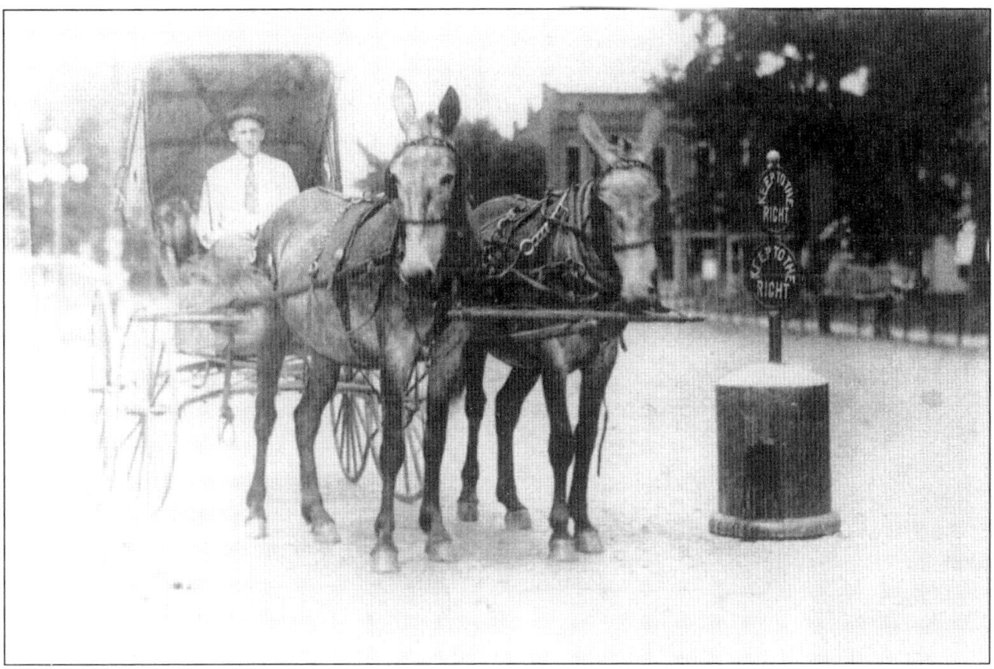

In June 1916, Mount Ayr traffic policeman Bird Gilliland had William Dowling make four "Keep to the Right" signs for placement around the square. (Courtesy of Mount Ayr Depot Museum.)

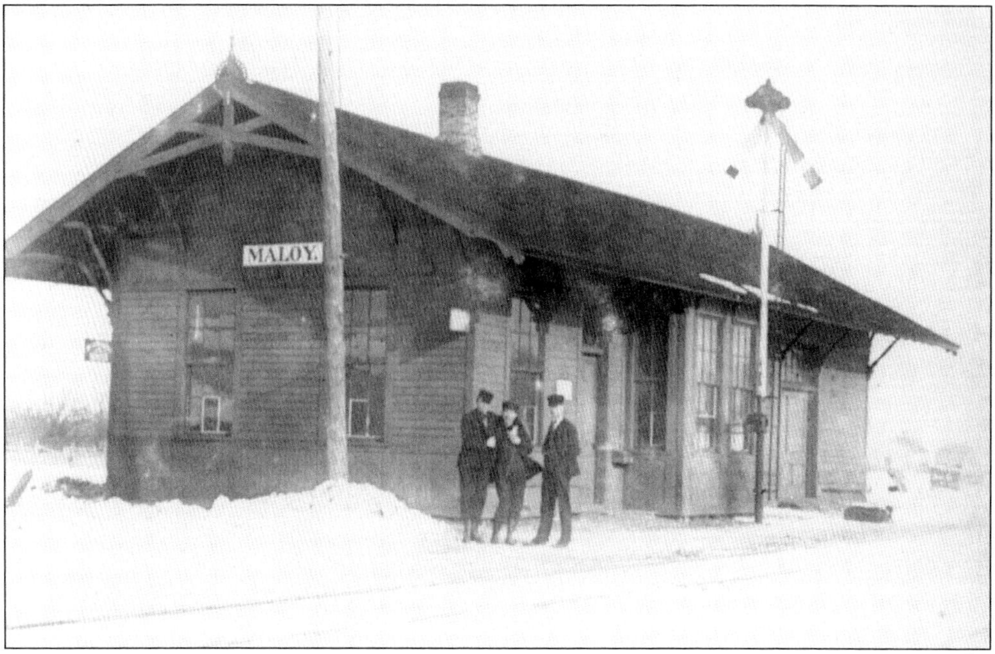

Maloy was named after David Maloy, a local farmer, and the town was still quite young when the Chicago, St. Paul, and Kansas City (CStP&KC) Railroad brought the trains in early in 1888. Being on a mainline railroad brought rapid growth to the little community. The CStP&KC became the Chicago Great Western Railroad in 1892. (Courtesy of Mount Ayr Depot Museum.)

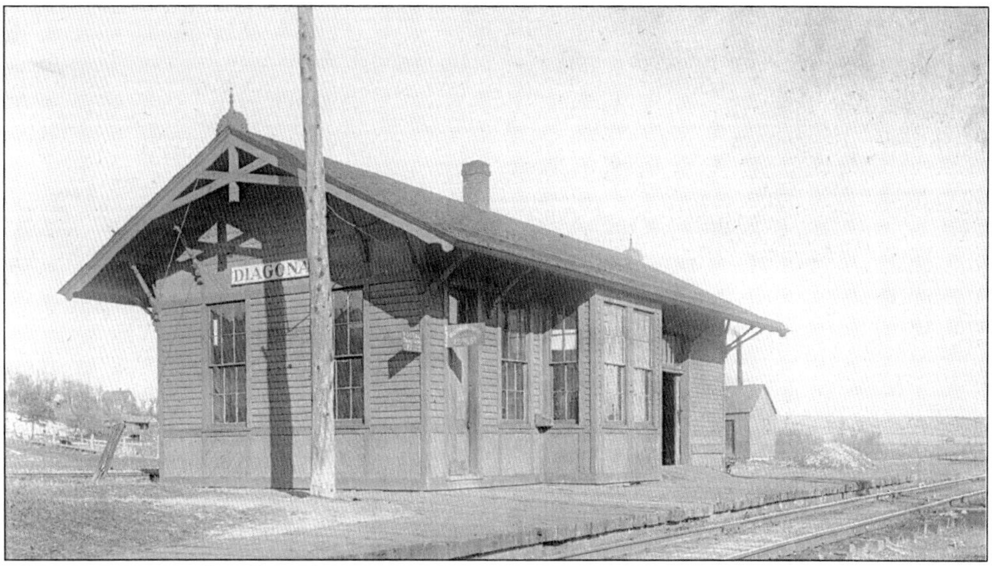

The CStP&KC Railroad put down its track as far as Knowlton in the fall of 1887. The line was completed to St. Joseph, Missouri, by May 1888, but full service did not begin until August 1888. In 1892, the CStP&KC was reorganized under the name Chicago Great Western Railroad Company (CGW). The depot pictured is a CGW Depot built north of the Burlington viaduct. In 1911, the depot was moved south of the viaduct, and in 1913 a second waiting room was added. The depot burned on the morning of March 18, 1939, and was replaced by a smaller depot in 1940. (Courtesy of Diagonal Printing Museum.)

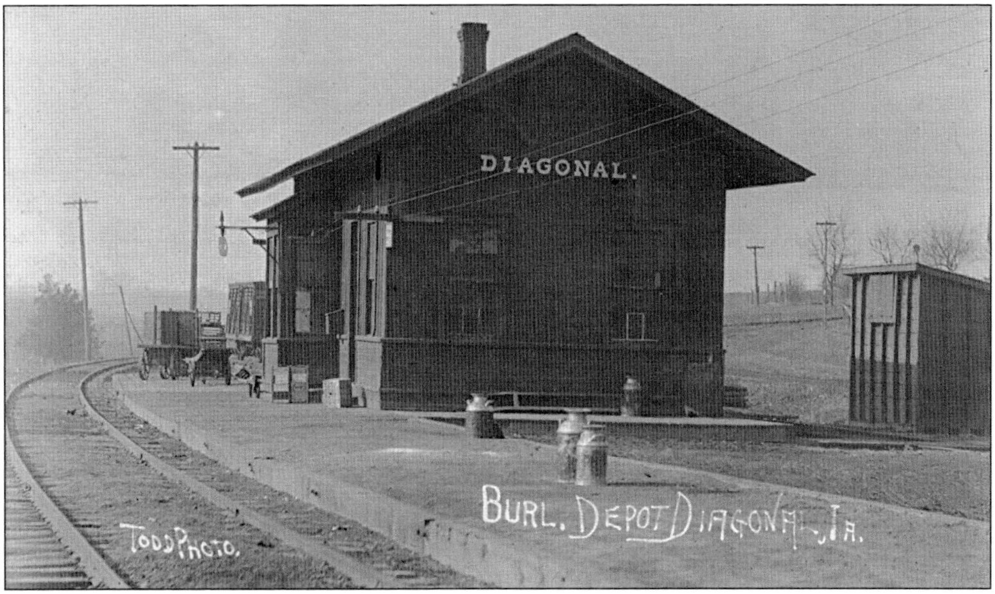

The K&W Depot at Goshen was moved to Diagonal in 1889. The entire town of Goshen moved a mile east so as to be at the only railroad crossing in Ringgold County; the new town of Diagonal was formed from this effort. By the time this c. 1915 photograph was taken, the CB&Q had purchased the line. The CB&Q discontinued service in 1945. (Courtesy of Diagonal Printing Museum.)

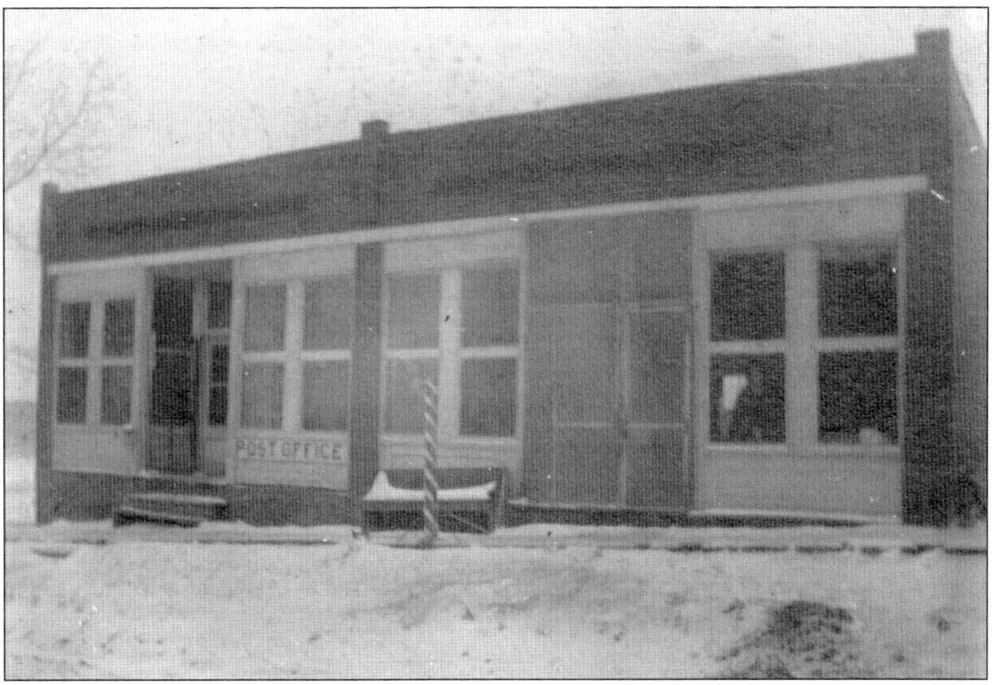

Pictured is Knowlton's post office and barbershop. The post office closed about 1920, and Knowlton forfeited its incorporation in 1926. After years of declining population and the transfer of businesses to Diagonal, Knowlton's high school was discontinued in the 1920s. (Courtesy of Diagonal Printing Museum.)

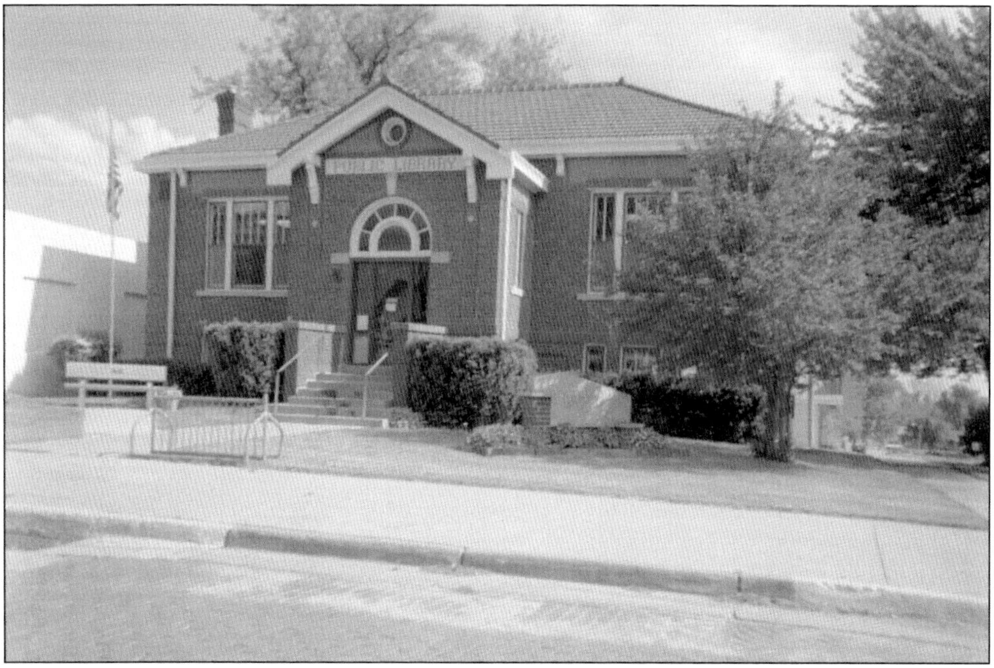

Carnegie libraries were established throughout the country during the early 1900s. Mount Ayr's Carnegie library opened November 15, 1916, and was dedicated on January 3, 1917. The library, located on the southwest corner of the square, features a comprehensive genealogical library. (Courtesy of Sharon R. Becker.)

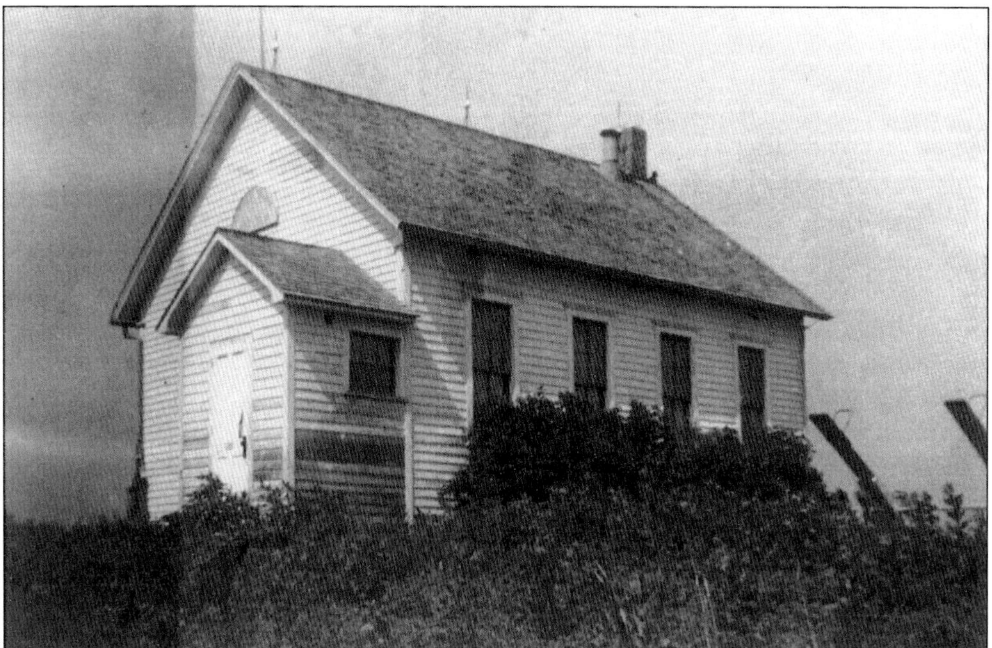

Fairview School was located about two miles southwest of Redding. This photograph was most likely taken in the 1940s or later. Notice the presence of lightning rods, rain gutters, and teeter-totters. The school is still standing. (Courtesy of Mount Ayr Depot Museum.)

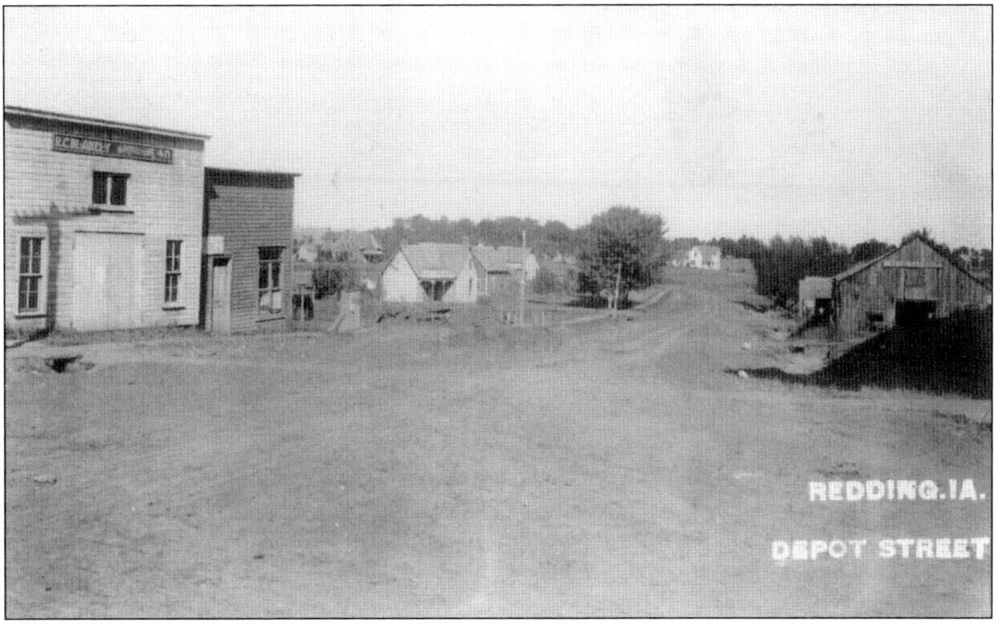

This view looks north from the northwest corner of the Redding town square toward the depot. The blacksmith shop is on the immediate left. The shadow on the right is being cast by the Opera House. (Courtesy of Friends of Old Redding.)

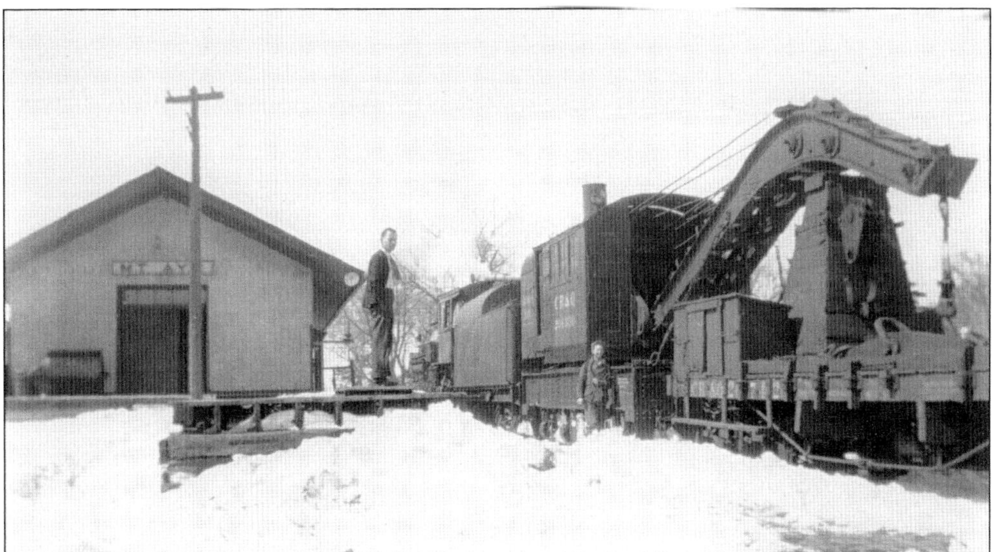

Harry Bisbey admires a derrick from the freight deck of the Mount Ayr Depot around 1931. Bisbey was the express agent at the depot and also assisted the station agent. Derailments were common on the Burlington road, especially during the 1930s when weather conditions were at their most extreme for Ringgold County. This train was obviously in town on a derailment call. (Courtesy of Mount Ayr Depot Museum.)

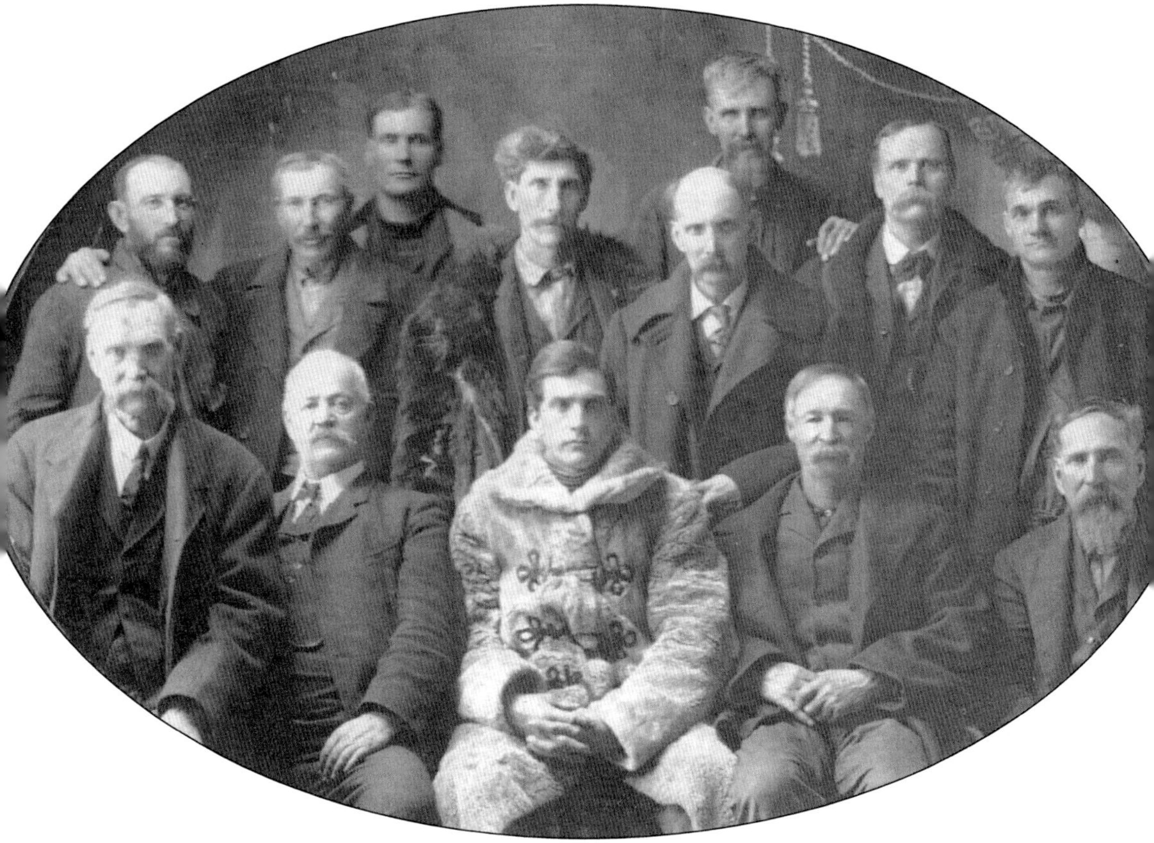

Men's fraternities such as IOOF and Masonic lodges were established in almost every Ringgold County town, along with Grand Army of the Republic posts for Civil War veterans. One such fraternity, believed to be the Odd Fellows, was established in Redding at the turn of the century. In this photograph are, from left to right, (first row) Sterling Goin, Dr. H.C. Bone, Berlie Goin, Allan Ramsey, and Isaac Goin; (second row) Jim Overholtzer, Tommie Goin, Bryan Goin, John Goin, William H. Young, and Jim Smith; (third row) Mr. Goin and Bill McIntosh. (Courtesy of Norma G. [Foland] Becker.)

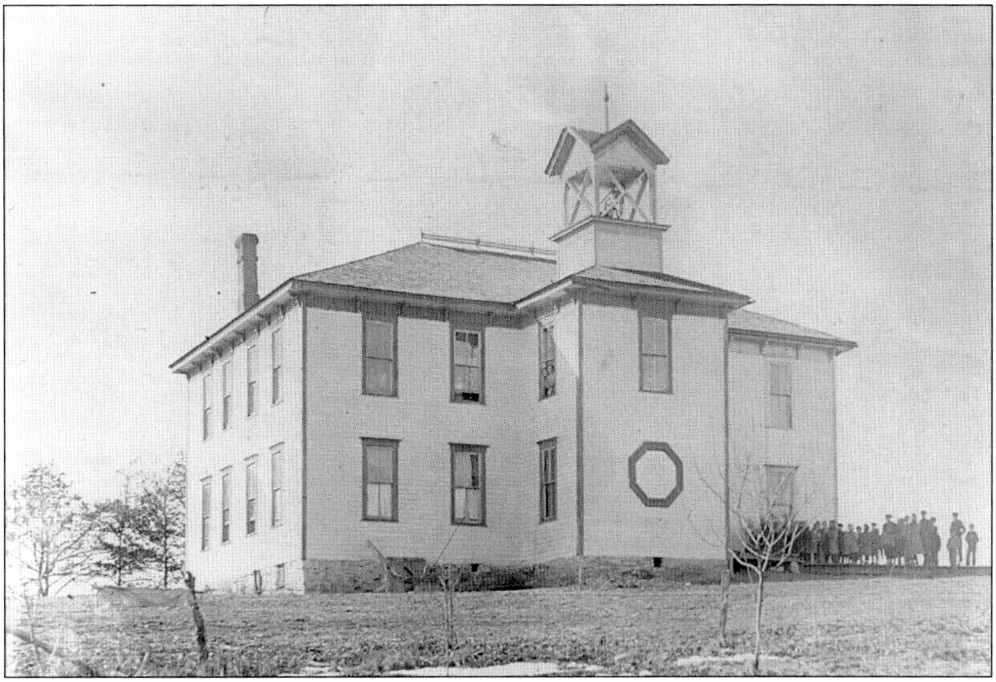

The Knowlton High School was built in 1894 and is believed to have had its first graduating class in 1900. The school became big enough to have both boys' and girls' basketball, but decreasing enrollment forced the school to close in the mid-1920s. (Diagonal Printing Museum.)

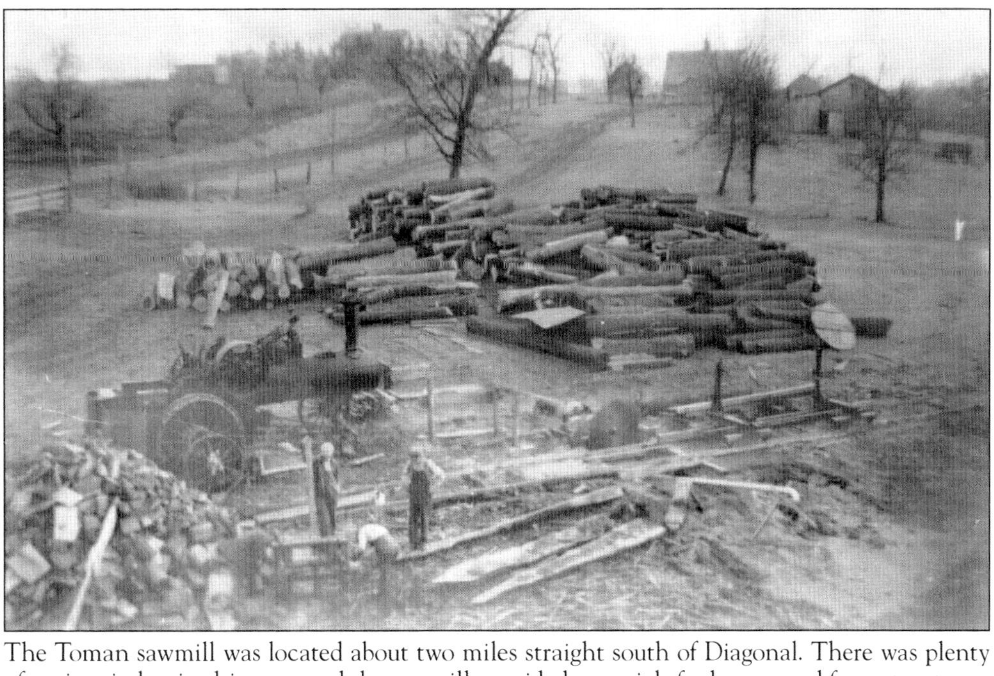

The Toman sawmill was located about two miles straight south of Diagonal. There was plenty of native timber in this area, and the sawmill provided materials for houses and farm structures. (Courtesy of Liz Wiley.)

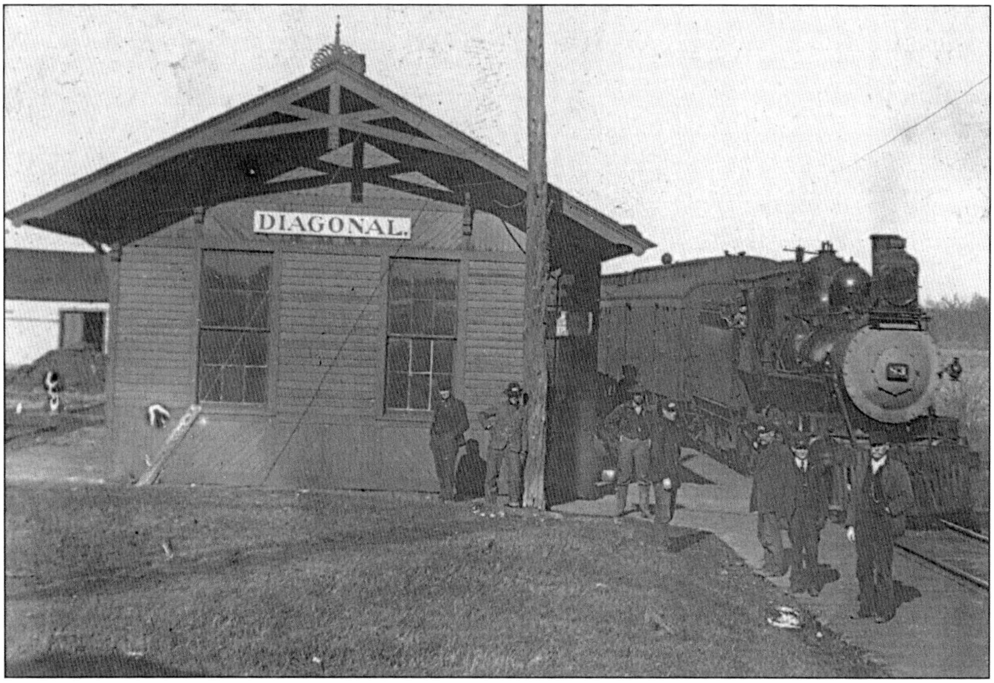

Engine No. 83 sits at the original Chicago Great Western Depot in Diagonal around 1908. This is probably southbound passenger train No. 5. This depot was the busiest station in Ringgold County. (Courtesy of Diagonal Printing Museum.)

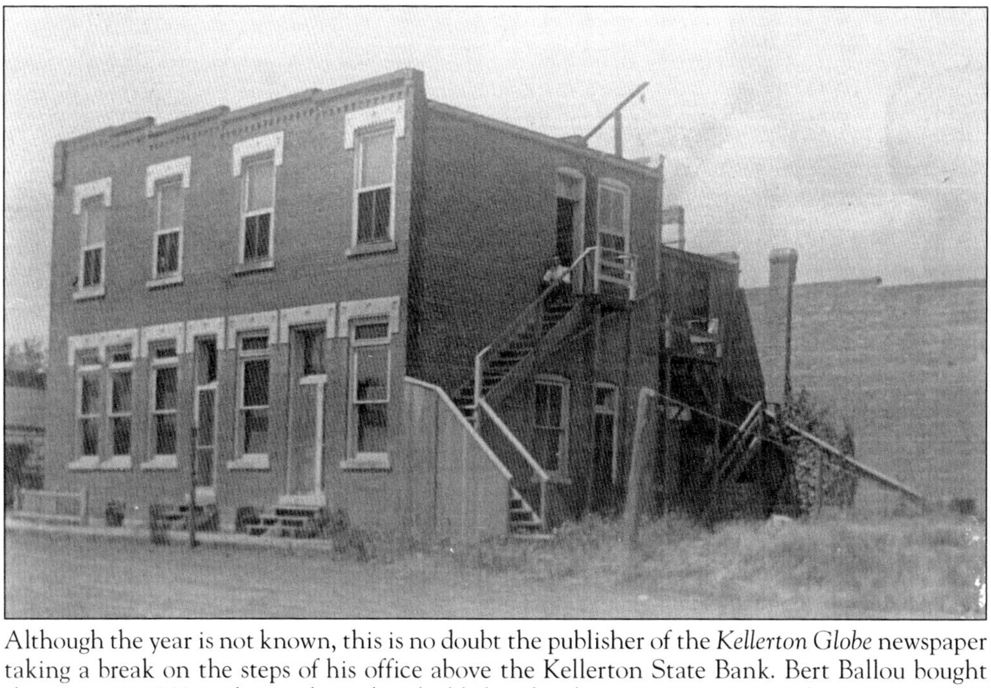

Although the year is not known, this is no doubt the publisher of the *Kellerton Globe* newspaper taking a break on the steps of his office above the Kellerton State Bank. Bert Ballou bought the paper in 1909 and served as editor/publisher for the next 50 years, so this is most likely Ballou. This structure still stands today and has been restored as an apartment building. (Courtesy of Rollie Jackson.)

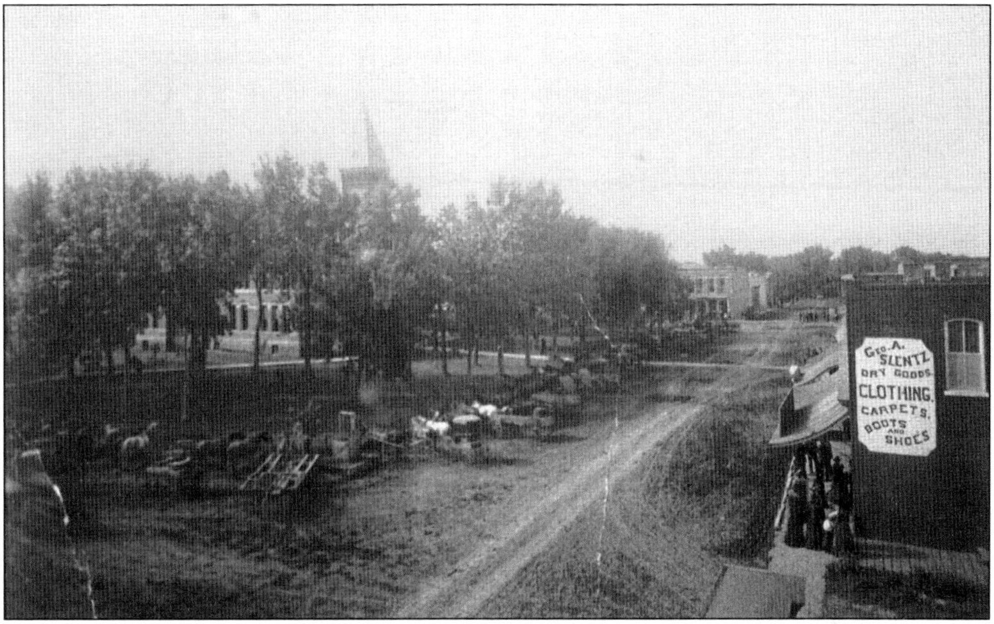

This view is of the east side of the Mount Ayr square, looking north, around 1890. At the time, the streets were not paved, and wooden planks served as sidewalks. The wells situated at the corners of the square were for both watering horses and for business use. On the immediate right is the dry goods store of George Slentz. The 102-foot-tall tower of the Ringgold County Courthouse can be seen above the treetops. (Courtesy of Mount Ayr Depot Museum.)

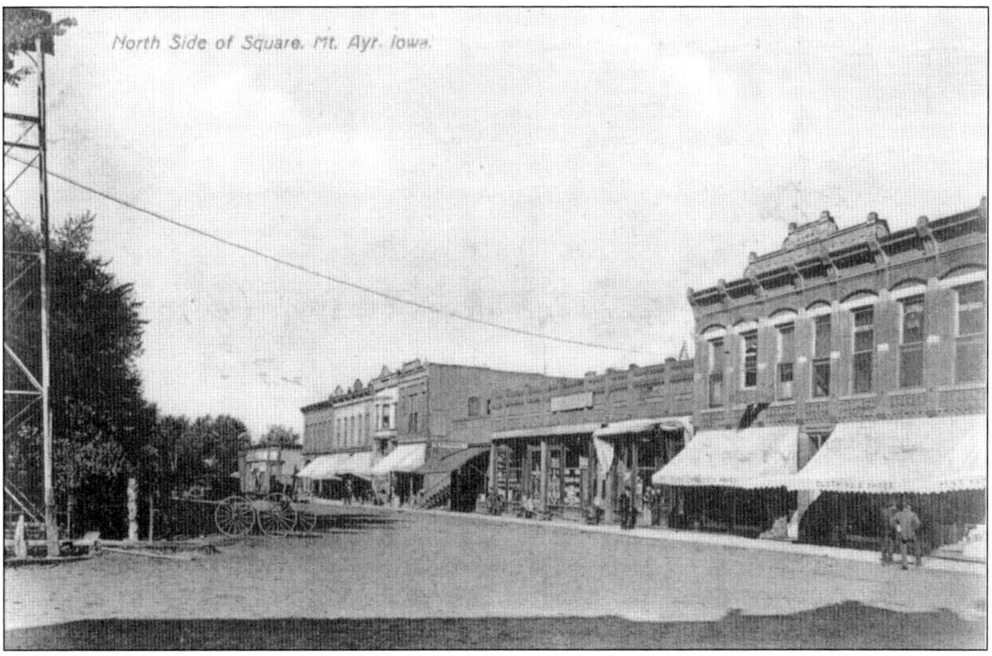

This postcard was postmarked in 1910 and depicts the north side of the Mount Ayr square. The Timby building (right) was home to M.E. Freeland's dry goods store. The upstairs held the law office of Lewis & Lewis as well as a dentist office. The bell tower to the left was used as a curfew warning and fire alarm. (Mount Ayr Depot Museum.)

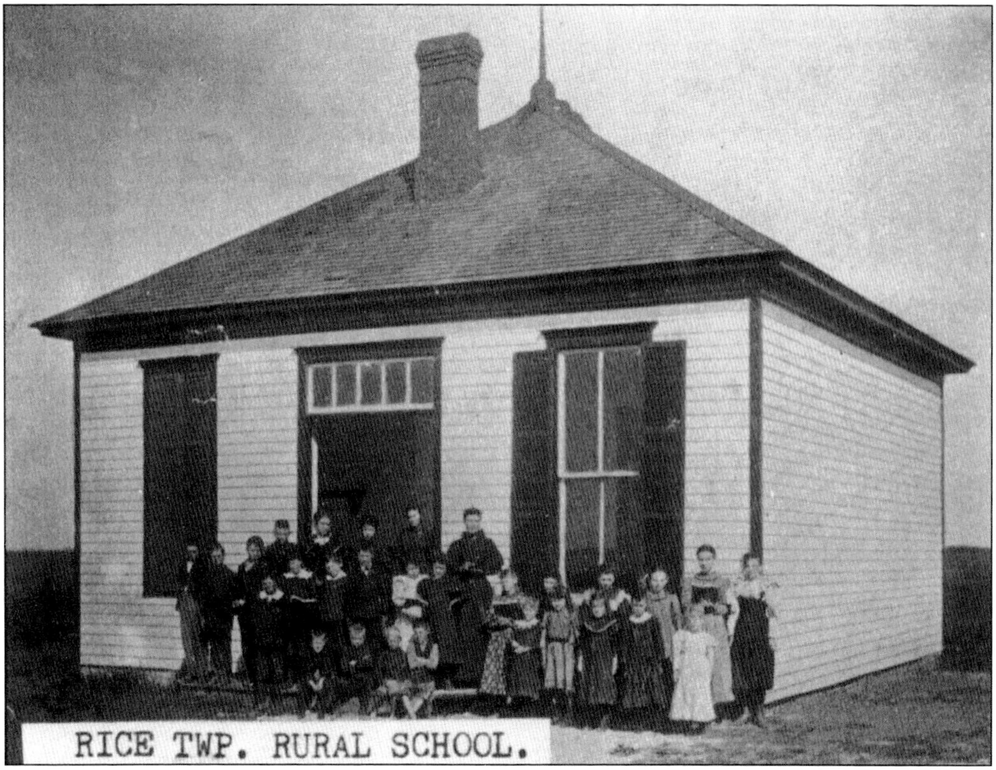

Eureka School, Rice No. 8, was located two and a half miles southeast of Delphos and was built in 1895 at a cost of $500. It was 26 feet by 27 feet and had a seating capacity of 40. This school was built with an experimental design that placed the windows on the north side to prevent direct sunlight from entering the classroom; the design was later abandoned. The building is still very new in this 1896 photograph. (Courtesy of Mount Ayr Depot Museum.)

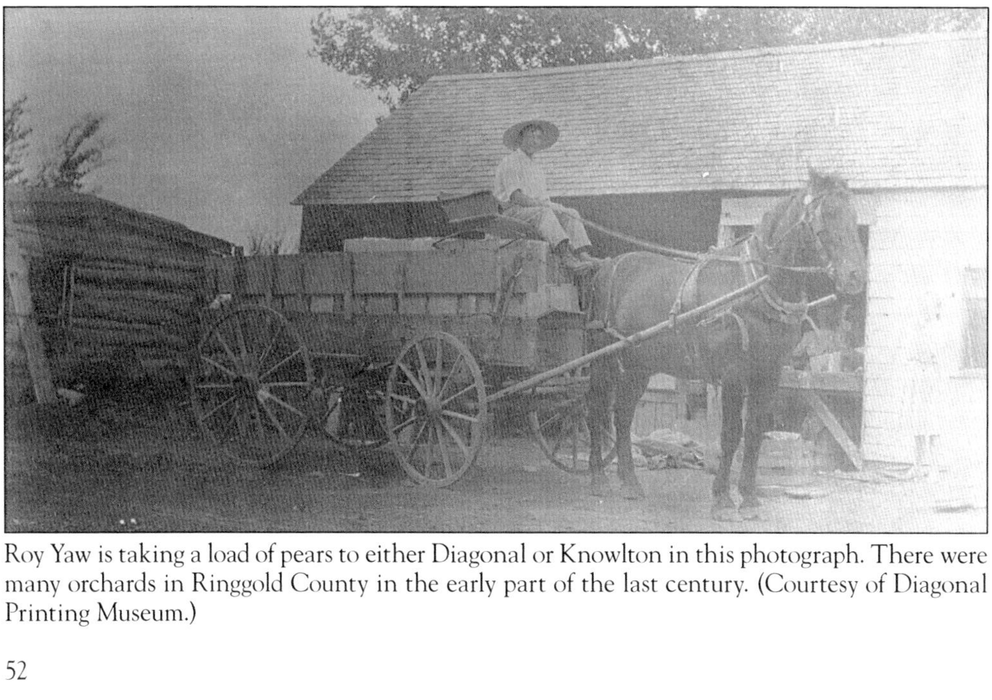

Roy Yaw is taking a load of pears to either Diagonal or Knowlton in this photograph. There were many orchards in Ringgold County in the early part of the last century. (Courtesy of Diagonal Printing Museum.)

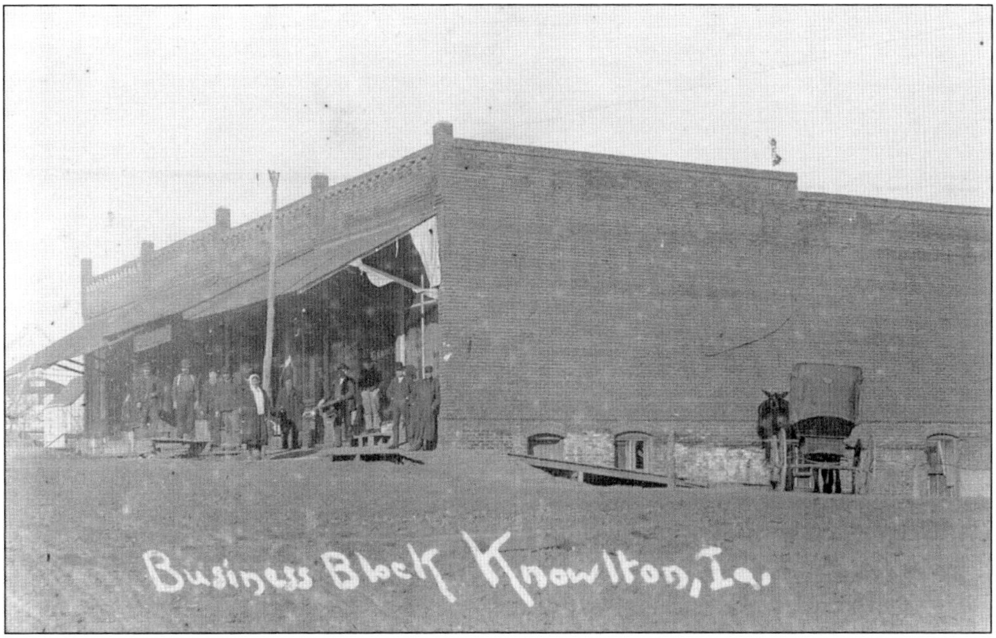

This photograph of Knowlton's business block was taken around 1910. The Yaryan store is nearest the corner. Knowlton was once a coaling station on the Chicago Great Western Railroad, but all that is left is the street in the picture. It is currently County Road J23. (Courtesy of Diagonal Printing Museum.)

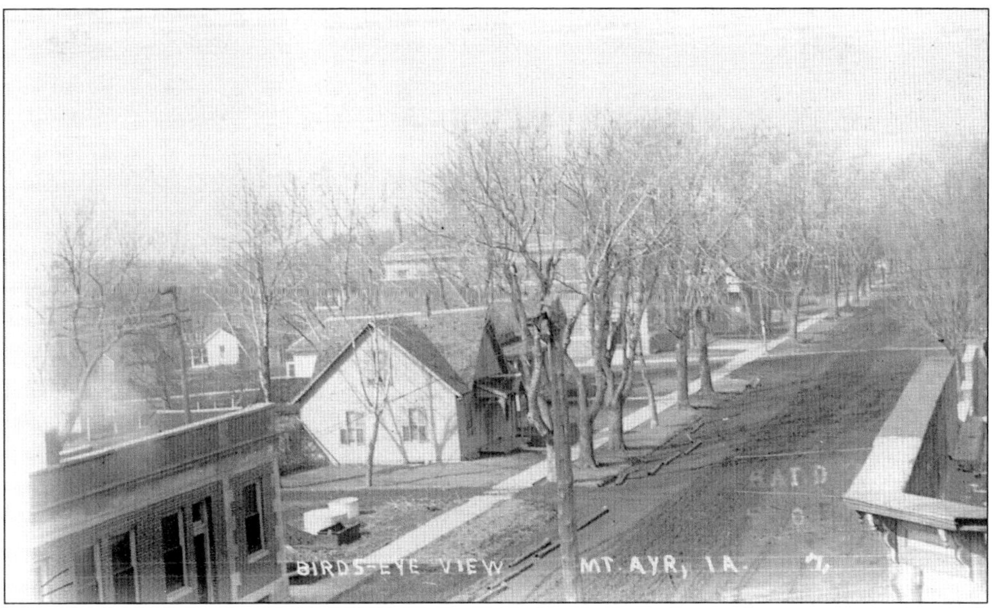

In this c. 1915 photograph is West Madison Street in Mount Ayr. Sewer pipe is about to be buried prior to the paving of Madison Street in 1916. The building to the near left is the Mount Ayr Bank; the house behind it is still standing. The building to the near right is the Z.T. Kinsell Hardware Store. The new Mount Ayr Methodist Episcopal Church can barely be seen through the trees in the center. (Courtesy of Mount Ayr Depot Museum.)

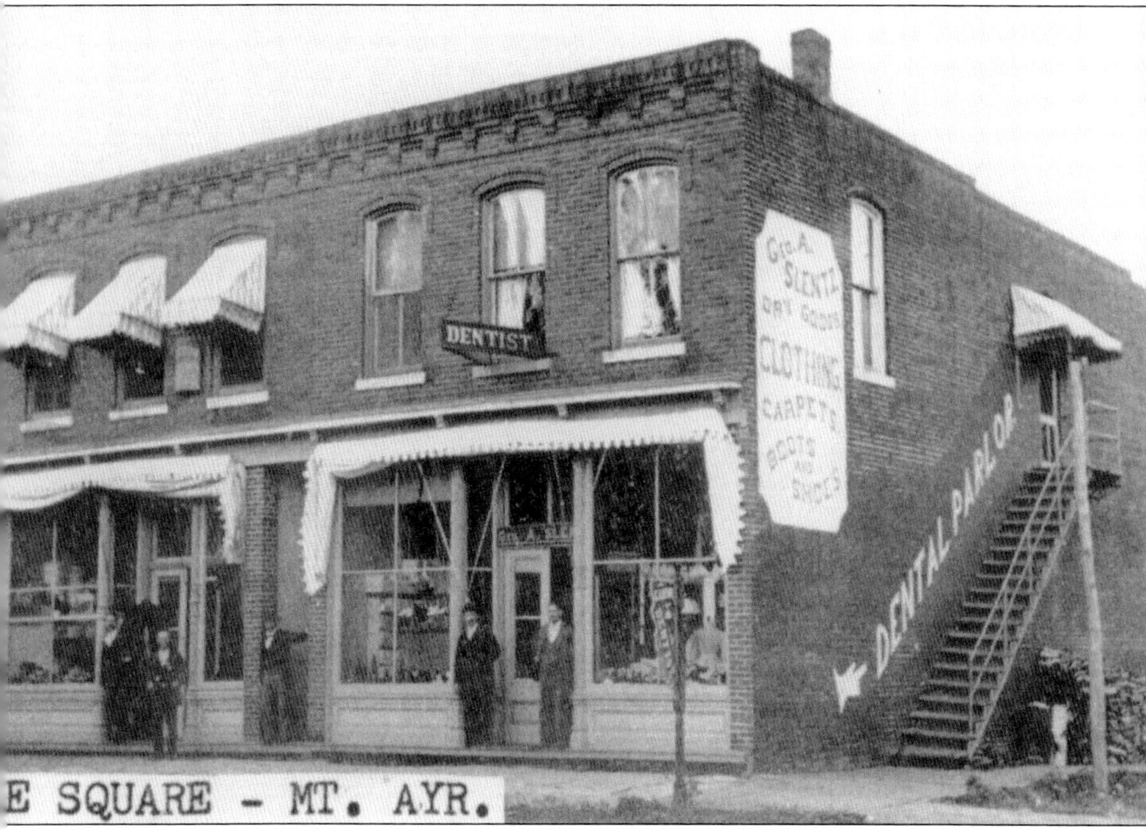

As Mount Ayr grew, business blocks like this one on the southeast corner of the Mount Ayr square sprang up. George A. Slentz occupied the building with his dry goods store seen here in 1895. Slentz came to Mount Ayr in 1878 as a teacher and principal of Mount Ayr Schools. By 1882, he had bought into the dry goods business and eventually had stores in Mount Ayr, Tingley, and Lesanville. (Courtesy of Mount Ayr Depot Museum.)

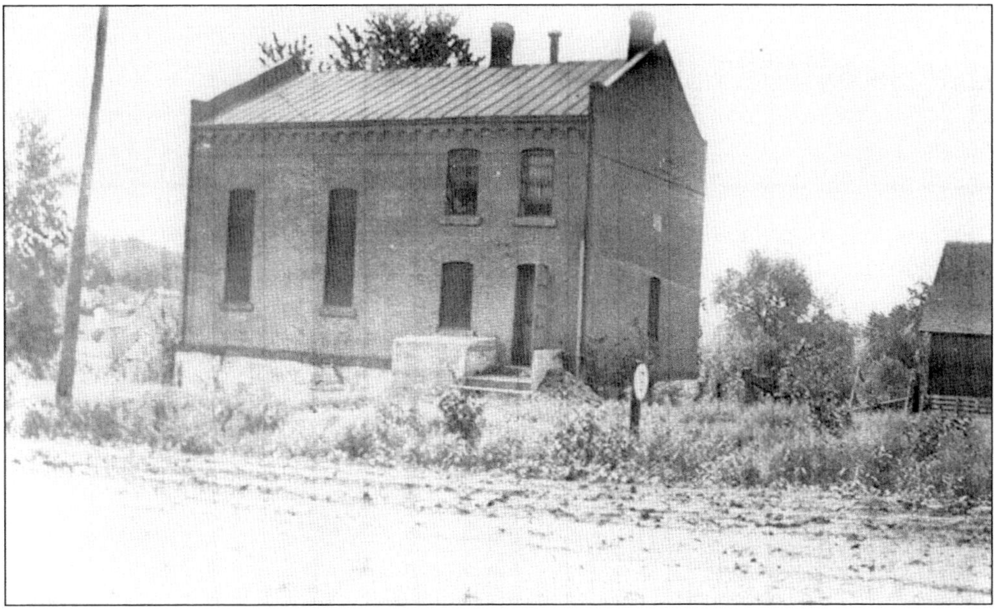

The Ringgold County Jail was built in 1895 of brick and stone at a cost of $4,113. It was 38 feet by 27 feet and served the county until 1927, when a new jail was built in the Ringgold County Courthouse. American Legion Post 172 bought the old jail for $1 on October 18, 1928. Today, the old jail serves as the Pedersen Law Office (below). The building was placed in the National Register of Historic Places in 1979. (Above, courtesy of Mount Ayr Depot Museum; below, Sharon R. Becker.)

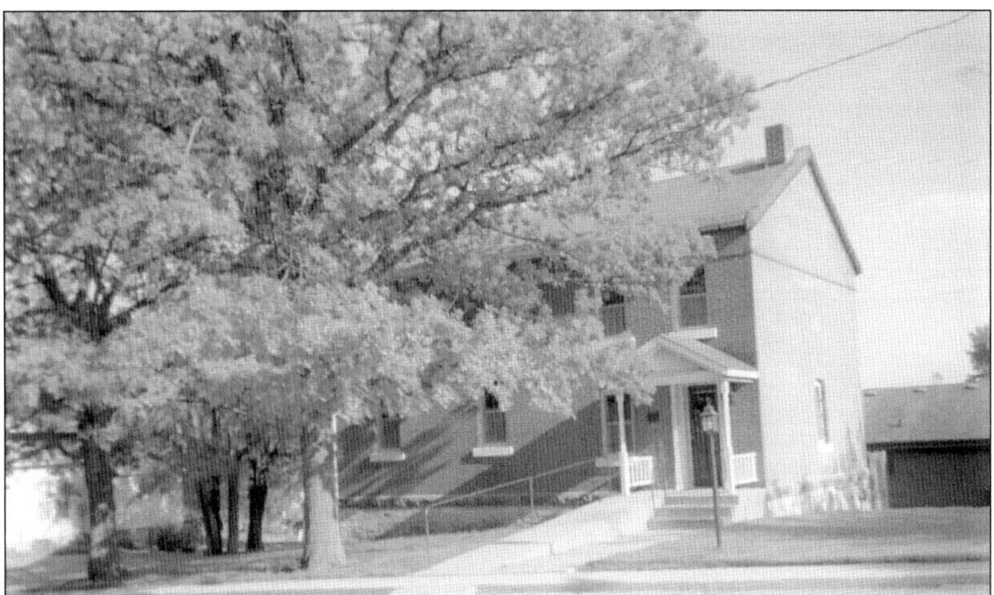

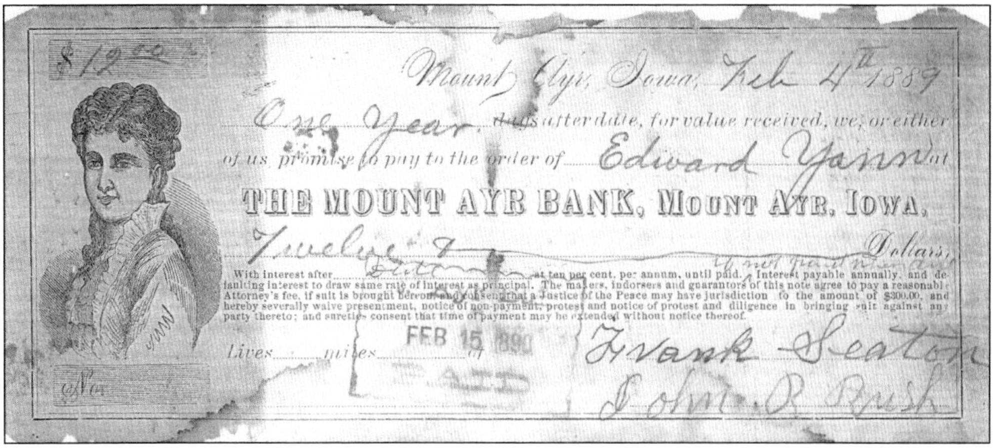

$12.00

Mount Ayr, Iowa, Feb 4th 1889

One Year days after date, for value received, we, or either of us promise to pay to the order of Edward Yann at

THE MOUNT AYR BANK, MOUNT AYR, IOWA,

Twelve & — Dollars,

With interest after date at ten per cent. per annum, until paid. Interest payable annually, and defaulting interest to draw same rate of interest as principal. The makers, indorsers and guarantors of this note agree to pay a reasonable Attorney's fee, if suit is brought thereon, and consent that a Justice of the Peace may have jurisdiction to the amount of $300.00, and hereby severally waive presentment, notice of non-payment, protest and notice of protest and diligence in bringing suit against any party thereto; and sureties consent that time of payment may be extended without notice thereof.

Lives ...... miles ...... of

FEB 15 1890

PAID

Frank Seaton

John R Rush

No.

This is an early promissory note issued by the Mount Ayr Bank, which was organized in 1880 by C.B. Morris and George Allyn. In 1885, Morris sold his interest to George's brother John Allyn. Frank Seaton came to Ringgold County from Pennsylvania about 1875 and settled in the southwest part of the county. (Courtesy of Delphos Museum.)

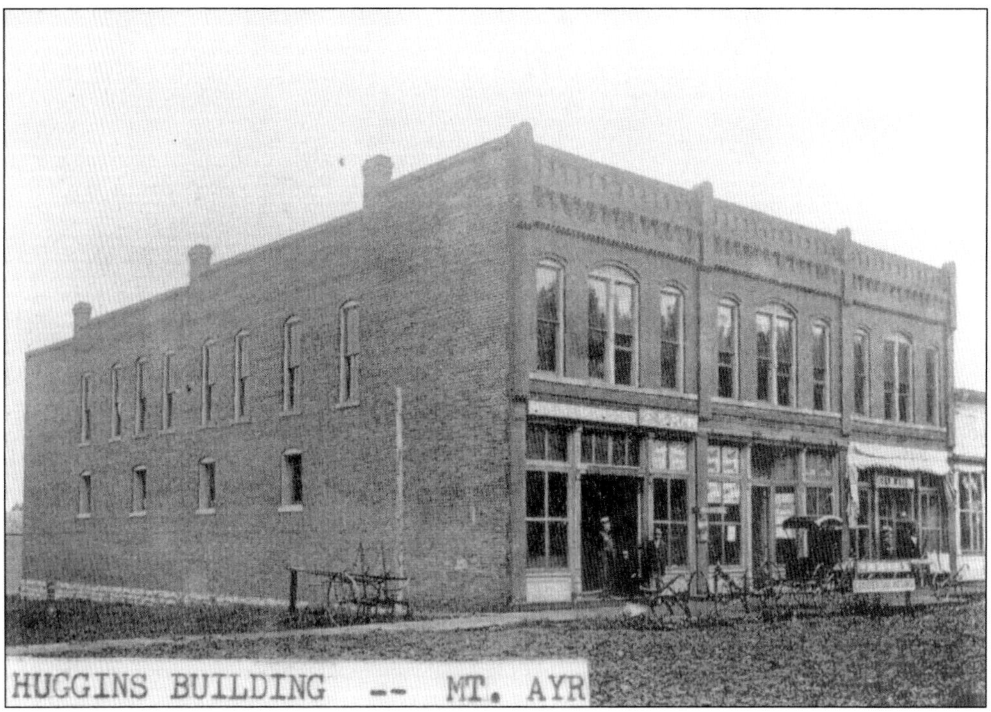

A.A. Huggins erected this building in 1892. It measures 66 feet by 100 feet, and it housed Huggins's farm-implement business. The building still stands and is located on the southwest corner of the Mount Ayr square. (Courtesy of Mount Ayr Depot Museum.)

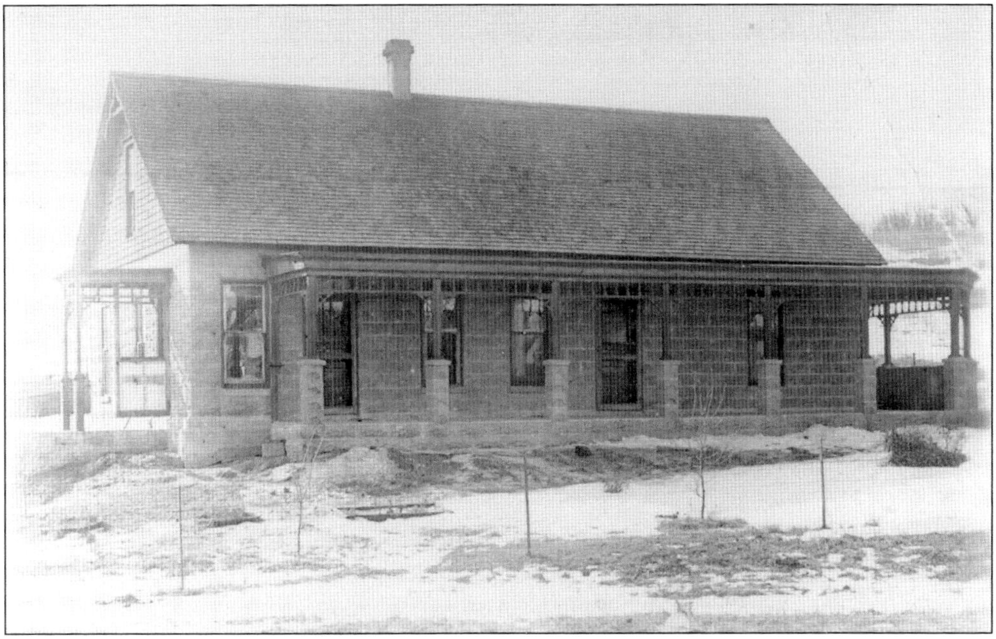

John Williams owned the foundry in Knowlton and had his home constructed of concrete blocks. Building material was probably the most important freight the railroads brought to the bustling county. (Courtesy of Diagonal Printing Museum.)

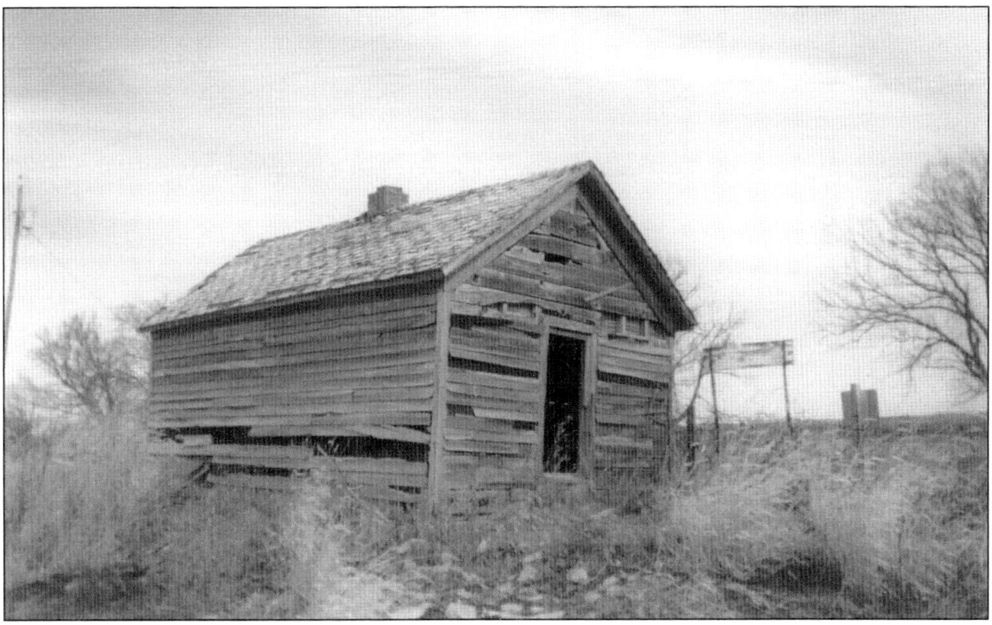

Dr. Allen Reynolds's office in the ghost town of Caledonia is pictured here in November 2006. This was the last building still standing in Caledonia before it was burned down in the spring of 2007. Reynolds is said to have retired in the 1930s, but electrical wiring, wool insulation, and metal roof edging, found in the ashes, suggests the building was used into the 1940s. Caledonia, like many Ringgold County towns, was bypassed by the railroads and perished. (Courtesy of Mike Avitt.)

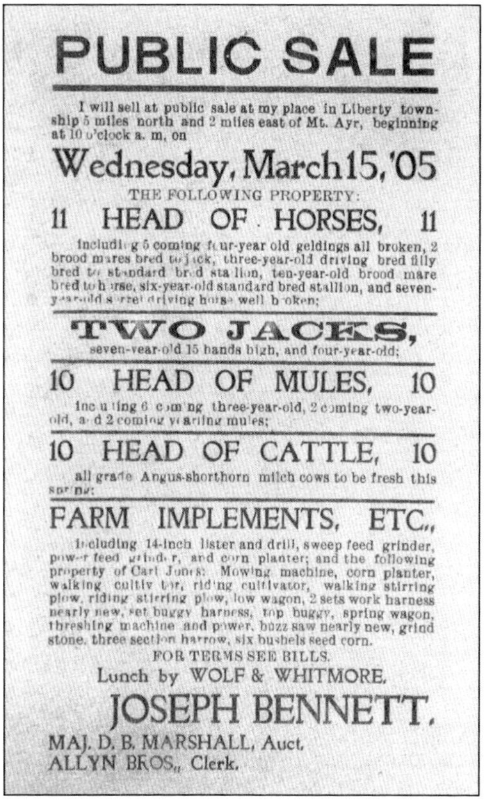

PUBLIC SALE

I will sell at public sale at my place in Liberty township 5 miles north and 2 miles east of Mt. Ayr, beginning at 10 o'clock a. m. on

Wednesday, March 15, '05

THE FOLLOWING PROPERTY:

11 HEAD OF HORSES, 11

including 5 coming four-year old geldings all broken, 2 brood mares bred to jack, three-year-old driving bred filly bred to standard bred stallion, ten-year-old brood mare bred to horse, six-year-old standard bred stallion, and seven-year-old sorrel driving horse well broken;

TWO JACKS,

seven-year-old 15 hands high, and four-year-old;

10 HEAD OF MULES, 10

including 6 coming three-year-old, 2 coming two-year-old, and 2 coming yearling mules;

10 HEAD OF CATTLE, 10

all grade Angus-shorthorn milch cows to be fresh this spring;

FARM IMPLEMENTS, ETC.,

including 14-inch lister and drill, sweep feed grinder, power feed grinder, and corn planter; and the following property of Carl Jones: Mowing machine, corn planter, walking cultivator, riding cultivator, walking stirring plow, riding stirring plow, low wagon, 2 sets work harness nearly new, set buggy harness, top buggy, spring wagon, threshing machine and power, buzz saw nearly new, grind stone, three section harrow, six bushels seed corn.

FOR TERMS SEE BILLS.

Lunch by WOLF & WHITMORE.

JOSEPH BENNETT.

MAJ. D. B. MARSHALL, Auct.
ALLYN BROS., Clerk.

Pictured is a sale bill from 1905 advertising a farm auction in Liberty Township. George and John Allyn were clerks for the sale. (Courtesy of Mount Ayr Depot Museum.)

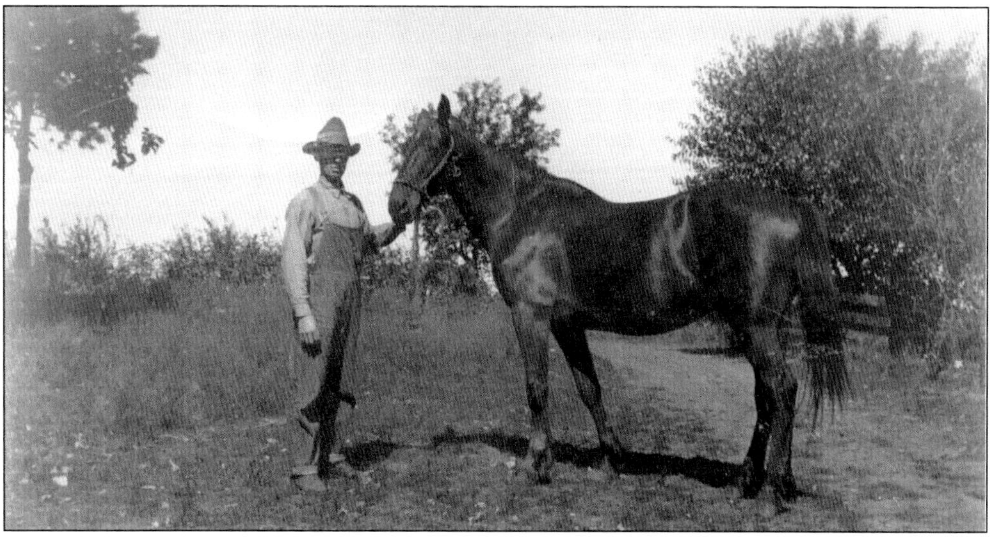

Ringgold County was well known for excellent draft and saddle horses. During the 1890s, several horse companies flourished throughout the county: the Liberty Township Horse Company, the Tingley Percheron Horse Association, the Mount Ayr Horse Company, and the Tingley Shire Horse Company. Tingley's annual Colt Show attracted quite a bit of interest and drew large crowds. Ringgold County attracted many horse buyers from Chicago, New York City, and other parts of the country. In this photograph is John Hanson of Tingley at age 58. (Courtesy of Dallas Riedesel.)

Three

Life in Ringgold County

As Ringgolders were engaged in worship, education, work, play, celebrations, policy making, and caretaking, many changes were taking place. The guardians of the county faced the difficulties of adverse weather conditions and unpredictable farm prices. There was war and disease, and there were fires. Still, the people persevered. Faithful and dedicated, they endured the periods of hardship and relished the simple pleasures of everyday life in the land they called home.

Advances in science, medicine, and technology came to the county, allowing the people to spend more time socializing and traveling. Historians recorded the county's history in print and image. The people loved their history and still do. They loved their town, church, school, or farm, and they still do.

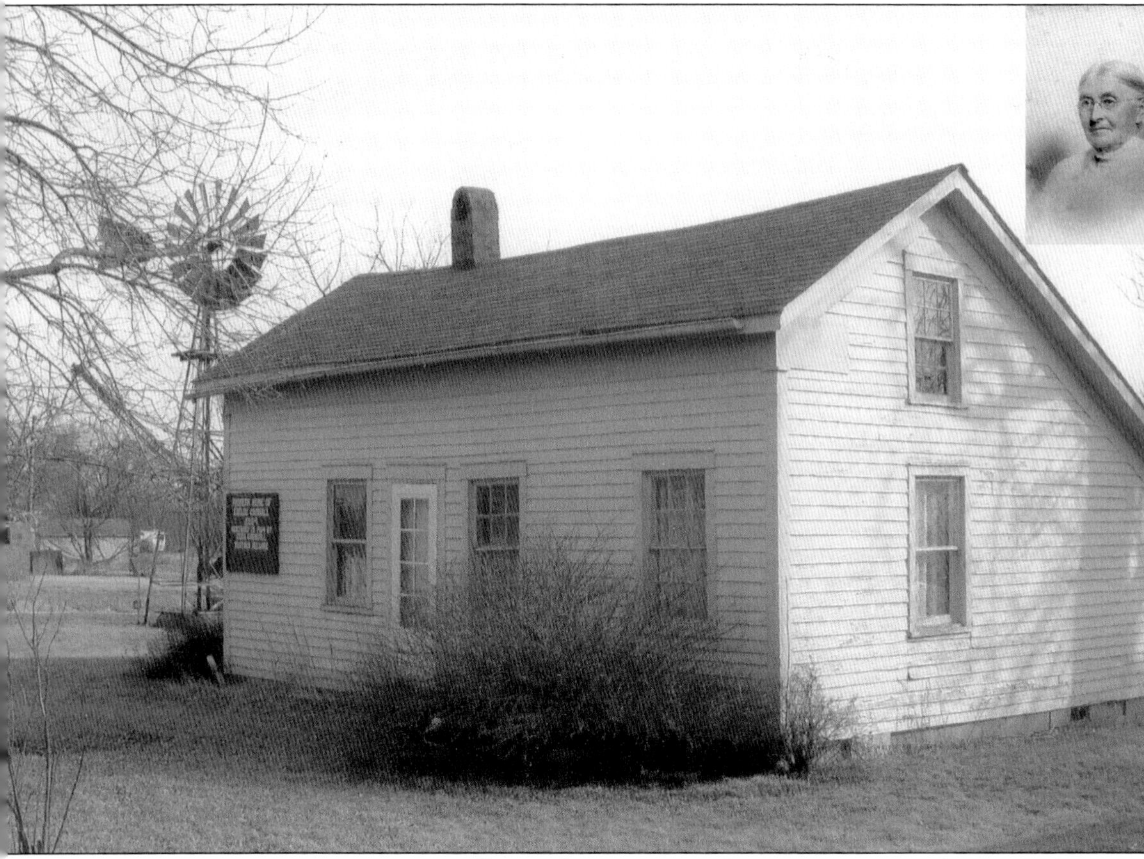

Emeline (Lucas) and Elihue Cornwall came from Bucyrus, Ohio, in August 1855 along with their young sons Avery and Herbert and Emeline's parental family. It was a long and hard journey, with Elihue becoming ill after he was caught in a hailstorm. The Cornwalls lived in a log cabin until they built their frame house in 1864. After Elihue's death in 1867, Emeline continued to reside at the house, where she raised the couple's six children. In 1970, the Cornwall family donated the building to the Ringgold County Historical Society. It is part of the Ringgold Pioneer Museum complex in Ellston. The inset photograph is from around 1910. (Photograph, courtesy of Mike Avitt; inset, Gene Dolson.)

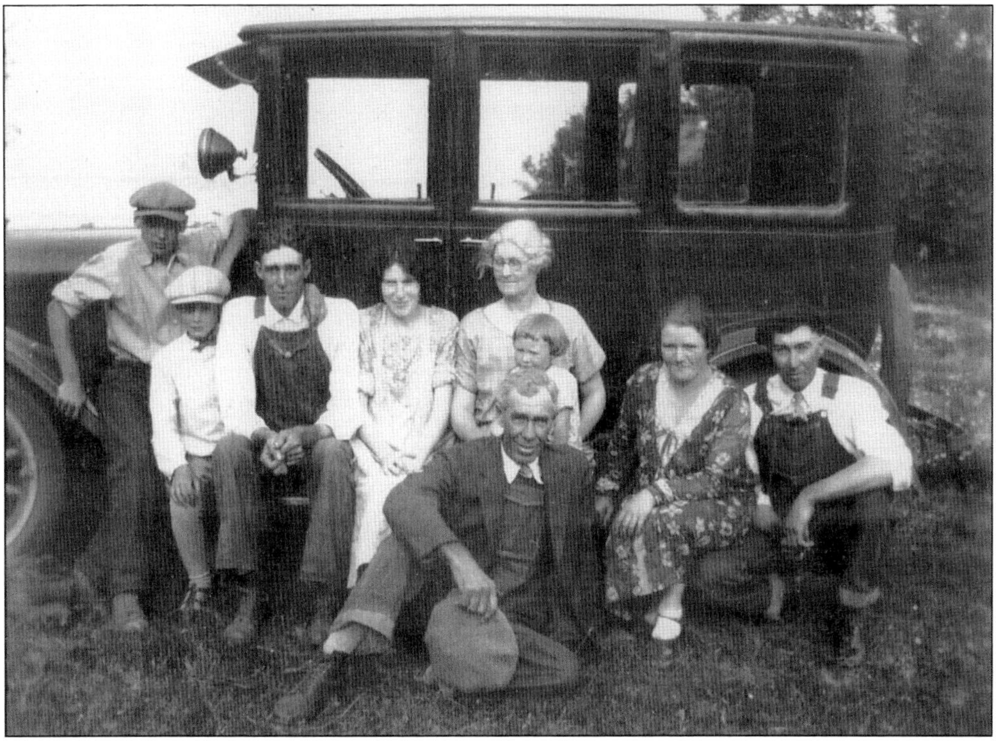

In 1932, when the Bramon family was visiting relatives in Seattle, Fred bought his black Dodge and drove the family back to their rural Delphos farm. Seated in front is Fred B. Bramon; behind him are, from left to right, unidentified, Gerald Bramon, Cleo Bramon, Elva (Swett) Bramon, Luella (Young) Bramon (holding Donella Bramon), Ruth (Lucas) Bramon, and Otto Bramon. (Courtesy of Norma G. [Foland] Becker.)

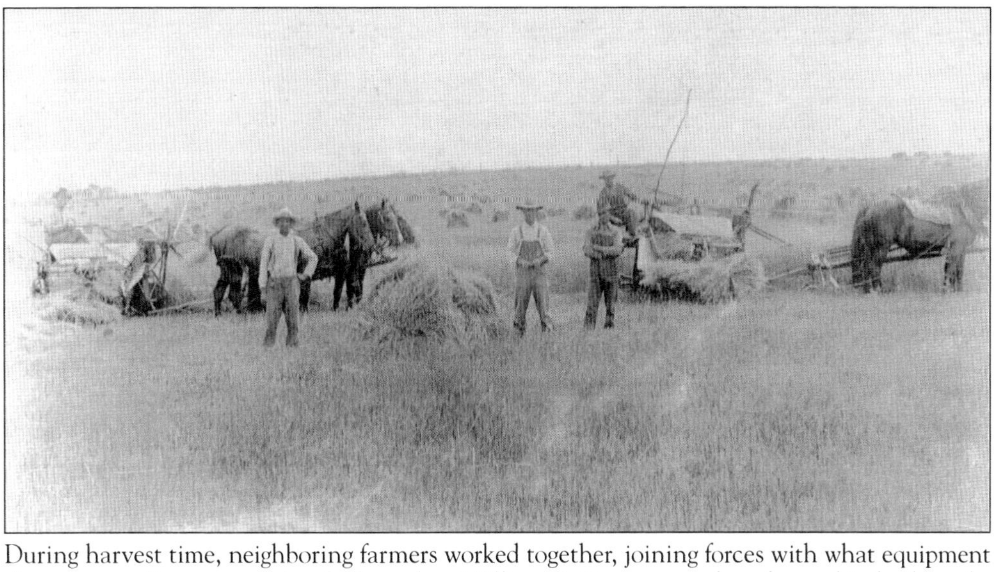

During harvest time, neighboring farmers worked together, joining forces with what equipment they possessed in a race against bad weather. William H. Young, seated on the oat binder, brought his crew to a rural Delphos oat field for the 1917 harvest. His son Fred Young is standing in the middle of the photograph. (Courtesy of Norma G. [Foland] Becker.)

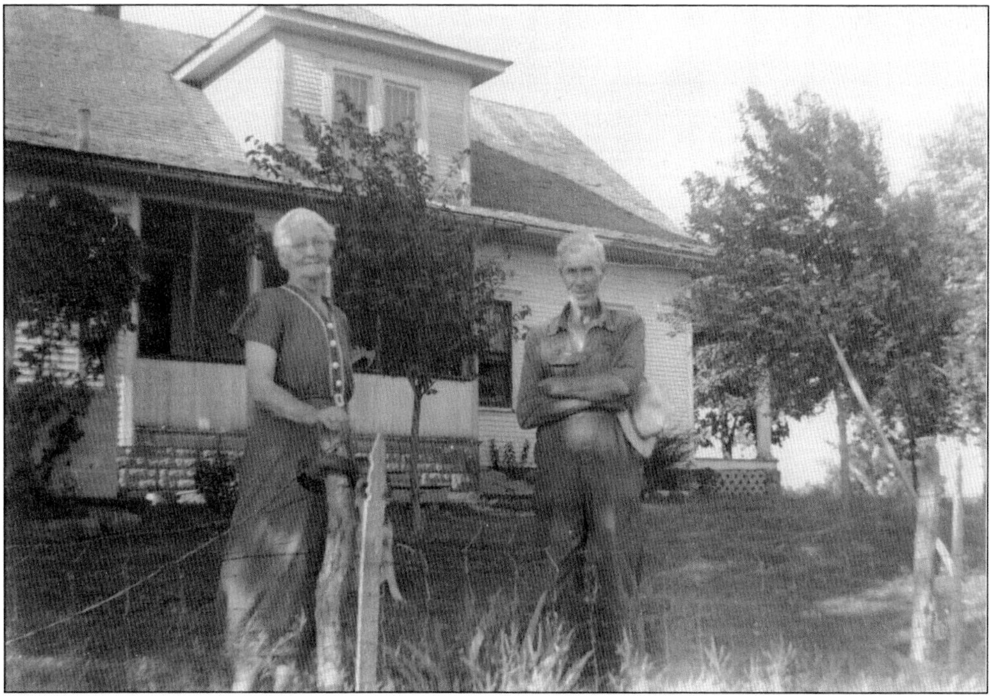

Many farmhouses included a front porch and a side or back porch where the family would come in from chores so as to not track through the house. The farm wife often occupied her time with a vegetable garden and flower gardens located around the house. In 1948, Luella and Fred B. Bramon lived on the farm northeast of Delphos. The house, although somewhat remodeled, stands today. (Courtesy of Norma G. [Foland] Becker.)

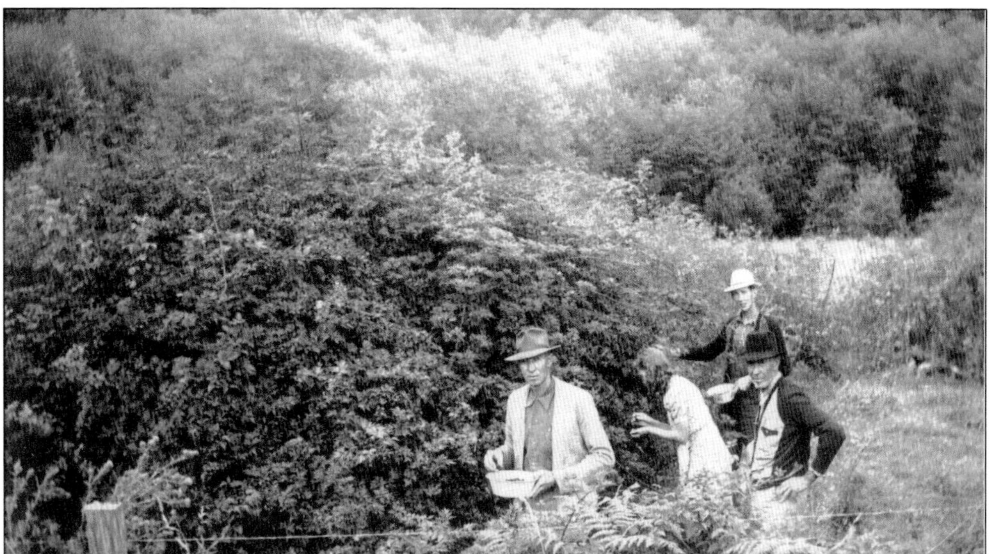

Many Ringgolders took advantage of the wild berry patches scattered throughout the county. A berry-picking expedition often involved the entire family, such as the Bramon family of rural Delphos. The berries were prepared and made into jellies, jams, preserves, or filling for pies. (Courtesy of Norma G. [Foland] Becker.)

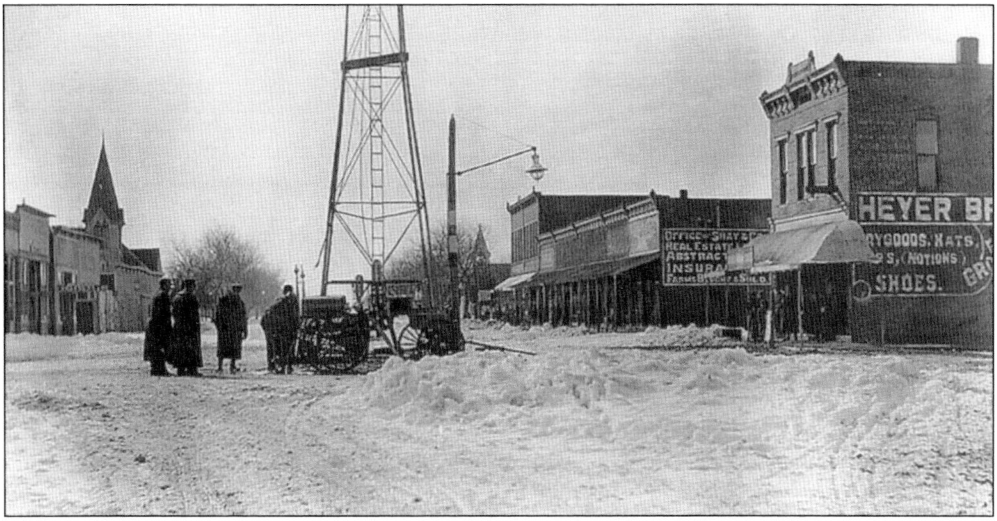

Fires destroyed many homes and businesses in Ringgold County's early days. Practically everything was made of wood, and firefighting consisted of nothing more than bucket brigades. Here, a group of volunteers in Tingley use an early firefighting water pump to put out a fire. They are drawing water from a well in the middle of the street. It was common for towns to dig wells in the street in business districts. Later, a bandstand was built over this well. (Courtesy Jane E. Lyle.)

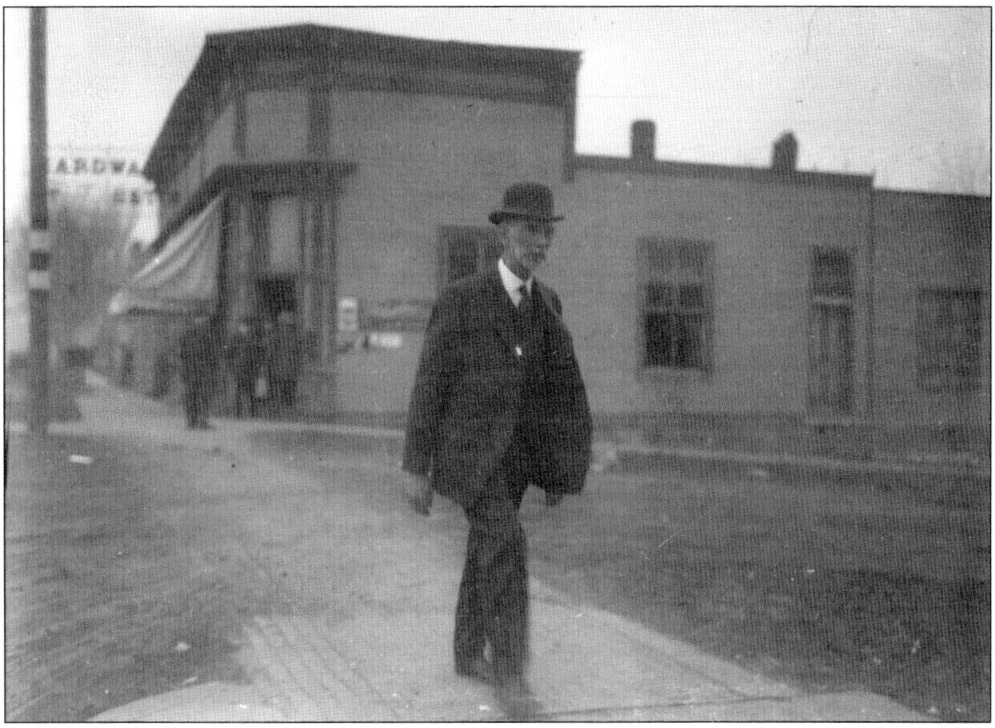

Before the streets were paved, many towns provided shoppers and visitors with crosswalks made of wood or concrete. This crosswalk on the northwest corner of the Mount Ayr square appears to be made of brick and concrete. It is rounded to accommodate wagon wheels. Behind the gentleman is the Z.T. Kinsell Hardware Store. That lot is now the home of the Mount Ayr Post Office. (Courtesy of Mount Ayr Depot Museum.)

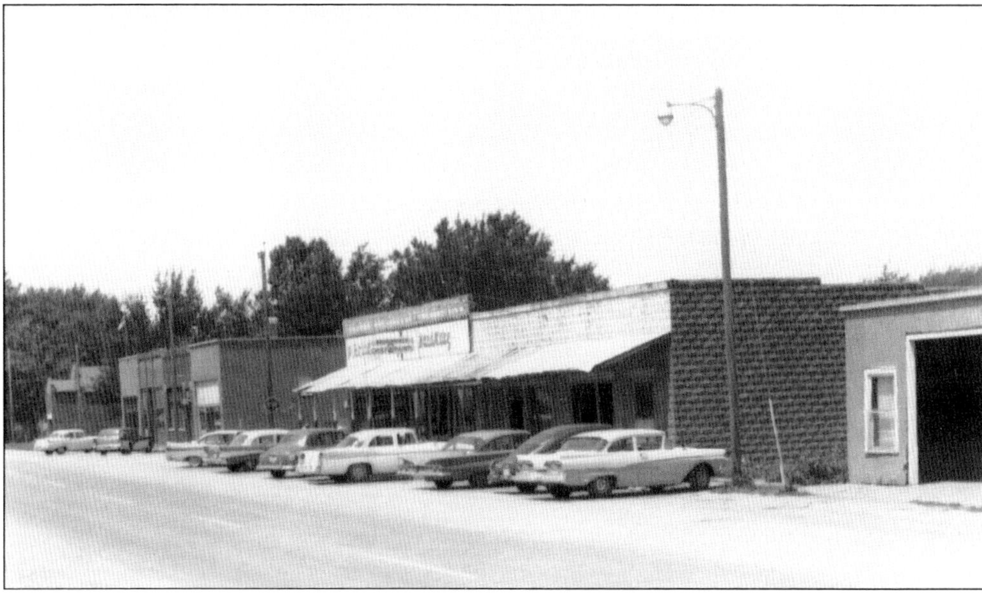

This is another busy day at the Breckenridge Store in Tingley around 1960. Bill Breckenridge started the store in 1921 and in 1923 moved to the location pictured. Many family members worked at the store over the years, and in 1960 Bill's son Billy and his wife, Minnie, took ownership of the store. Billy and Minnie operated the store until 1991, selling groceries, hardware, and dry goods. Not many stores deliver groceries to their customers' homes, but the Breckenridge Store did. (Courtesy of Mount Ayr Depot Museum.)

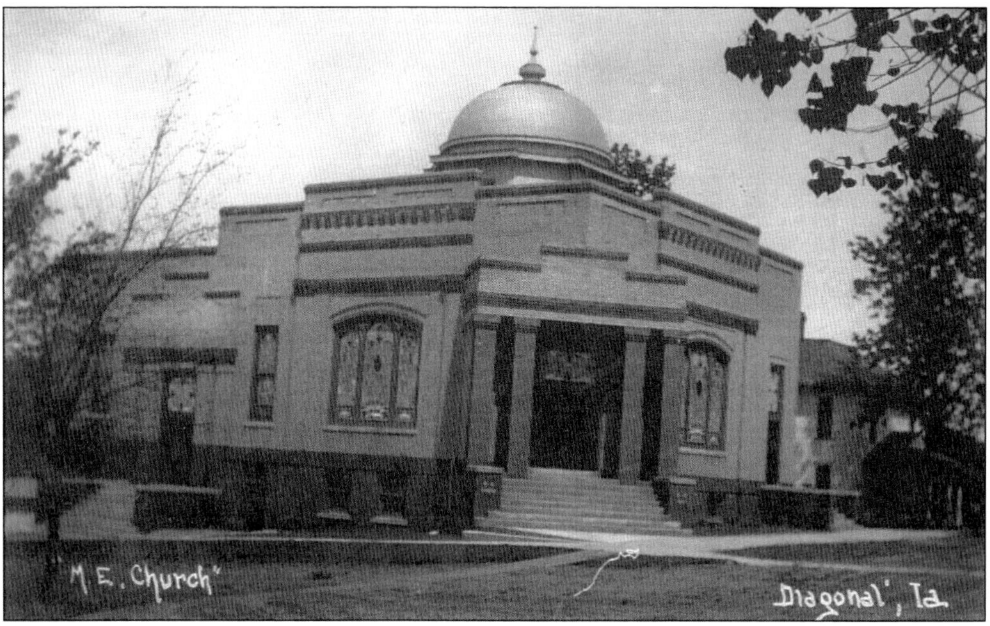

The Goshen Methodist Episcopal Church was moved to Diagonal in 1890. During the summer of 1905, an infestation of woodpeckers forced the removal of the church spire. A cornerstone for a new brick church was placed on the Fourth of July 1911, and dedication services were held November 17, 1911. The church dome was removed in 1971. Today, the church serves as the United Church of Diagonal. (Courtesy of Mount Ayr Depot Museum.)

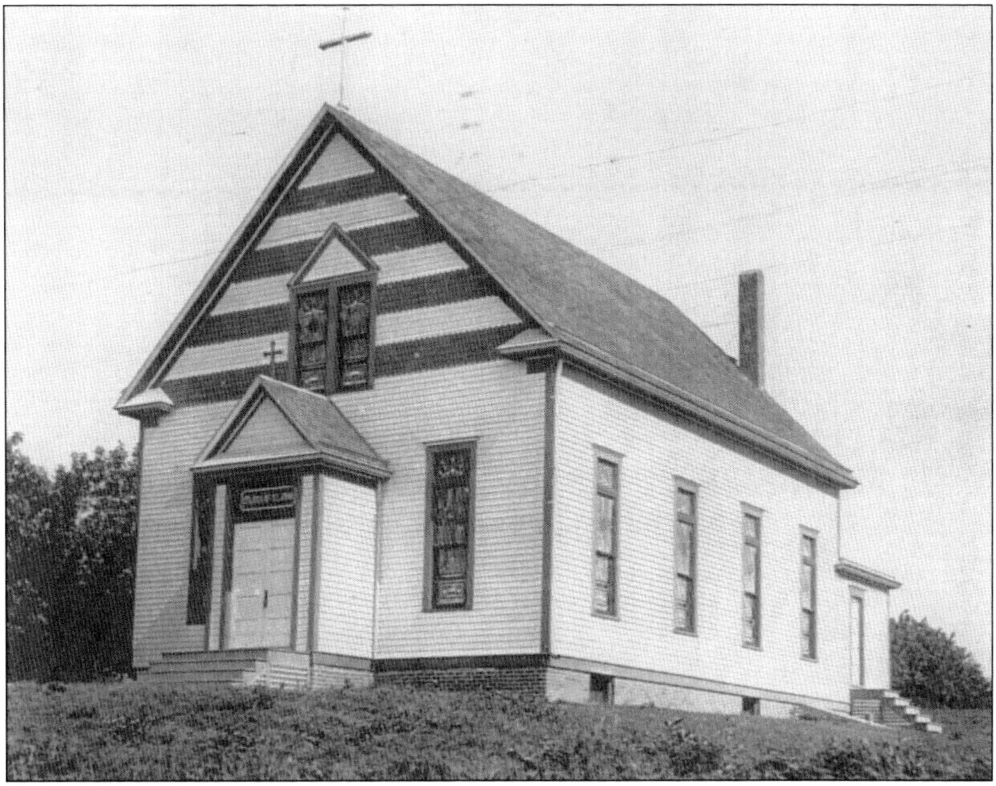

St. John's Catholic Church building was dedicated on May 10, 1911, and served Diagonal until it was closed in the fall of 1969. Fr. Maurice J. Culhane, an Irish immigrant, served the parish well for over 46 years. (Courtesy of Mount Ayr Depot Museum.)

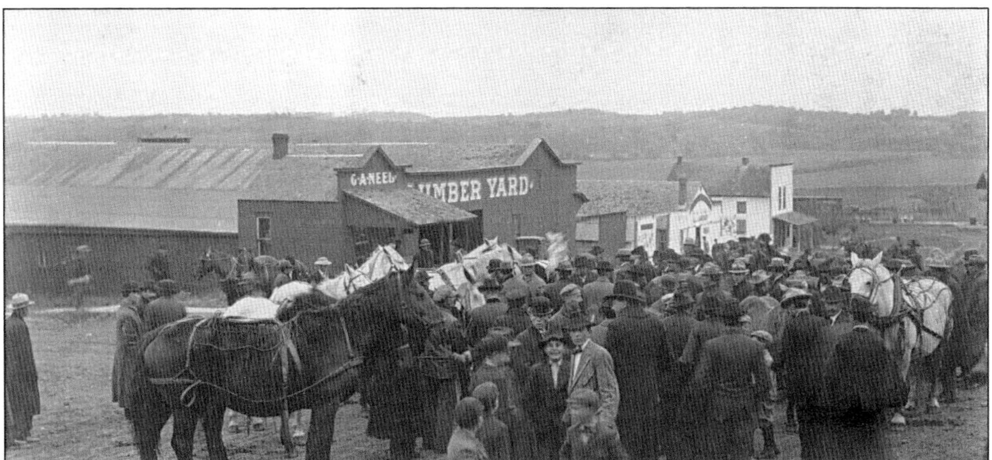

The Farmer's Institute was moved from Mount Ayr to Diagonal in January 1909. A frame auditorium with a seating capacity of 1,000 was constructed, and festivities were held annually in October. A stock show was included, along with other categories, including corn, stock judging, culinary, fancywork, and educational departments. This photograph of the institute was taken on the southeast side of Main Street in Diagonal in 1910. In 1919, the Farmer's Institute included a parade with the festivities. (Courtesy of Diagonal Printing Museum.)

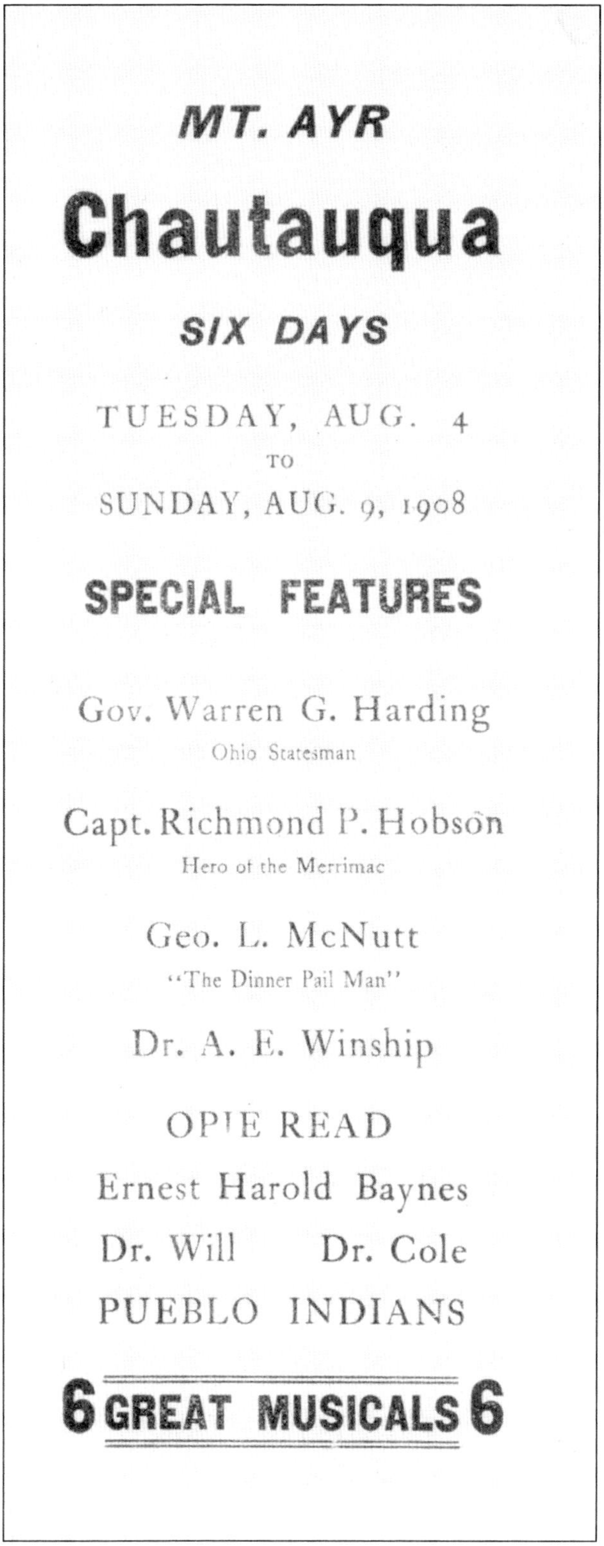
MT. AYR

Chautauqua

SIX DAYS

TUESDAY, AUG. 4
TO
SUNDAY, AUG. 9, 1908

SPECIAL FEATURES

Gov. Warren G. Harding
Ohio Statesman

Capt. Richmond P. Hobson
Hero of the Merrimac

Geo. L. McNutt
"The Dinner Pail Man"

Dr. A. E. Winship

OPIE READ

Ernest Harold Baynes

Dr. Will Dr. Cole

PUEBLO INDIANS

6 GREAT MUSICALS 6

Advanced tickets for the Mount Ayr Chautauqua were only $1.50 in 1908, and that covered all six days. Even though future US president Warren Harding was a speaker, the biggest crowd (about 2,000) was for Richmond P. Hobson, the "Hero of the Merrimac." Hobson was awarded the Medal of Honor for his heroism during the Spanish-American War. He achieved the rank of rear admiral and also served as a congressman from his home state of Alabama. Chautauquas were entertaining, but the primary purpose was to enlighten people in matters religious, moral, cultural, and political. (Courtesy of Mount Ayr Depot Museum.)

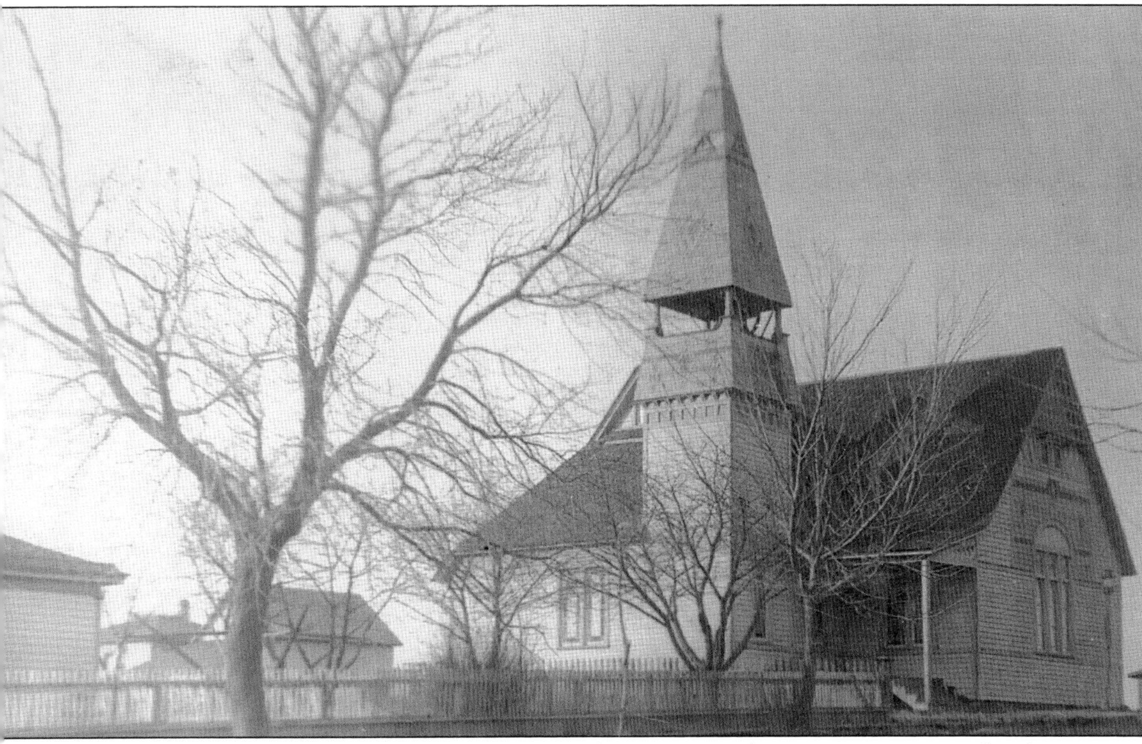

Diagonal's Presbyterian Church was dedicated in February 1890. The congregation united with the Methodist and Christian Church into the United Church of Diagonal in February 1978. The church building no longer stands. (Courtesy of Diagonal Printing Museum.)

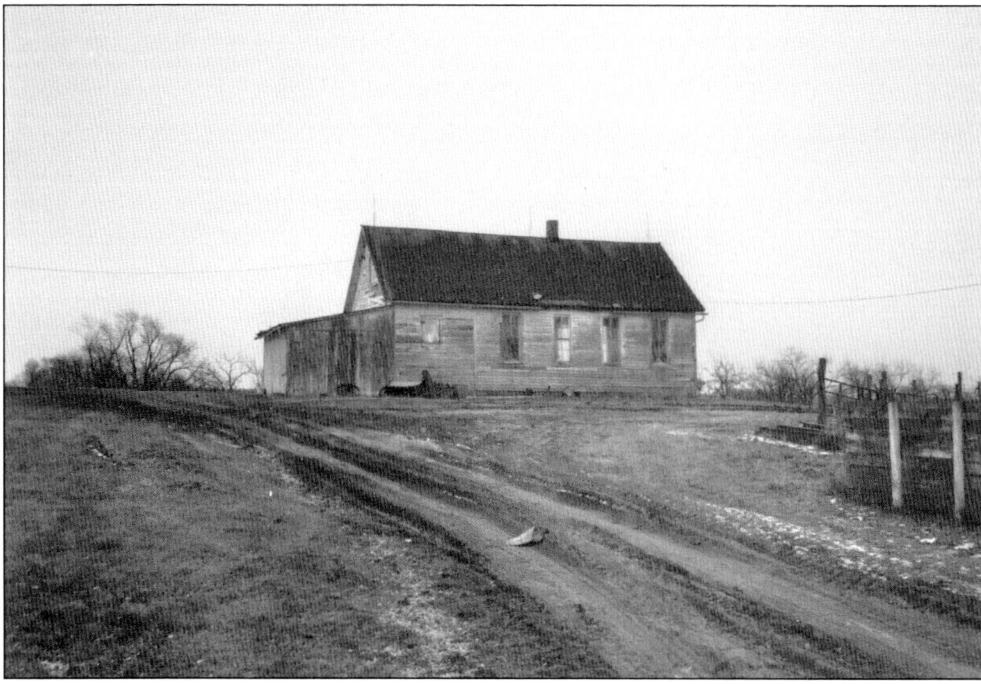

The Jackson Hill School (Monroe No. 8) sits in its second location about two and a half miles north of Kellerton on the Matt Daughton farm. This photograph was taken just before the school was moved to the Ringgold County Fairgrounds in 1992. There, it was restored inside and out (below) by Bob and Kay Sickels and a host of volunteers. (Above, courtesy of Bob and Kay Sickels; below, Sharon R. Becker.)

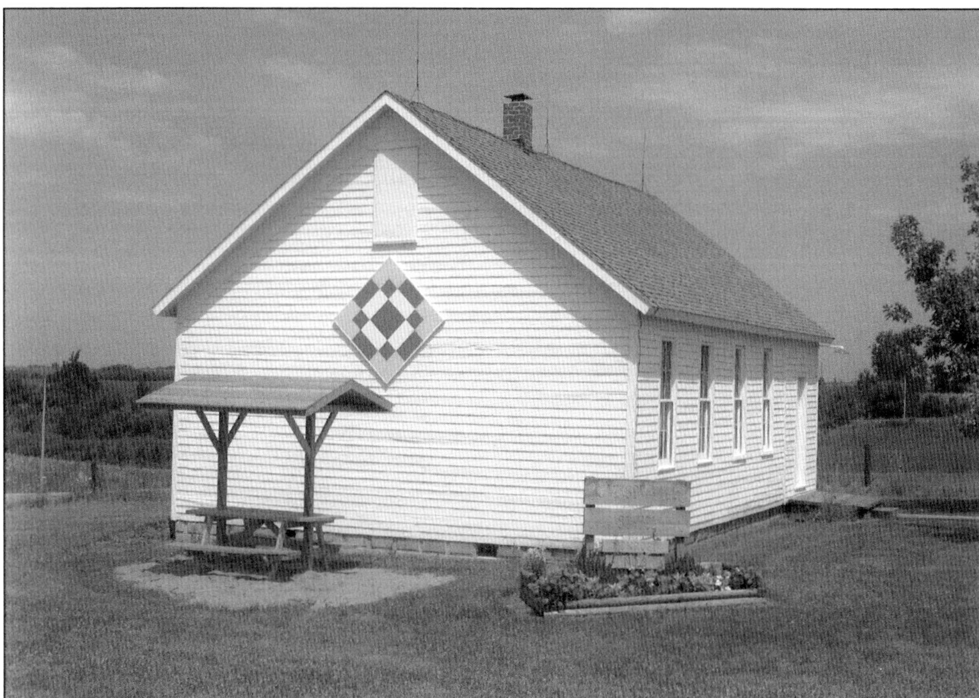

Leland and Lucile Jackson (pictured) owned and operated the Ellston Locker until the business was sold to Jim and Martha Smith. The Smiths sandblasted and tuck-pointed the entire building in 1980. (Courtesy of Mount Ayr Depot Museum.)

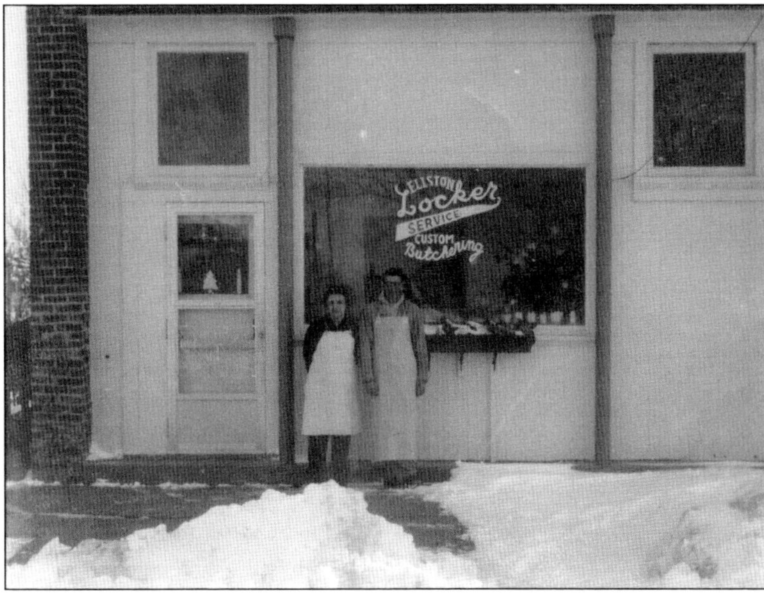

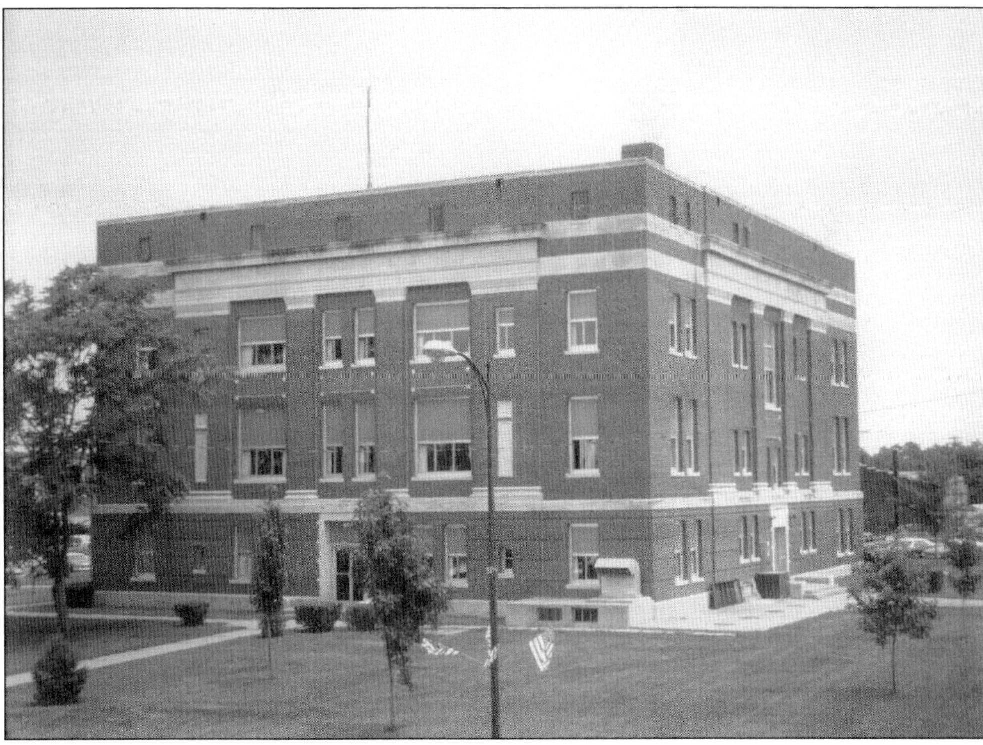

Here, Earl Wheelan has photographed the Ringgold County Courthouse on July 4, 1976, the nation's 200th birthday. He took the photograph from the Mason's building on the southwest corner of the square. (Courtesy of Mount Ayr Depot Museum.)

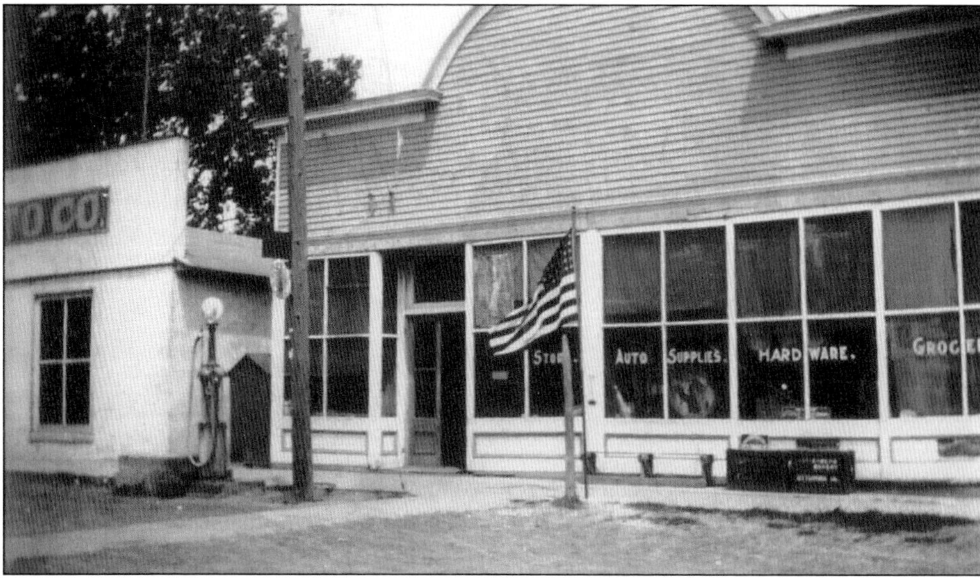

An early gas pump sits between the Redding Auto Company (left) and a hardware store on the north side of the Redding square. (Courtesy of Friends of Old Redding.)

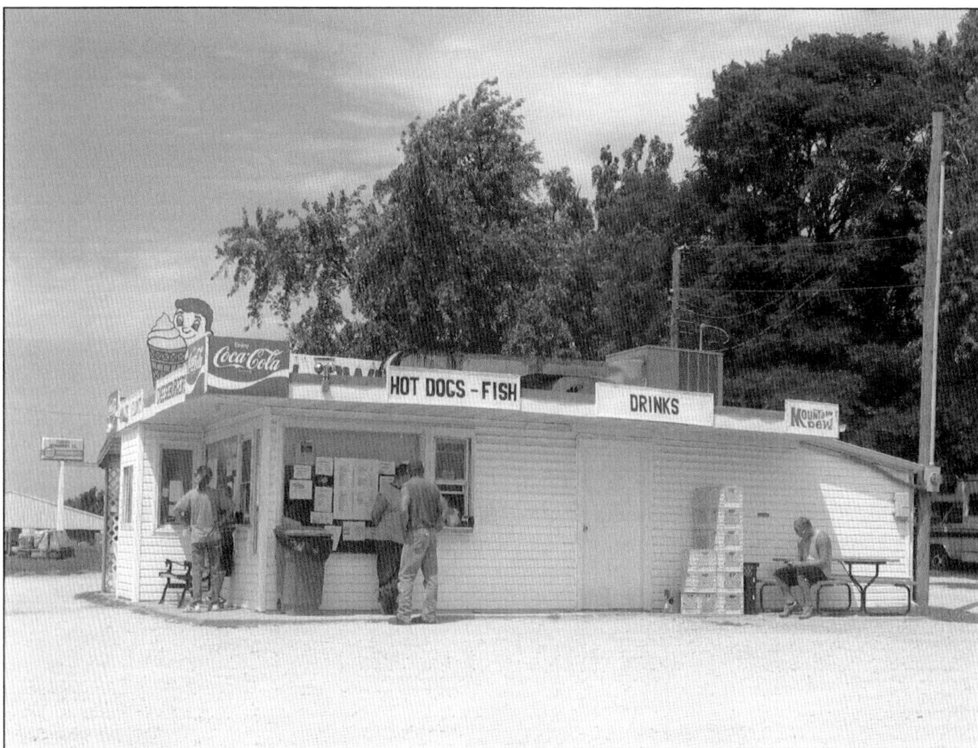

Mount Ayr's Dairy Sweet, located along Highway 2, has been a landmark and a favorite place to refresh one's soul and treat one's taste buds for generations of children of all ages. (Courtesy of Sharon R. Becker.)

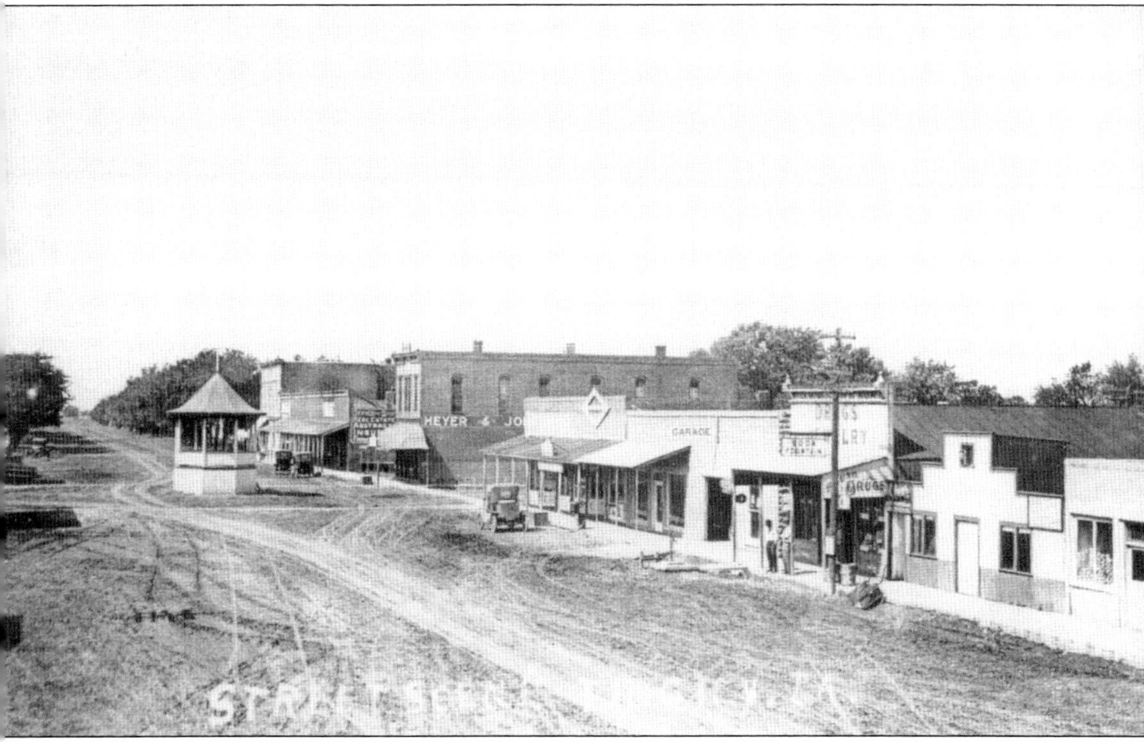

Tingley was platted in 1881, and the trains came in 1882. The town grew quickly and wood-frame business buildings lined the main road that went through town. A fire in 1894 was so consuming that more than half the businesses were lost. The town responded by erecting beautiful wood-frame and brick business buildings before even two years had passed. This view is of the north side of Main Street around 1915. (Courtesy of Mount Ayr Depot Museum.)

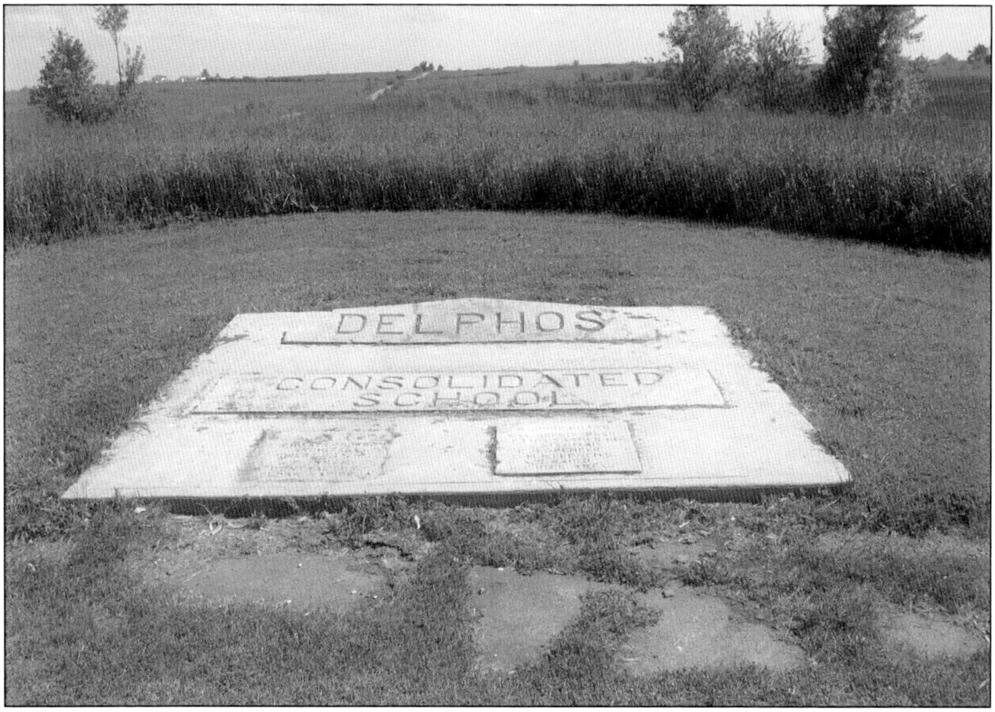

Many of Ringgold County's schools suffered from decreasing enrollment and eventually closed. The only reminder that a grand two-story brick schoolhouse once stood in Delphos is this plaque. (Courtesy of Sharon R. Becker.)

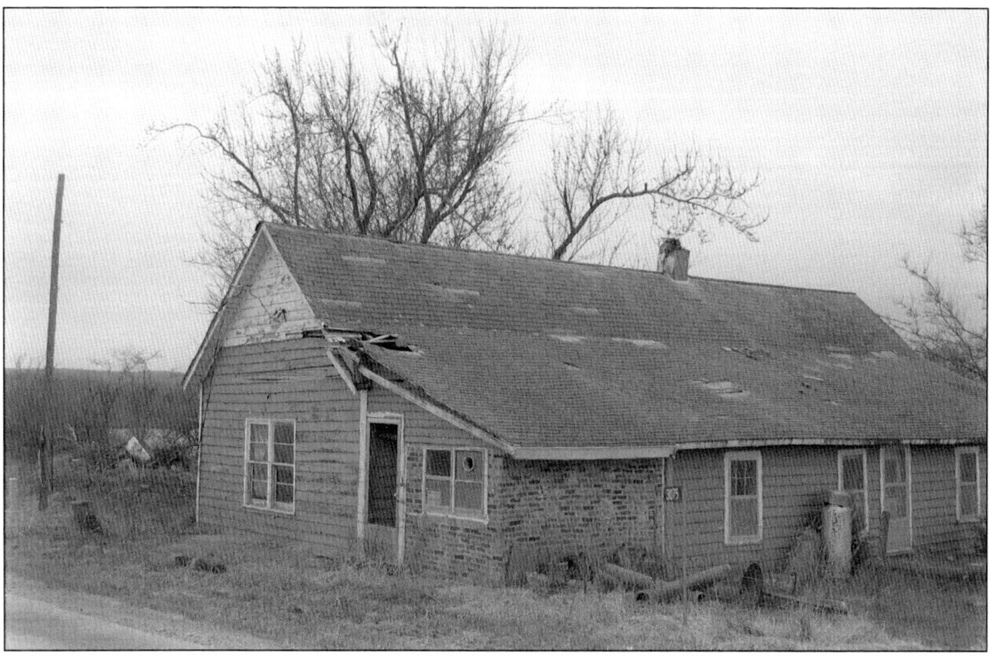
Watterson was a rural community located south of Mount Ayr; it never was a town. The hub of the community was the Watterson Store, pictured here. (Courtesy of Mike Avitt and Sharon R. Becker.)

From left to right, Dean, Bill, Vic, and Vern Shields have a friendly family visit at the Watterson Store around 1950. The store was a gathering place for locals and visitors alike in the Watterson community. (Courtesy of Vernadean Hacker Rocha.)

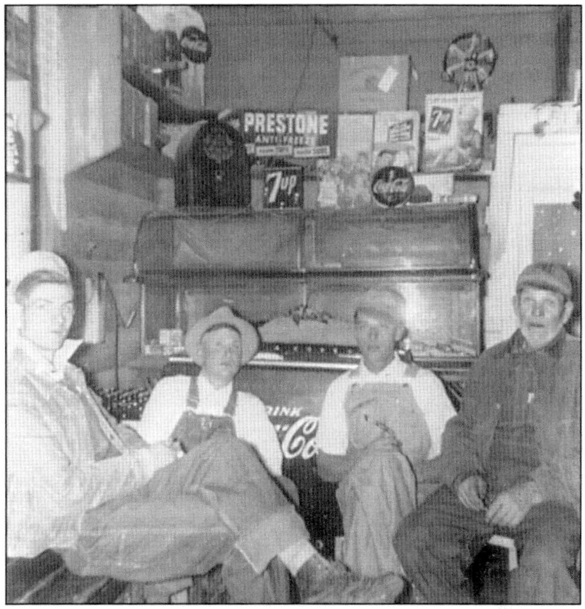

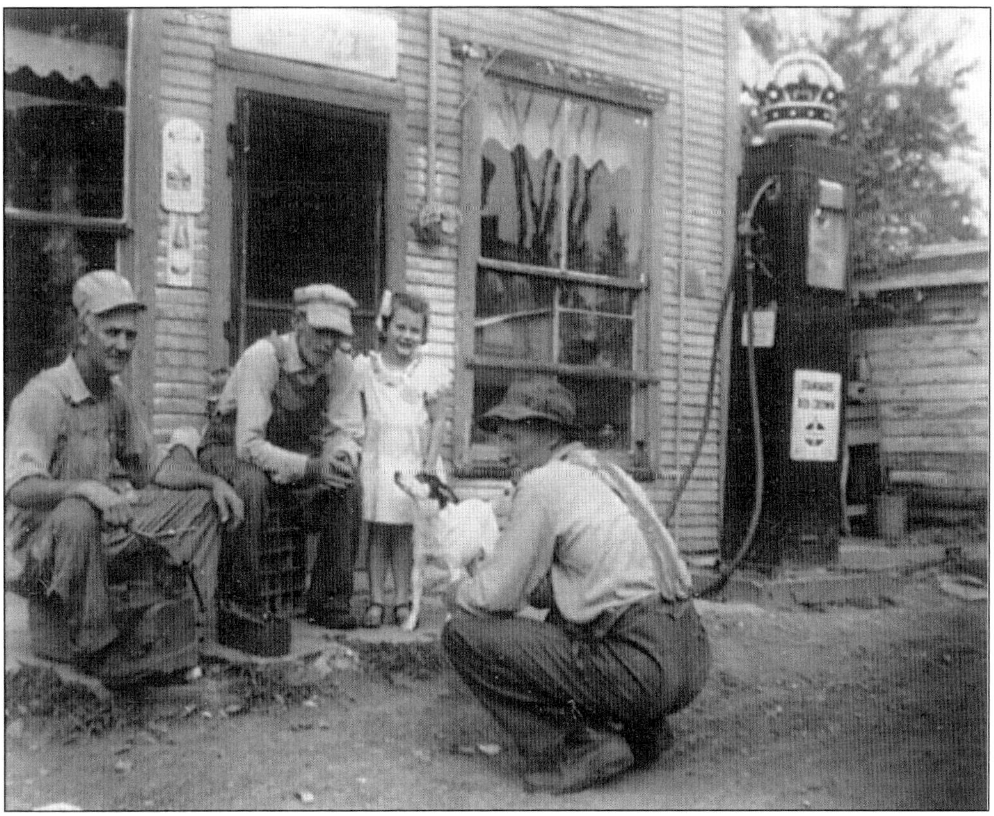

Neil Johnston (squatting) relaxes in front of the Watterson Store around 1950. Behind him are, from left to right, Vern Hacker, Vern Shields, and Vernadean Hacker (with her dog Stubbie). Shields has found a comfortable seat on an empty, wooden pop-bottle case. Hacker and his wife, Vera, were owners of the store. (Courtesy of Vernadean Hacker Rocha.)

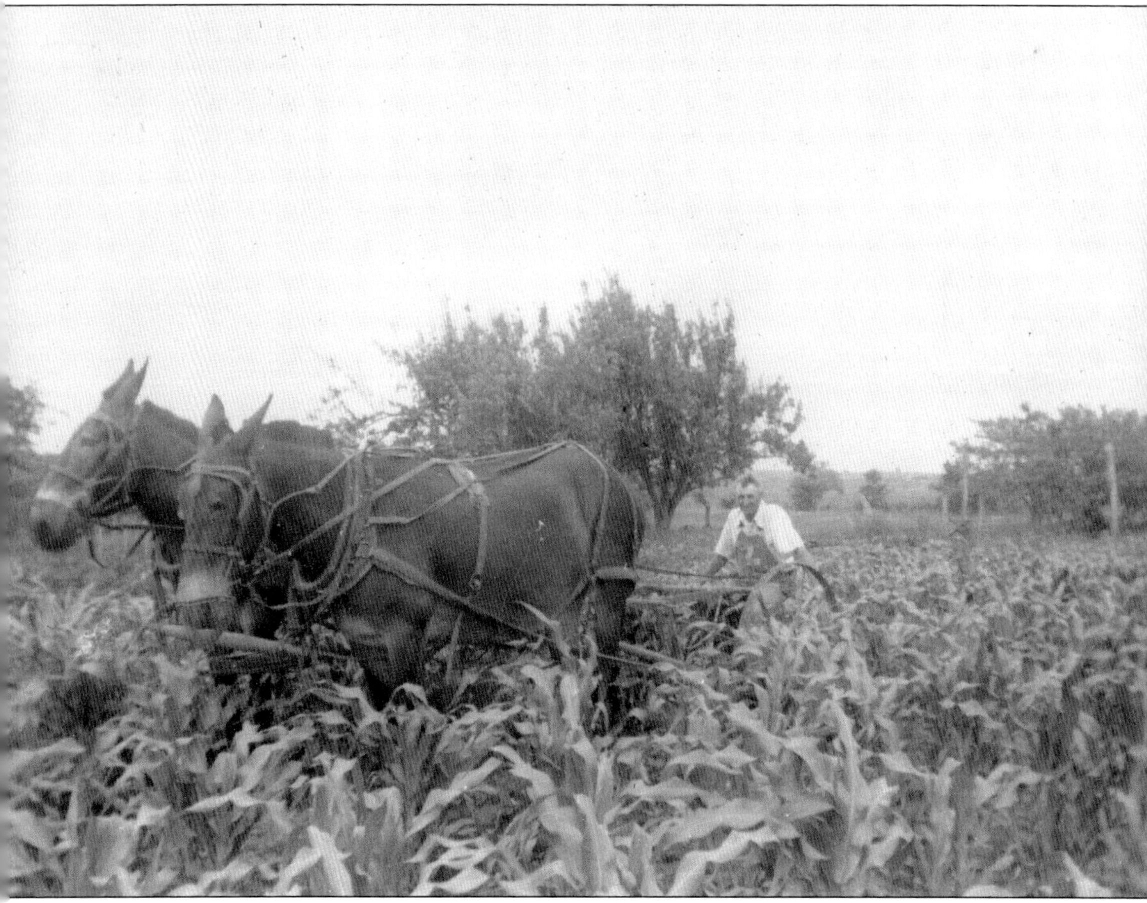

Draft animals often became important members of a farm family. Mules Bill and Dave were no exception. They helped the Bramon family farm northeast of Delphos and later served on the Homer Foland farm, located northeast of Grand River. Here, Bill, Dave, and Homer cultivate corn in 1951. When they weren't working, the mules gave many a child a ride around the barn lot. (Courtesy of Norma G. [Foland] Becker.)

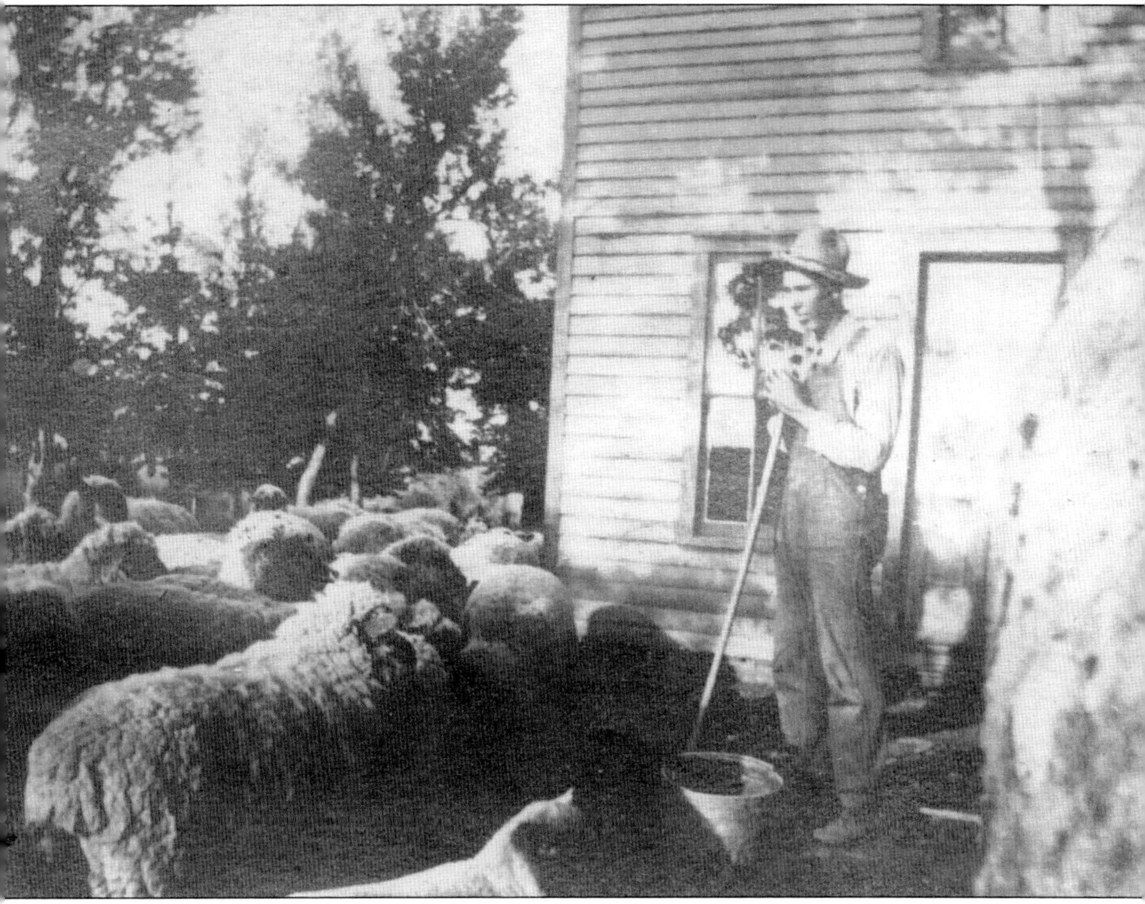

In this 1919 photograph are Fred B. Bramon and his flock, northeast of Delphos. Capt. Andrew Johnston and Charles K. Grimes were among Ringgold County's early sheep producers. Prior to the Civil War, wolves were a constant threat, which caused the county to impose a bounty. Due to the large payment of bounties, one local joked that the farmers were raising wolves to cash in on the bounty. During the Civil War, flocks provided much-needed wool for blankets and uniforms. (Courtesy of Norma G. [Foland] Becker.)

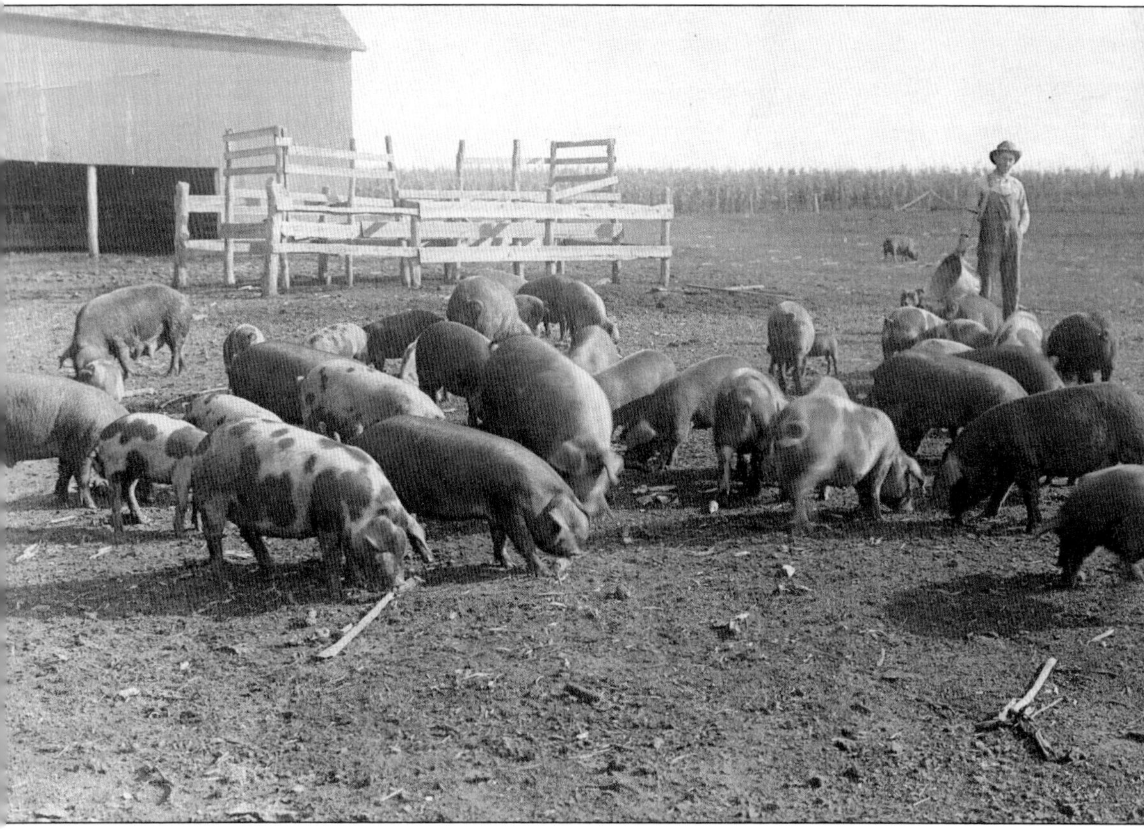

Daniel Tidrick, of Liberty Township, was among the early Ringgold County farmers who introduced Poland China hogs into the county. During the 1870s, hog production in the county was almost wiped out with the introduction of a herd law in 1870 that was followed by an outbreak of swine cholera in 1876 and 1877. The law required farmers to erect fencing, which at times cost more than what the land initially cost. The introduction of barbed wire and woven wire solved this problem for most farmers. Fred B. Bramon raised a mixed herd of Poland China hogs on his rural Delphos farm. (Courtesy of Norma G. [Foland] Becker.)

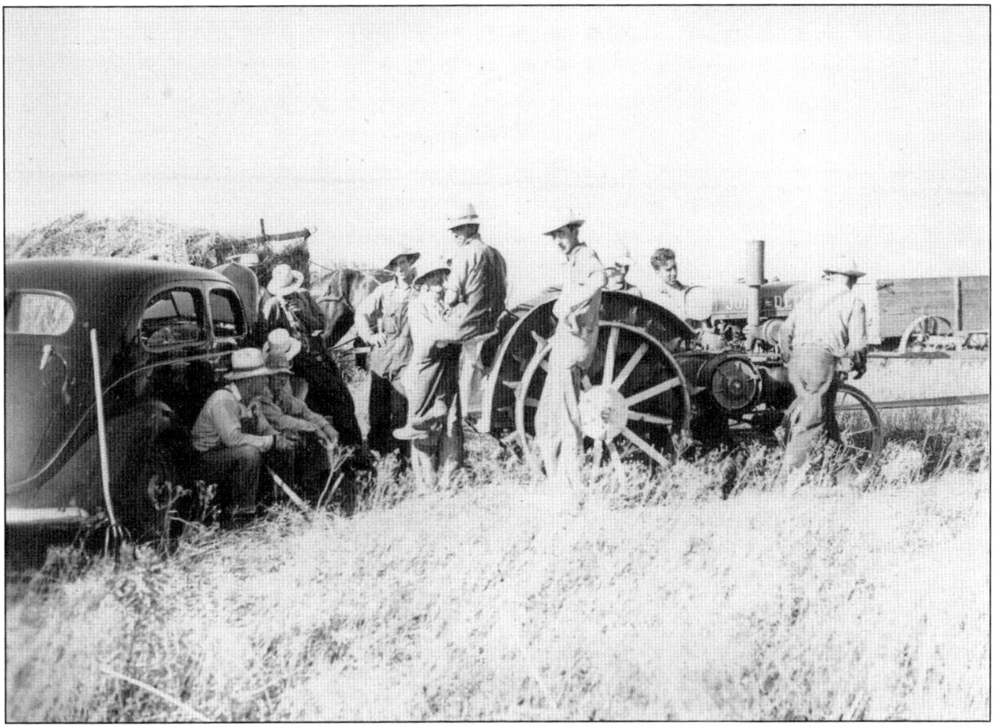

Osman Liniger purchased the first threshing machine in the county in 1862 for $500, which he paid entirely with cash. Sy Crosley bought a "down power" threshing machine, which was operated by four of five teams of horses. As motorized farm equipment began to replace horse-drawn and powered farming methods, farmers pooled what equipment they owned with their neighbors to communally bring in a harvest. One such group has gathered in rural Delphos in the 1930s, with the host farmer's wife preparing a large spread to feed the hungry men and boys. (Courtesy of Norma G. [Foland] Becker.)

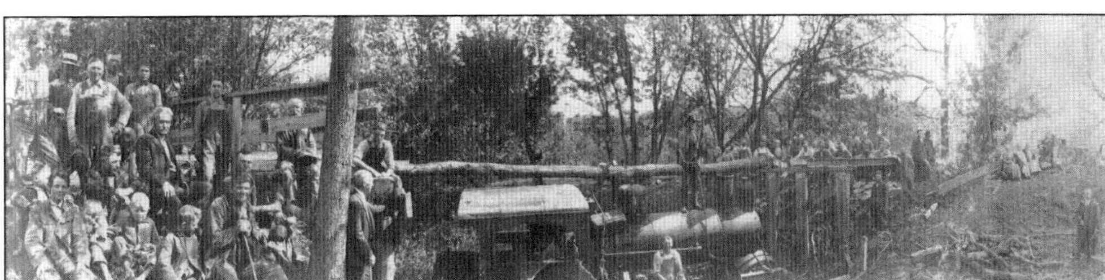

Earl Dugan's threshing machine fell through a bridge in Lotts Creek in 1923. The bridge had to be dismantled to get the threshing machine upright and pulled out by horses. A crowd gathers to watch this unusual event. (Courtesy of Ron Mackey.)

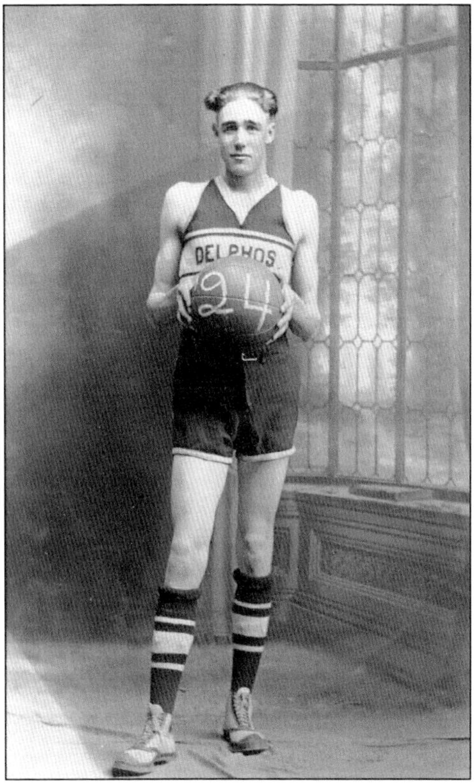

Basketball was a very popular among the people of Ringgold County. A basketball game between neighboring towns packed the high school gymnasiums and provided a good evening's worth of entertainment. In the early 1900s, many schools did not have a high school gymnasium, so games would be played in the town's opera house. Emotions ran high during Ringgold County's high school basketball tournament. Coach Omar "Pop" Varner was a successful basketball coach, taking his Diagonal Maroons to the state tournament, where they won the championship in 1938 and took second place in 1939. When coach Varner was at Delphos Consolidated School, two of his ballplayers were Cleo Bramon (left) and Otto Bramon (below). (Both, courtesy of Norma G. [Foland] Becker.)

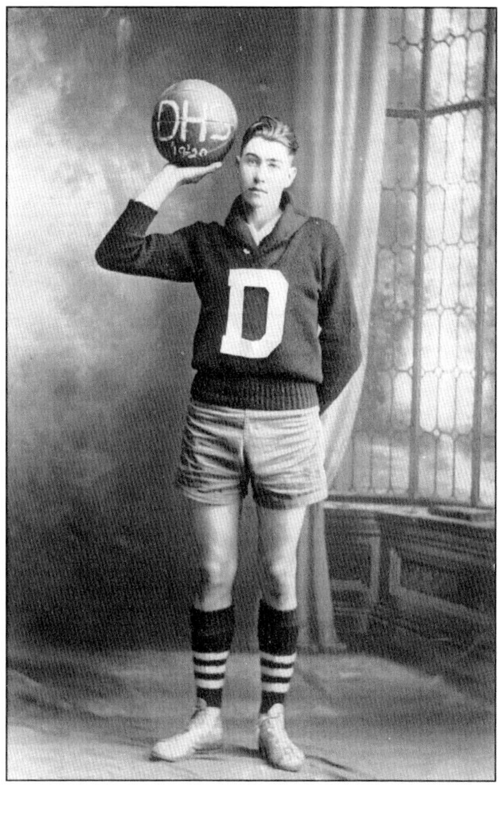

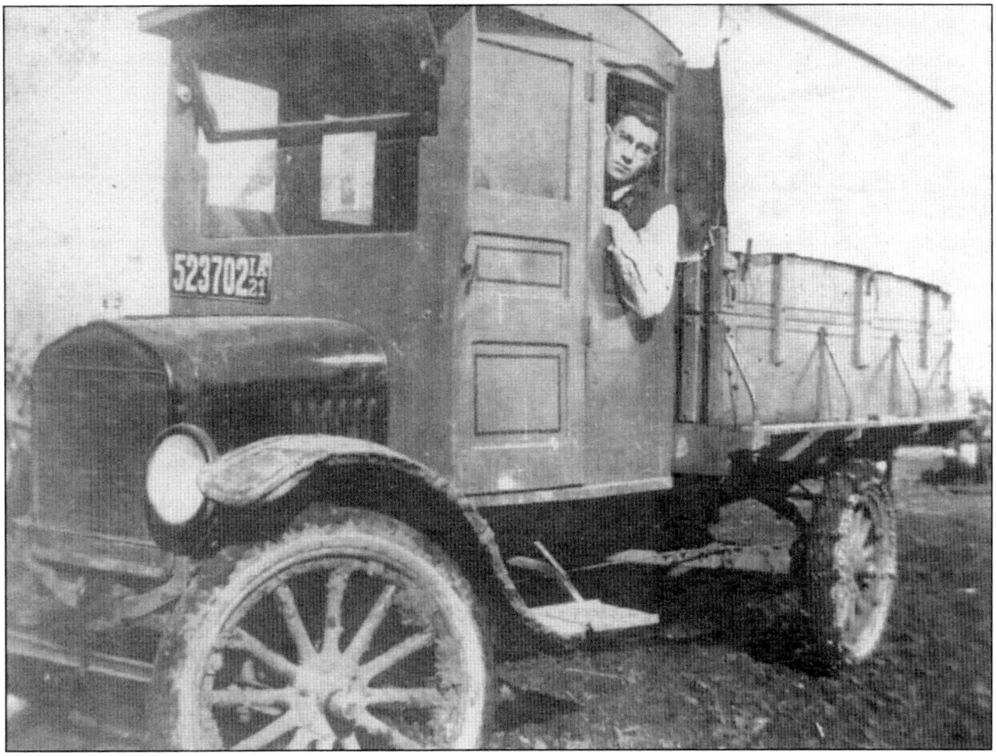

As Ringgold County improved the roads, school districts used horse-drawn hacks for the transportation of schoolchildren. Later, the hacks were replaced by school trucks and eventually by school buses. In 1931, Otto Bramon drove the school truck for the Delphos Community School. (Courtesy of Norma G. [Foland] Becker.)

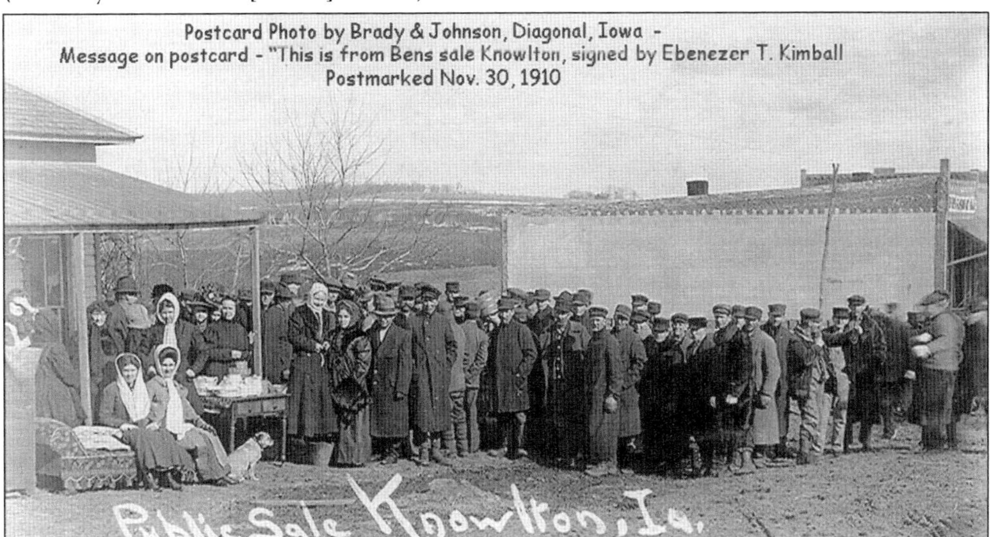

A bundled-up crowd gathers for a public auction in Knowlton. The sun is shining, and the dirt street is dry (or frozen). Public sales still draw big crowds today. However, they are held indoors in the winter. The message on the postcard reads, "This is from Ben's sale, Knowlton" and is signed by Ebenezer Kimball and postmarked November 30, 1910. (Courtesy of Delbert Spencer.)

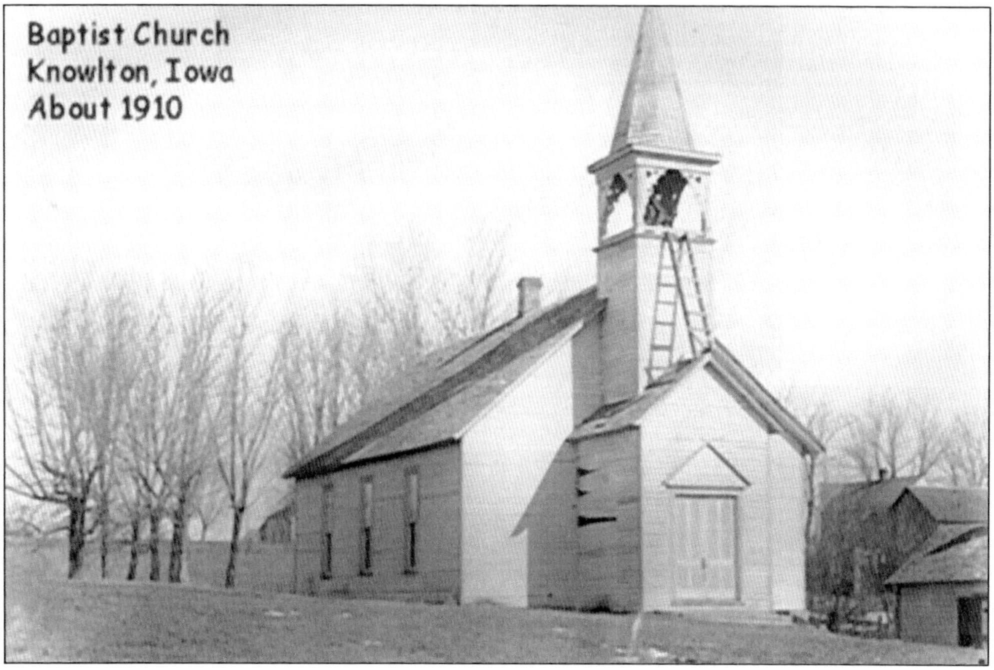

The Baptist Church at Knowlton is pictured as it appeared in 1910. It looks as though some repairs are underway. (Courtesy of Mount Ayr Depot Museum.)

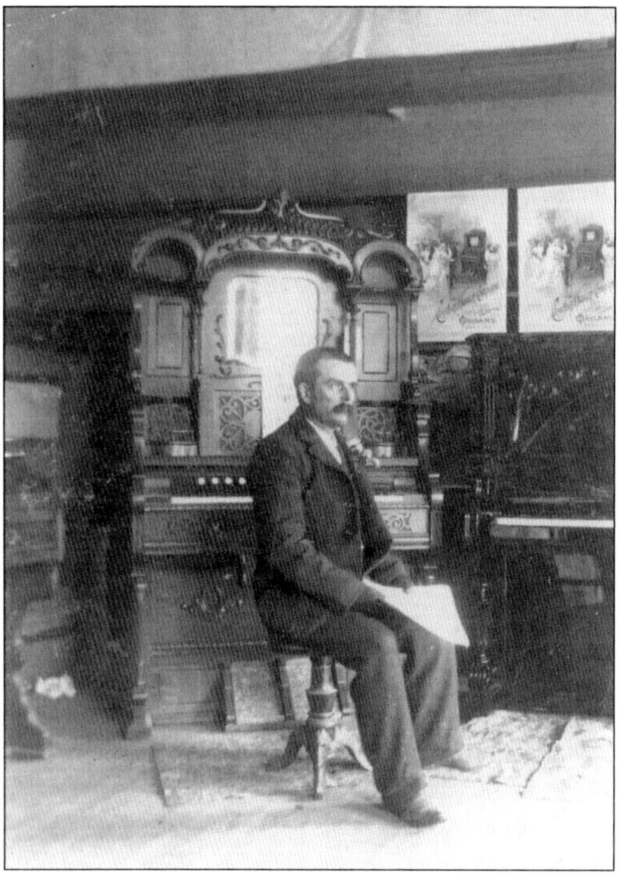

This photograph is of Reger's Music Store in Mount Ayr. William Albert Reger, son of Methodist minister Rev. Alfred Alphaeus and Frances A. (Ludington) Reger, was born in Wheeling, West Virginia. William owned a music store and served as Mount Ayr's postmaster from 1882 to 1886. (Courtesy of Mount Ayr Depot Museum.)

Della (Fogle) Vanderpool accompanies soloist Thelma (Foland) Palmer in this c. 1922 photograph. Before television, video games, and DVDs, family entertainment usually involved gathering around the piano in the parlor. (Courtesy of Norma G. [Foland] Becker.)

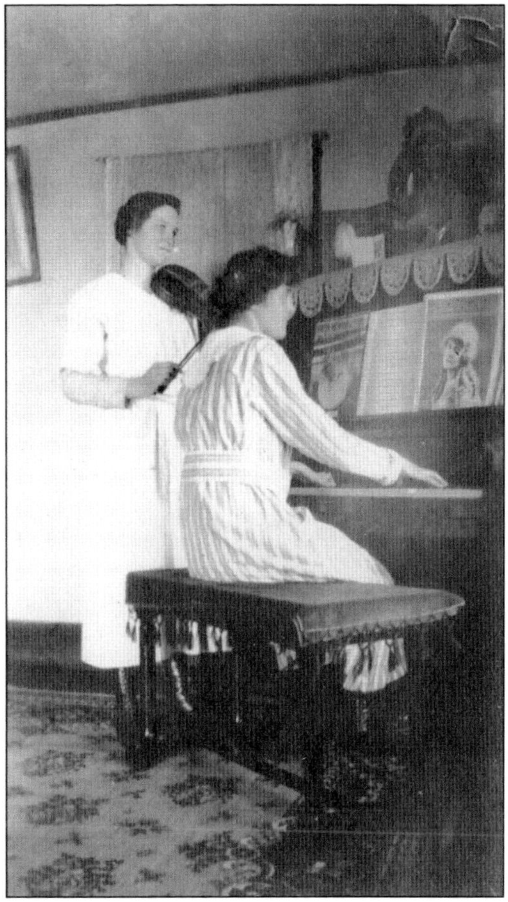

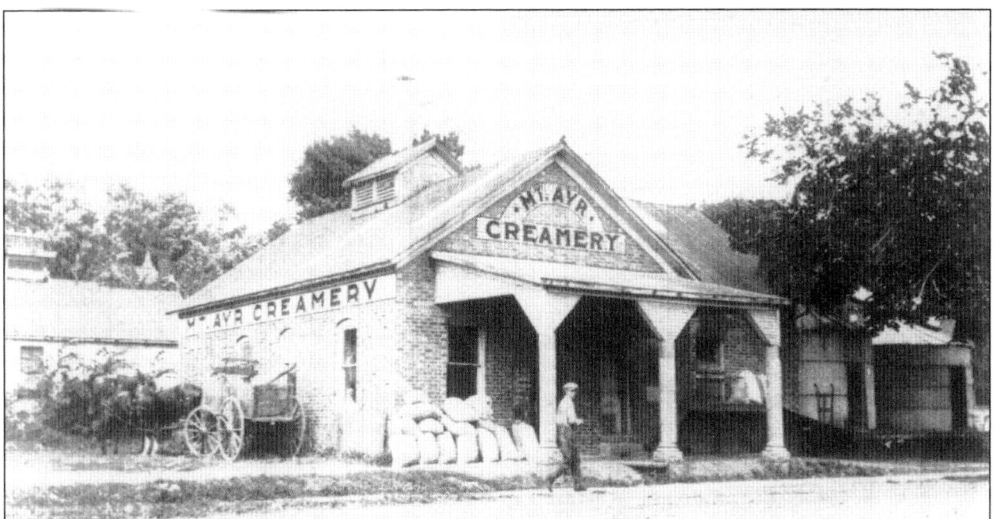

Farmers would bring their cream into town and sell it at a creamery. Mount Ayr's creamery was located northwest of the square. Today, this building is Jamie's Coffee Mill. (Courtesy of Sharon R. Becker.)

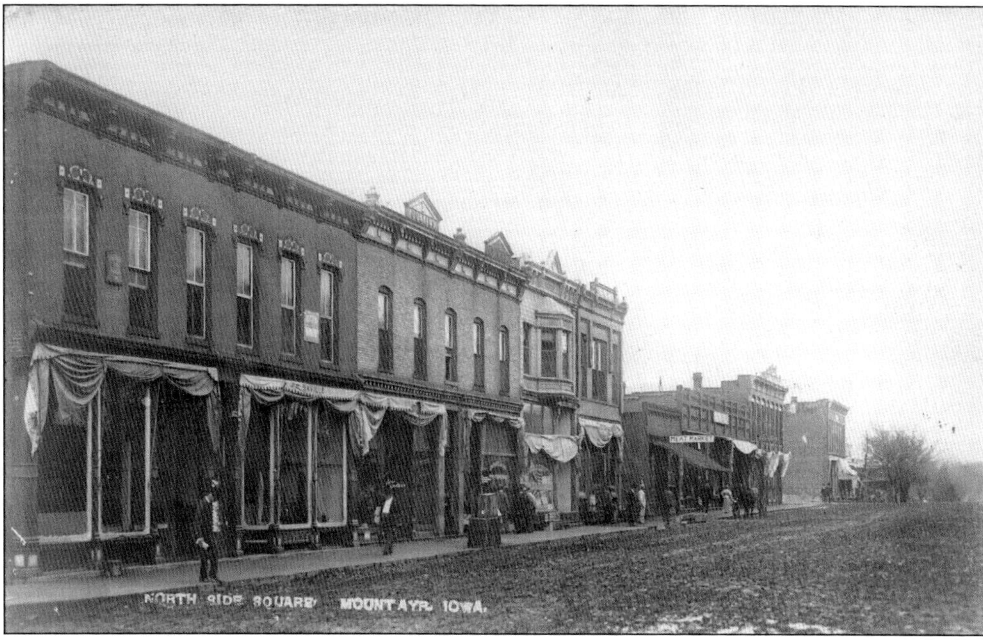

Before electricity, running water, and paved streets, business was quickly expanding on the north side of the Mount Ayr square. By the early part of the 20th century, investors and businessmen like A.A. Huggins, J.A. Saville, Amos "Fatty" Collins, H.H. Wilson, and William Timby (two of his buildings appear here) had built the north side of the square into an impressive block of retail and service stores. All of these buildings were constructed before 1900 and most are still standing today. (Courtesy of Mount Ayr Depot Museum.)

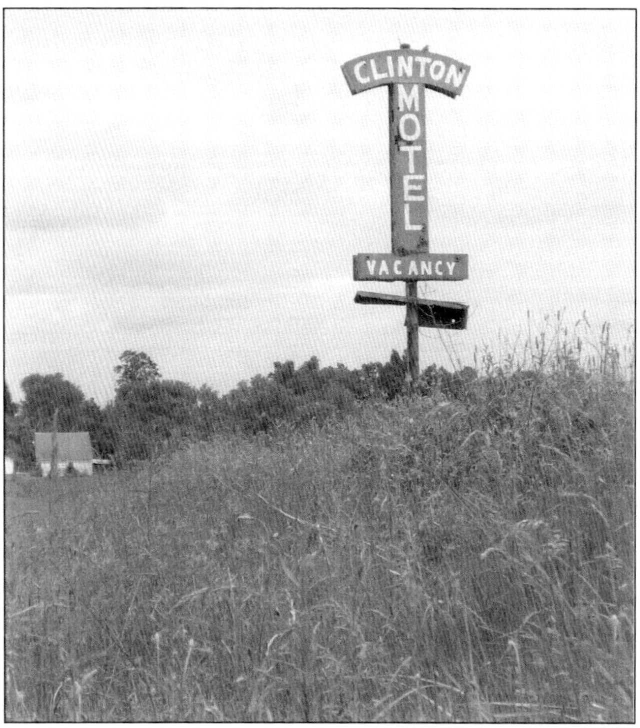

McCullough Motor Company constructed the Clinton Motel in 1950. Located on Highway 2 in Mount Ayr, the motel was named after Clinton Rice, the adopted son of McCullough Motor Company owner Mabel McCullough Rice. After 54 years of service, the motel closed in September 2004. The building was moved by the Amish residing in the area, converting segments into a farm building and starter homes for newlyweds. In June 2010, all that remained was the motel's vacancy sign. (Courtesy of Sharon R. Becker.)

In 1946, Ron Abbott was photographed on Plum Creek Farm riding his mare Beauty as her mule colt stands close by. Plum Creek Farm was located north of Diagonal. (Courtesy of Ron Abbott.)

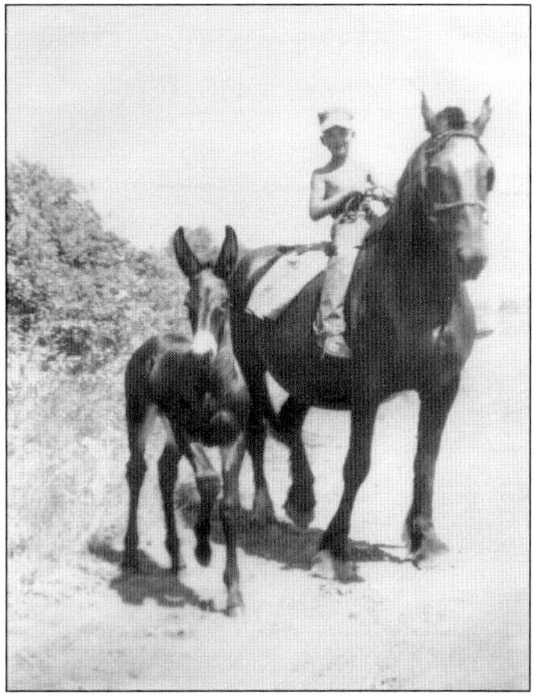

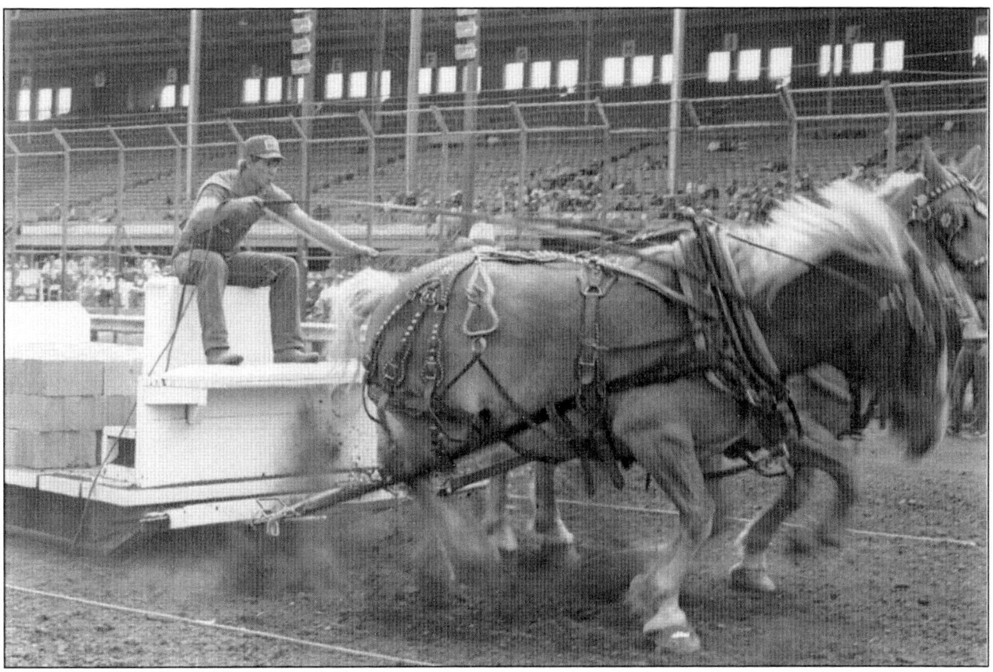

Fairs have long held the interest of Ringgold County residents. The Ringgold County Fair Association was organized in June 1859, with the first fair held the following fall on the courthouse square. The first Tingley Tournament and Street Fair was held in August 1900 with a foal and colt show added in 1906. Many Ringgold County citizens competed not only in the county fair but also in the Iowa State Fair, winning high honors and prizes. In 1985, Brian Wimer competed in the draft horse–pulling contest at the Iowa State Fair. (Courtesy of *Mount Ayr Record-News*.)

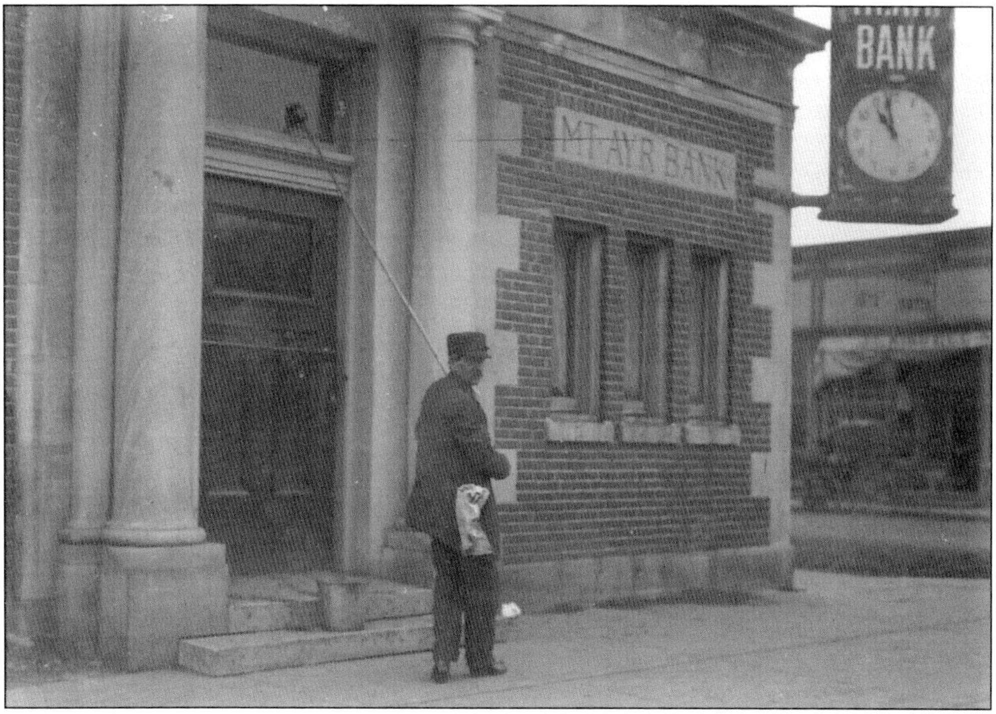

A photographer catches a window washer by surprise at the Mount Ayr Bank around 1913. This bank was built in 1912 and became Mount Ayr State Bank in 1915. The name changed again in the 1930s, this time to Security State Bank. Kinsell Hardware can be seen across the street. (Courtesy of Mount Ayr Depot Museum.)

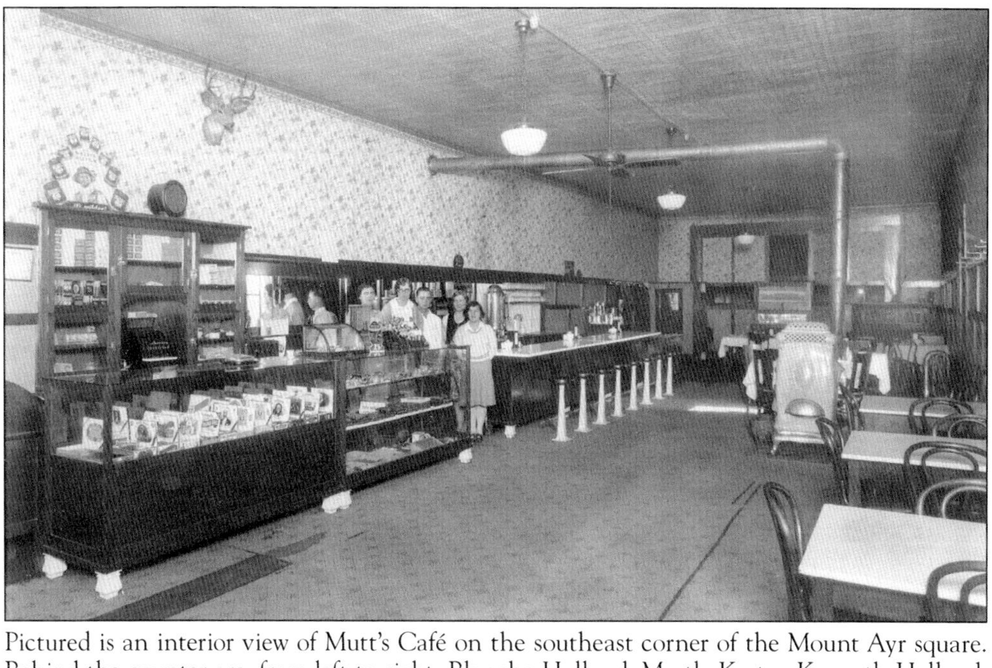

Pictured is an interior view of Mutt's Café on the southeast corner of the Mount Ayr square. Behind the counter are, from left to right, Blanche Holland, Myrtle Kaster, Kenneth Holland, Wilma Kelly Ellis, and Celeste Caldwell. (Courtesy of Mount Ayr Depot Museum.)

The Mount Ayr *Record-News* was formed in 1907 with the merging of the *Twice-A-Week News* and the *Ringgold Record* newspapers. Pictured on North Taylor Street are, from left to right, Rev. J.H. Tedford, Sam Spurrier, Stanton Tennant, Alex Maxwell, Hattie Kelley, A.B. Worley, Carroll Spurrier, and James Lawhead. Sam Spurrier was owner of the *Record-News* at this time, and Reverend Tedford was the past owner of the *Ringgold Record*. (Courtesy of Mount Ayr Depot Museum.)

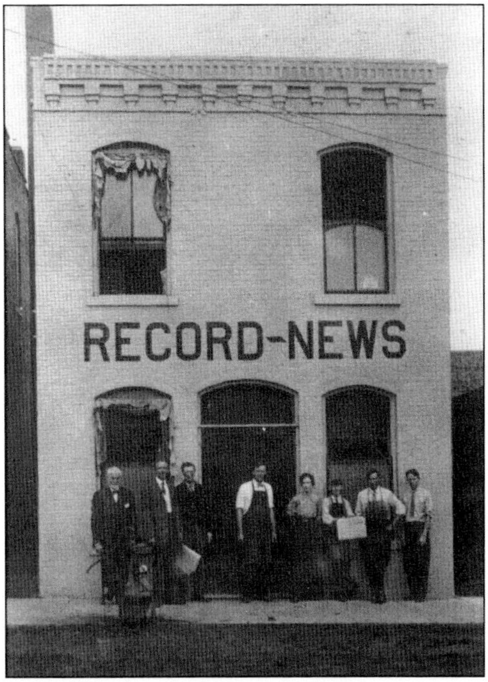

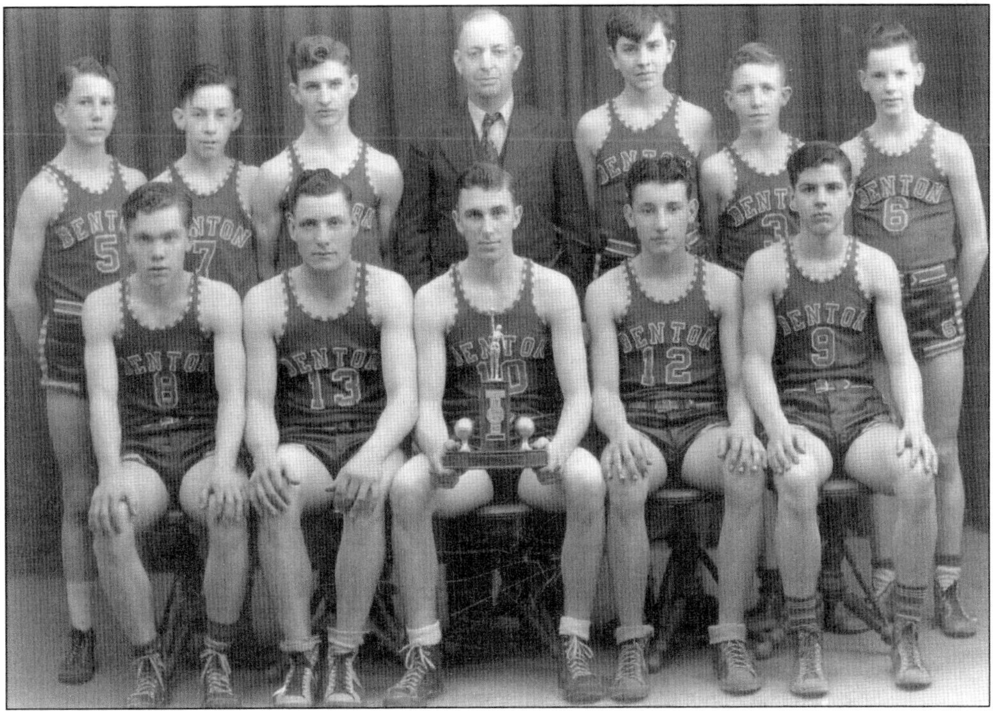

In a time when Maloy and Diagonal dominated high school boys' basketball, the Benton boys outplayed and outscored their opponents to win the 1940 Sectional Tournament. Pictured are, from left to right, (first row) Don Dillenburg, Russell Adams, Gene Cross, Keith Cole, and Herb Dillenburg; (second row) Joe Dalton, Bob Fisher, Eldon Dillenburg, coach Harry Cole, Darrell Smith, Merle Butler, and Dudley Watts. (Courtesy of Benton Museum.)

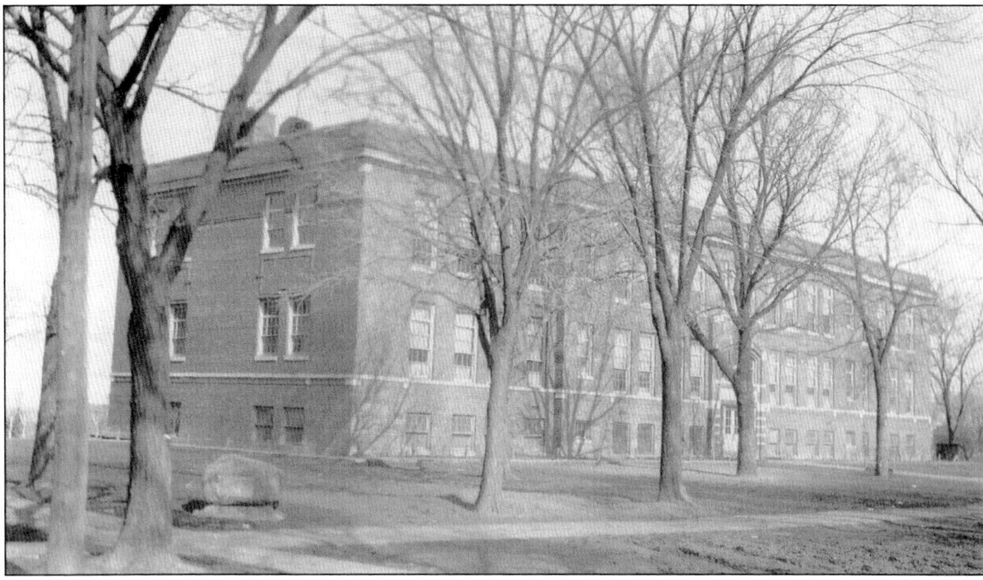

A modern brick high school was built in Mount Ayr between 1912 and 1913. The new school was 157 feet by 51 feet, with an annex of 72 feet by 33 feet. Complete with running water, electricity, and a gymnasium, the building was constructed for about $40,000 and opened for classes on September 1, 1913. A need for more classroom space necessitated the construction of an addition and a new gymnasium in 1936. The school pictured was torn down in 1978. (Courtesy of Mount Ayr Depot Museum.)

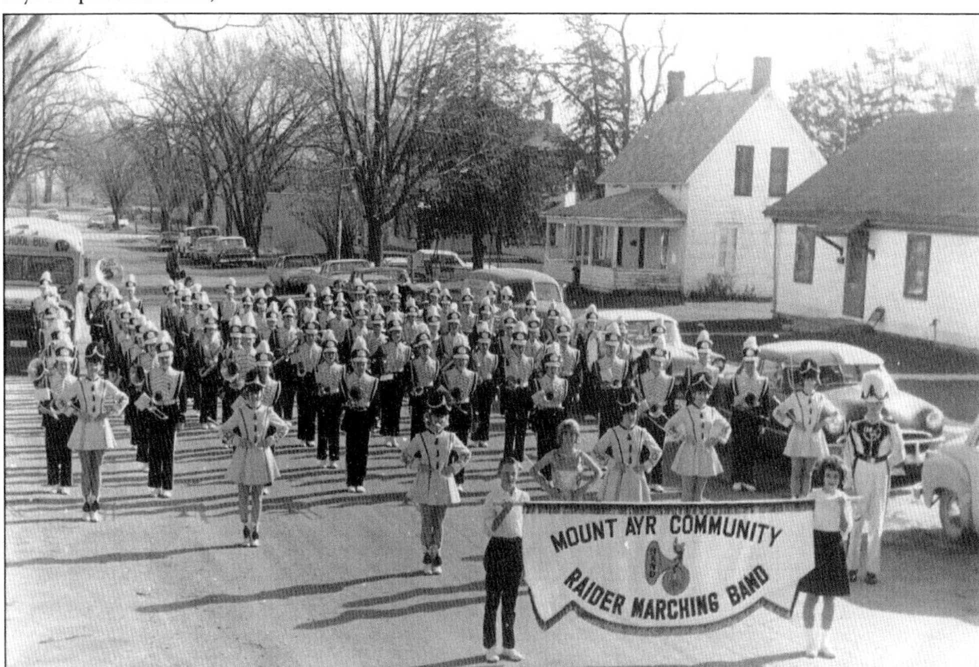

The Mount Ayr High School marching band practices its routine on East Adams Street in the mid-1960s. The band was under the direction of Merrill Perry. (Courtesy of Mount Ayr Depot Museum.)

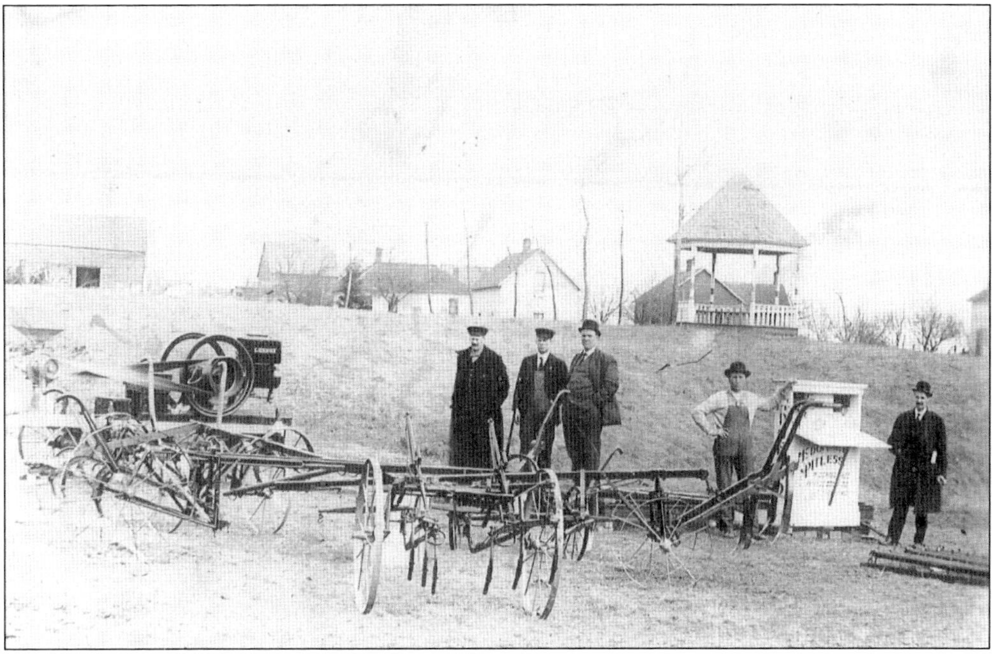

Folks gather for an agricultural implement display at Benton around 1905. One of the items shown is a pitless scale, manufactured by the McDonald Brothers Pitless Scale Company located in Pleasant Hill, Missouri. These scales were used for weighing mail and other items before they were loaded onto trains. (Courtesy of Benton Museum.)

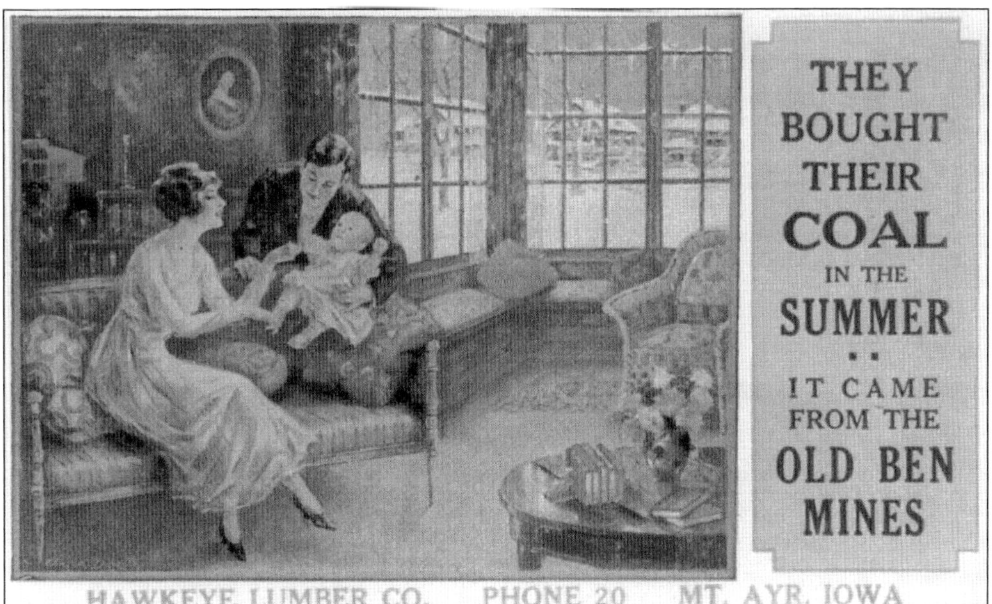

Coal from different mines burned differently. This is why merchants often advertised what mine the coal came from. Coal was a relatively inexpensive source of home heating, and coming by rail it was easy to obtain. This advertisement came in the form of an ink blotter. (Courtesy of Mount Ayr Depot Museum.)

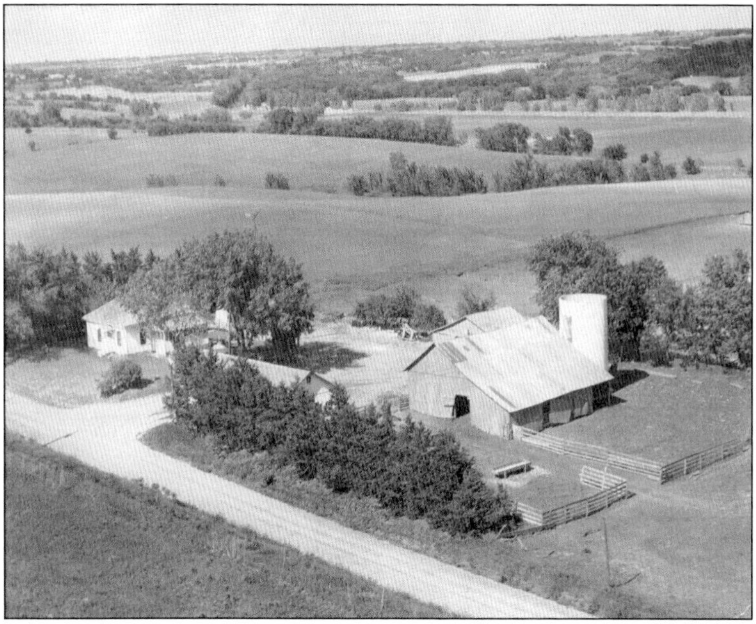

The Donald Butt farm, located southwest of Diagonal, is photographed here from the air in the 1950s. Donald was instrumental in obtaining antique farm equipment for the Pioneer Center Museum in Ellston. He was a leading authority on agricultural history in Ringgold County. (Courtesy of Arlene Sobotka.)

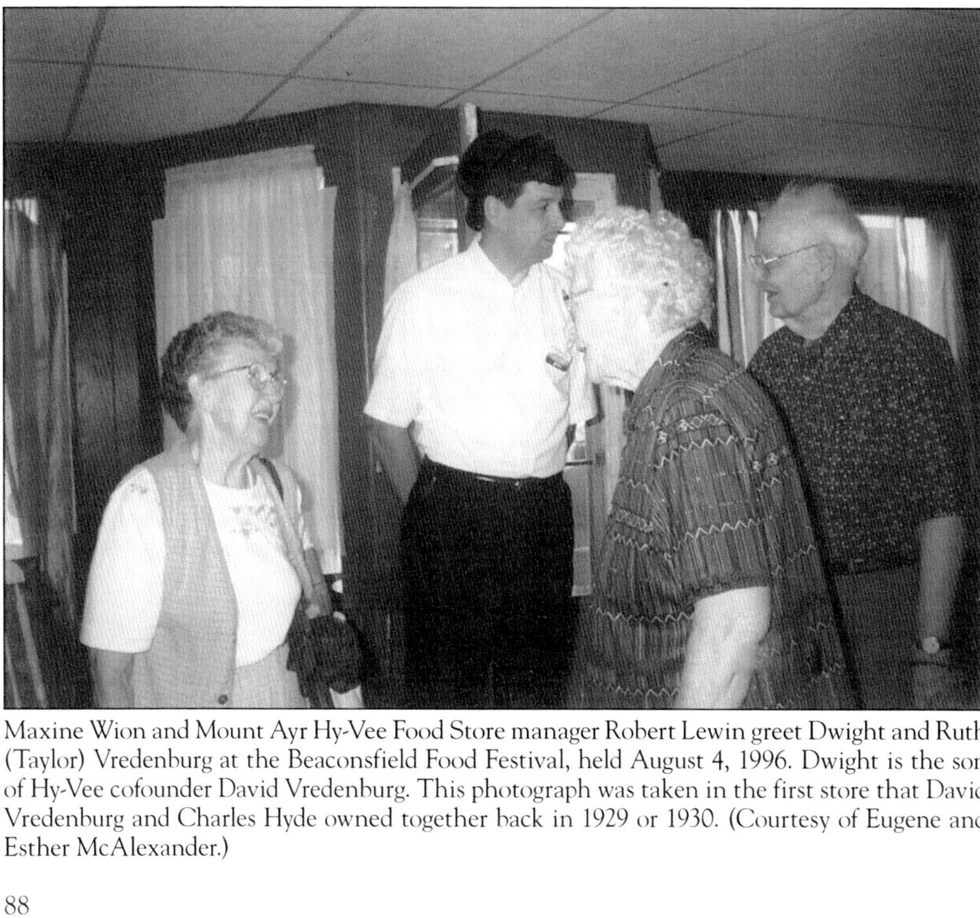

Maxine Wion and Mount Ayr Hy-Vee Food Store manager Robert Lewin greet Dwight and Ruth (Taylor) Vredenburg at the Beaconsfield Food Festival, held August 4, 1996. Dwight is the son of Hy-Vee cofounder David Vredenburg. This photograph was taken in the first store that David Vredenburg and Charles Hyde owned together back in 1929 or 1930. (Courtesy of Eugene and Esther McAlexander.)

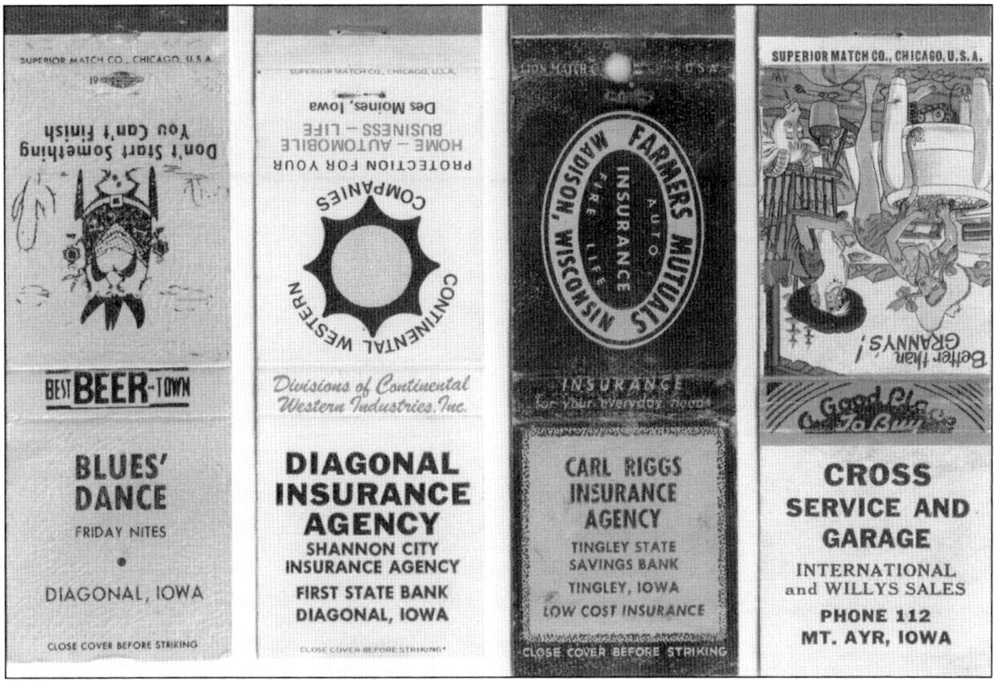

Most merchants in Ringgold County provided their customers with gifts, such as calendars, thermometers, ballpoint pens, ink blotters, ice scrapers, coin purses, and key tags. All these gifts had the name of the business on them as well as additional information like telephone numbers and addresses. By far the most common of these advertising gifts was the matchbook. They are almost nonexistent today. (Courtesy of Mount Ayr Depot Museum.)

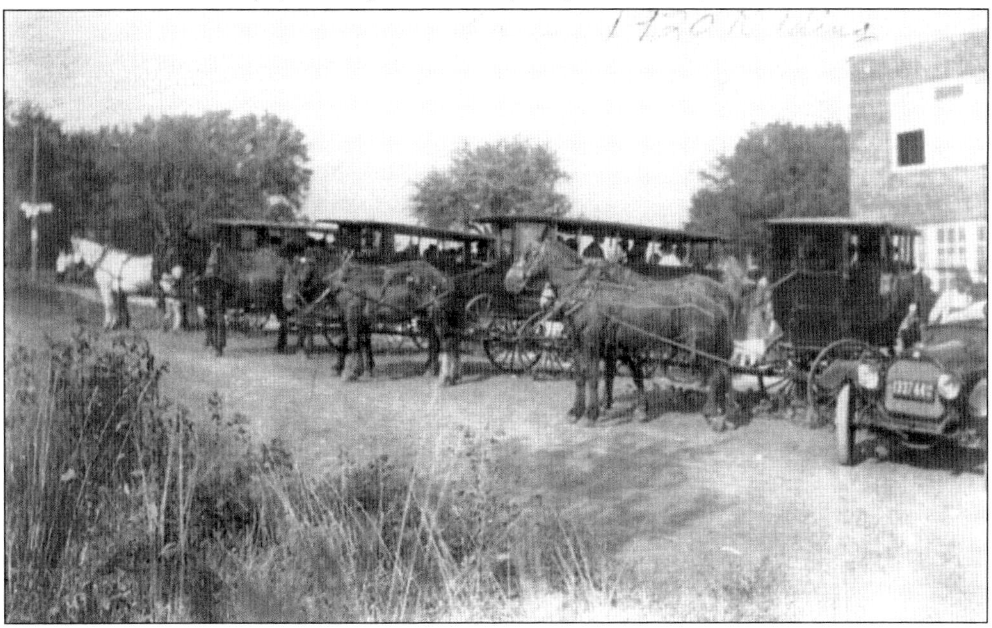

School hacks are lined up to load students at the Redding High School in 1920. Besides walking or riding a horse, this is how rural students got to and from school before the advent of buses. (Courtesy of Mount Ayr Depot Museum.)

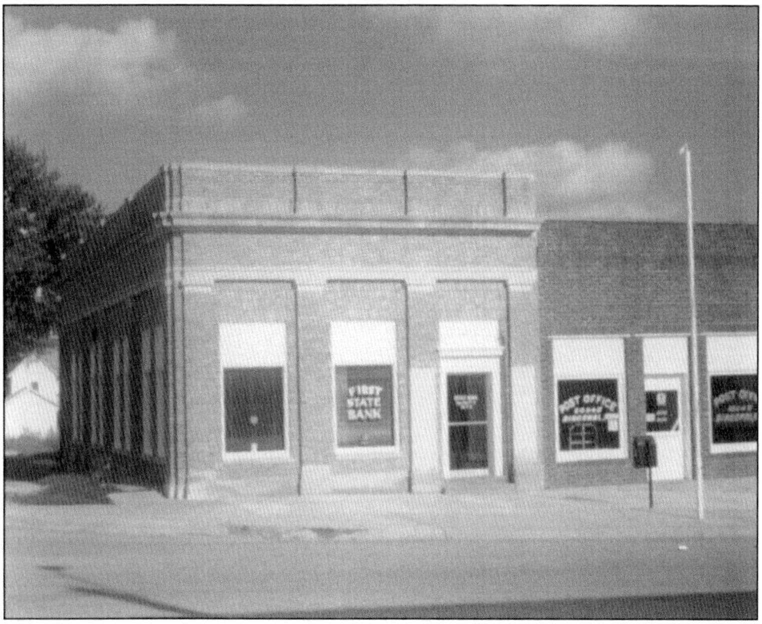

This is a 1975 photograph of the First State Bank in Diagonal. This was the site of the last bank robbery in Ringgold County. On June 20, 1986, a lone robber entered the bank and held up teller Ginny Zimmerman. The crime was never solved. (Courtesy of Diagonal Printing Museum.)

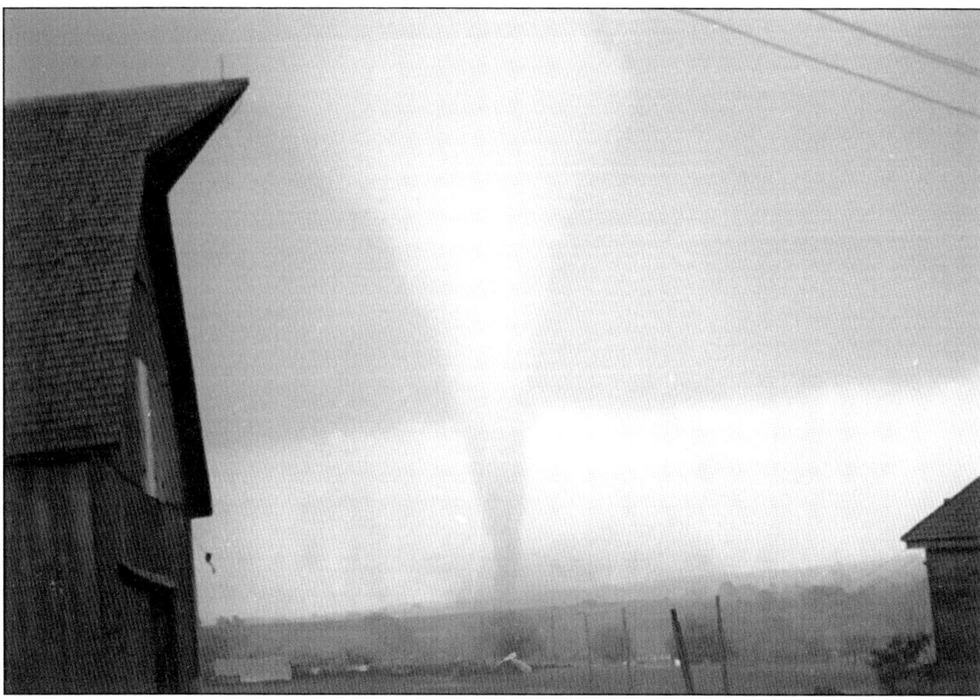

Dan Barker took this photograph of a tornado on May 23, 1981, about one and a half miles west of Benton. The tornado cut across the county from west-southwest to east-northeast and did tremendous damage to the Jerry Wimer farm and Loch Ayr, both located about two miles north of Mount Ayr. (Courtesy of LaViece Barker.)

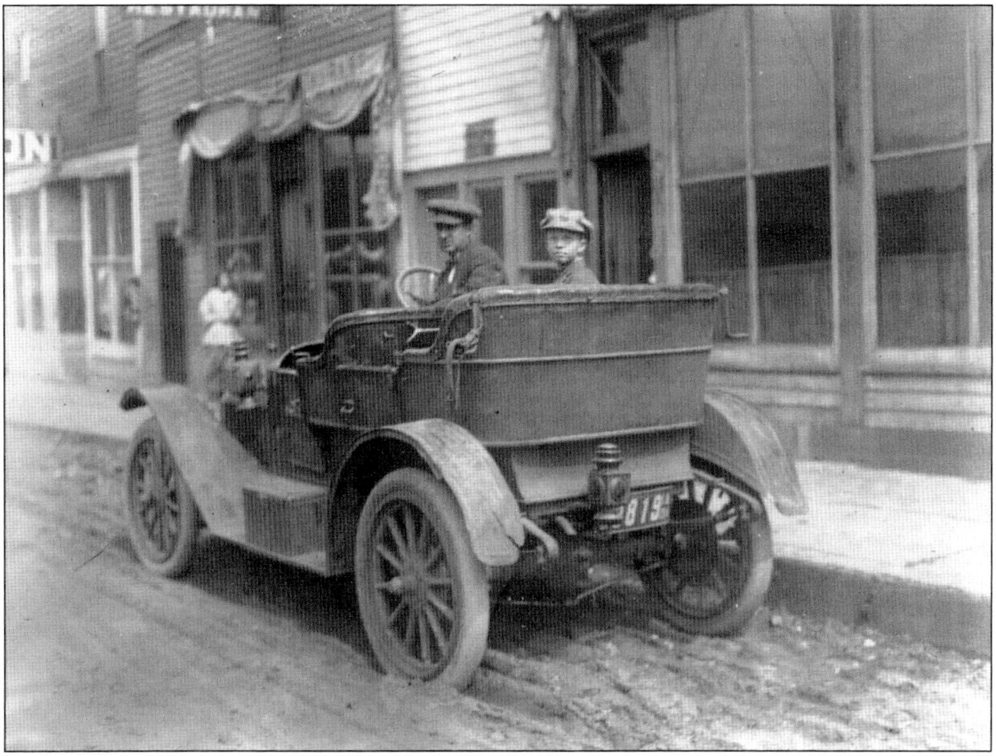

Two early motorists are parked on North Taylor Street in Mount Ayr around 1914. This street would be bricked in 1916. Behind the travelers are a restaurant and the Bonton, an early motion picture theater. These lots are occupied today by the Farm and Home Store. (Courtesy of Mount Ayr Depot Museum.)

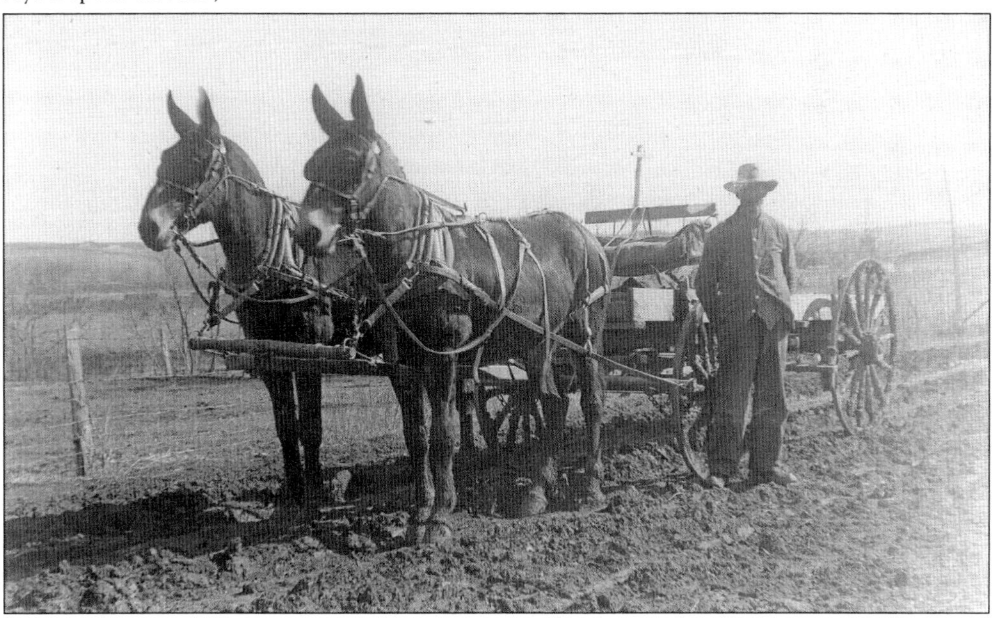

Sidney Butt poses with his mules about two miles north of Knowlton somewhere near his farm. The Chicago Great Western tracks can barely be seen in the distance. (Courtesy of Arlene Sobotka.)

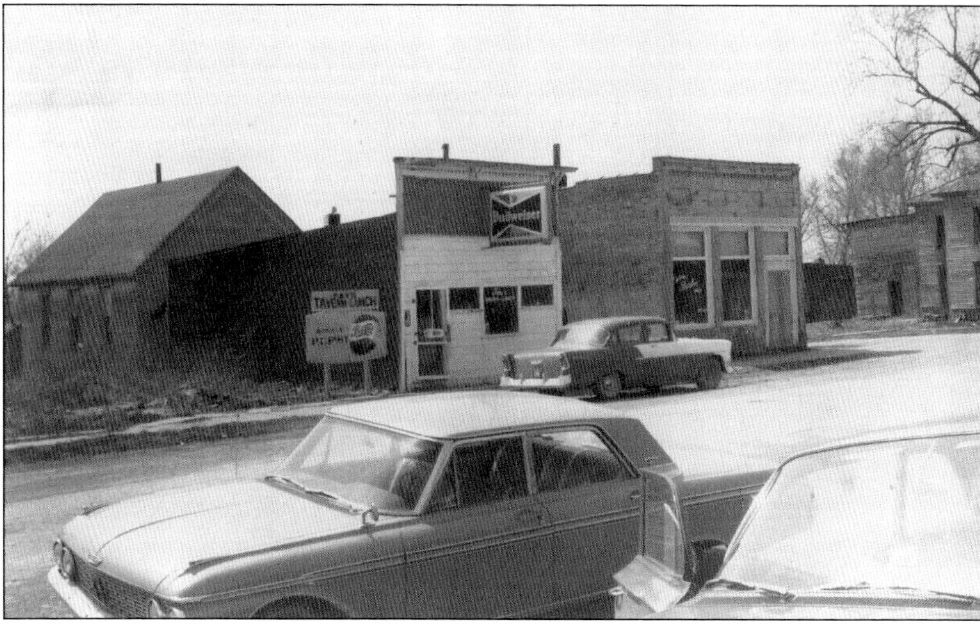

Around 1950, the Willow Shade (Tingley No. 9) Country School was attached to the rear of Joe Fay's Tavern in Ellston. The addition was used as a pool hall. To the right of the tavern is Paul Jackson's Barber Shop. Dick Simpson started his tonsorial career here in 1963 after his apprenticeship in Clarinda. Dick opened his shop on the south side of the Mount Ayr square on May 3, 1964, and is Ringgold County's only barbershop today. To the far right is the Ellston Hotel. It was dismantled and hauled to the Roy Huntsman farm in the mid- or late 1960s. (Courtesy of Doug Strange.)

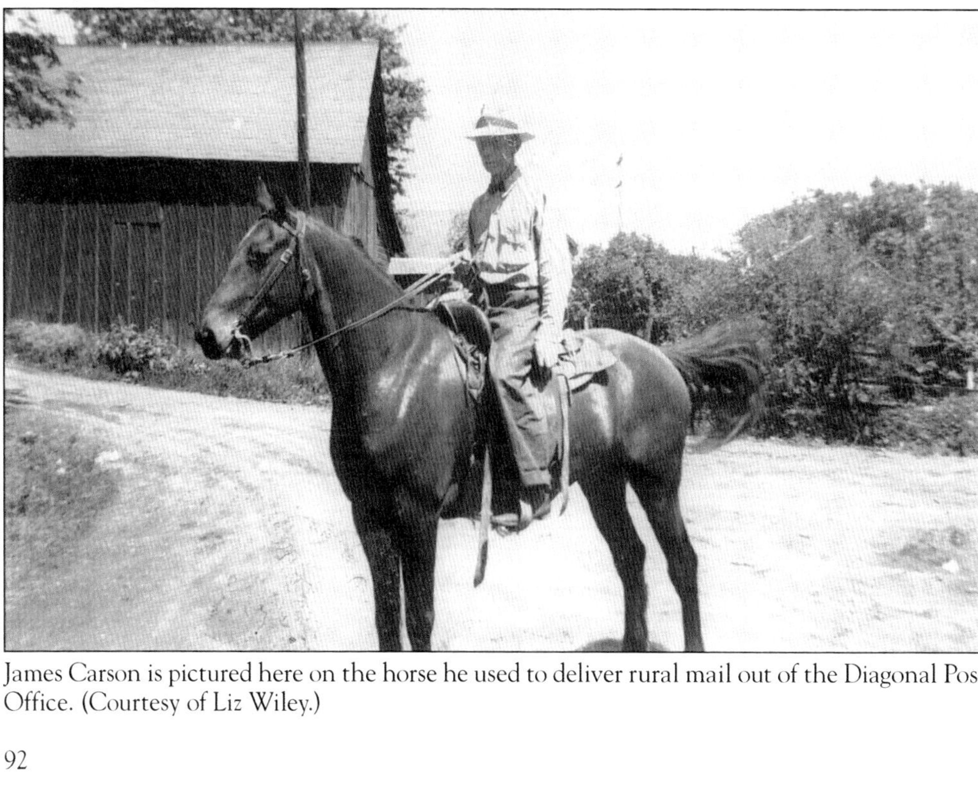

James Carson is pictured here on the horse he used to deliver rural mail out of the Diagonal Post Office. (Courtesy of Liz Wiley.)

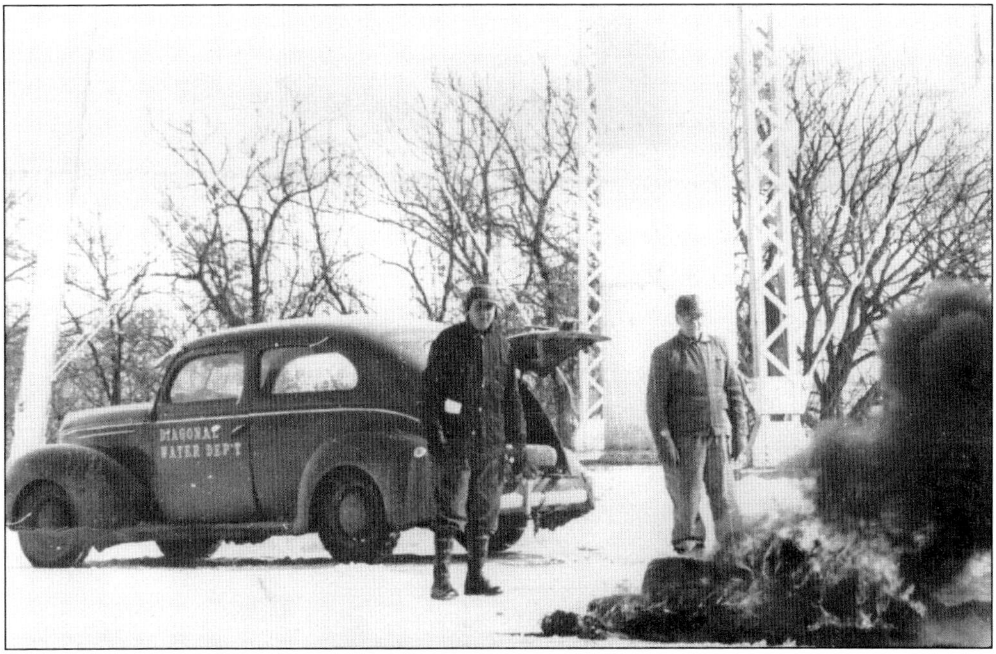

Diagonal Water Department employee Grant Stamper (left) is burning some tires in an apparent attempt to thaw something out. (Courtesy of Liz Wiley.)

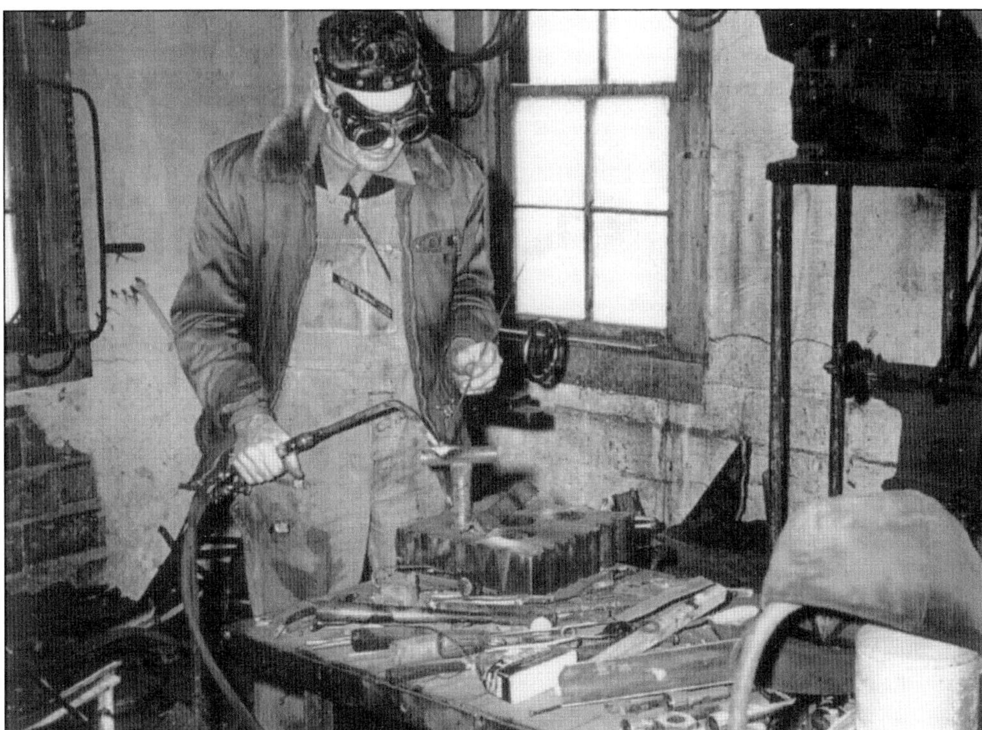

Andy Yashack toils in the Yashack Welding Shop in Diagonal. The shop was across the street and south of Boyer's Bar. (Courtesy of Liz Wiley.)

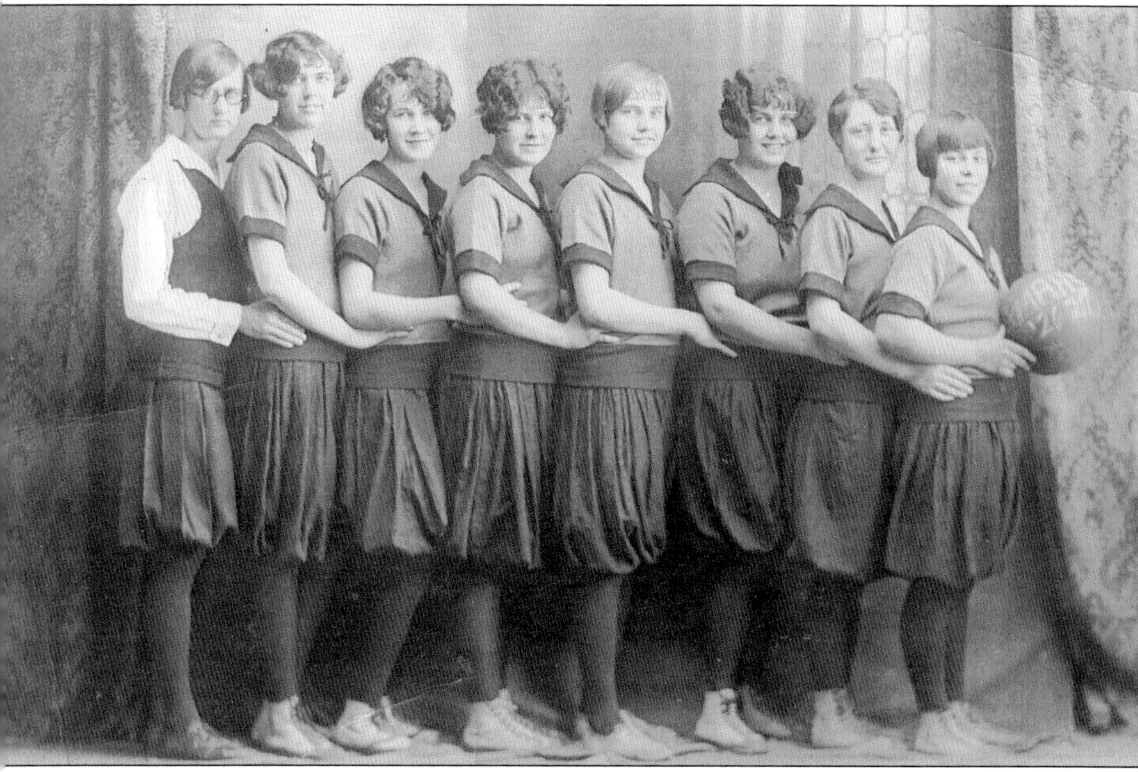

By the 1920s, the Mount Ayr girls' basketball schedule allowed for competition against other schools. Before that, the different classes played each other in a tournament. This postcard is of the girls' 1926–1927 team. The team included, from left to right, Esther Boyer (coach), Neva Sloan, Lorene Bagley, Orpha Combs, Mary Dinkel, Anna White (captain), Lois Combs, and Oma Dickerson. (Courtesy of Mount Ayr Depot Museum.)

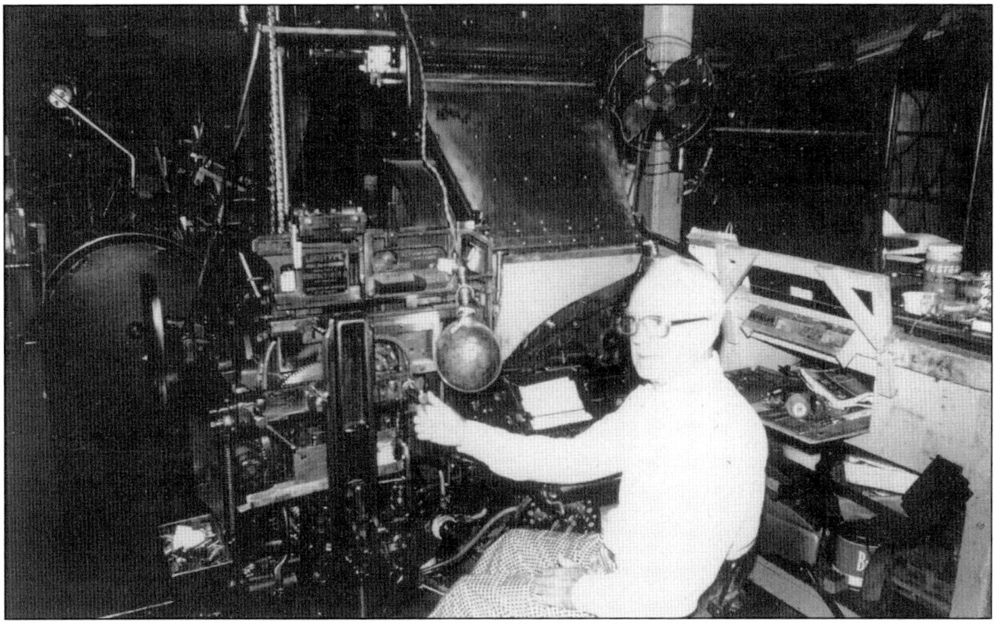

Diagonal Reporter publisher Harold Turnbull operates a linotype machine, which the newspaper bought in the 1920s. Harold was hired on as an apprentice in April 1922, when he was 16 years old. He bought the newspaper in 1934 and retired from the business in 1972 after 50 years with the *Diagonal Reporter.* (Courtesy of Liz Wiley.)

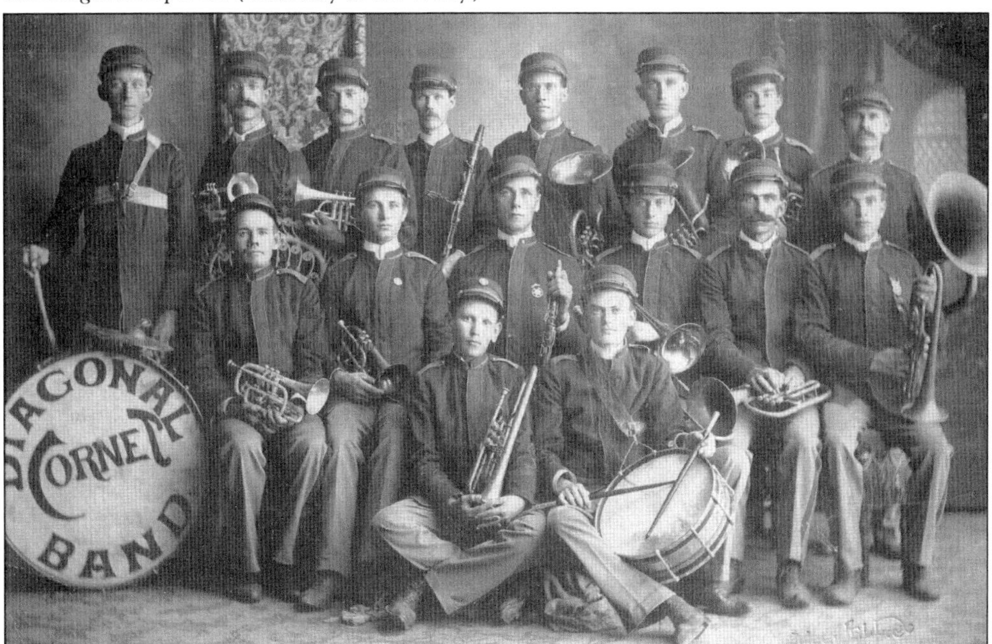

Seen in the early 1900s, the Diagonal Cornet Band poses for the camera. Pictured are, from left to right, (first row) Paine and Jimmie Todd; (second row) Hal Yaw, Frank Slavik, Jerry Zaruba, Frank Talley, Clarence Gard, and Frank Fogle; (third row) Harry Todd, Dr. L.D. Rink, Alva Paine, Edgar Todd, Elmer Shaw, Linn Wood, Glen Canfield, and Ray Brattain. (Courtesy of Diagonal Printing Museum.)

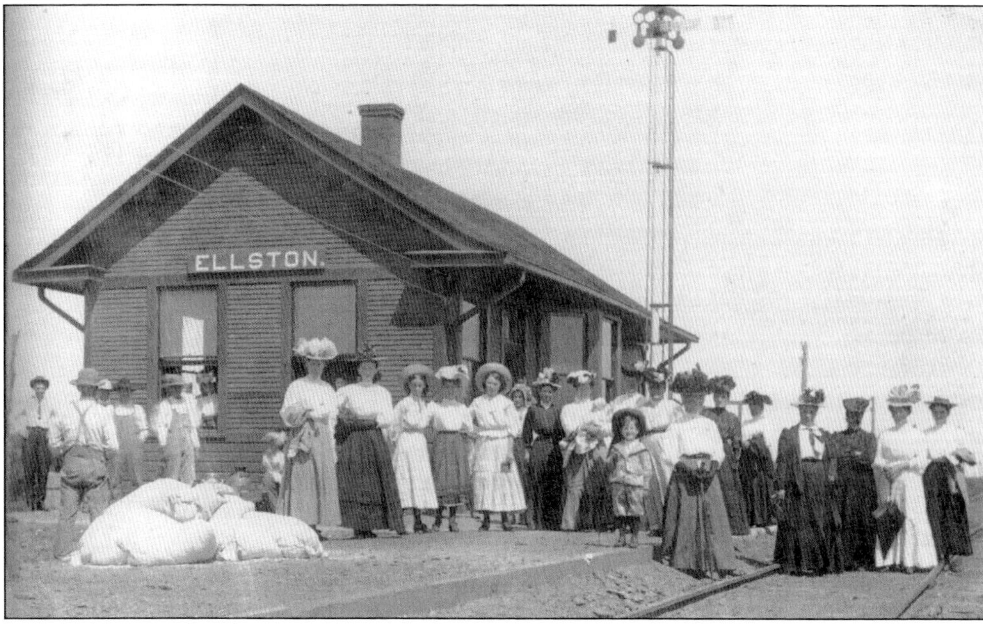

It is not known what the special occasion was at the Ellston Depot in 1908, but it was common for large events to be held there. Political dignitaries and famous orators sometimes took train trips to reach small-town folk before the days of radio. To the east lay Beaconsfield, and the next stop west was Tingley on this railroad line. (Courtesy of Mount Ayr Depot Museum.)

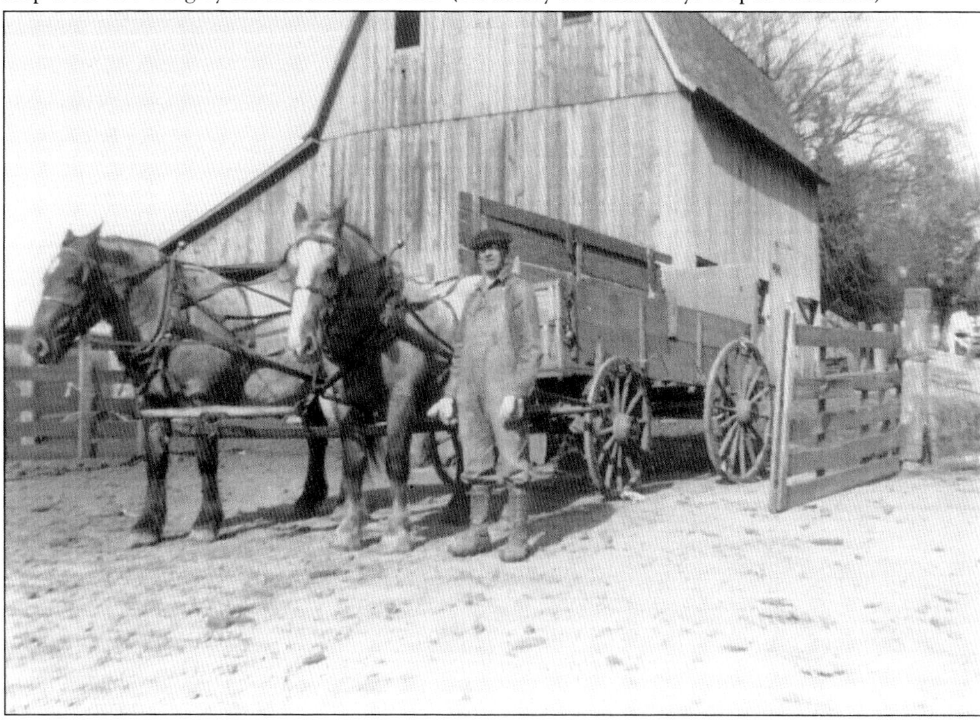

Pictured is Robert O'Grady with his team and wagon. Robert attended Pumptown, a rural school northeast of Ellston, and later bought a farm two miles northeast of Ellston. All five of his children graduated from Ellston High School. (Courtesy of Rod and Deb Bastow.)

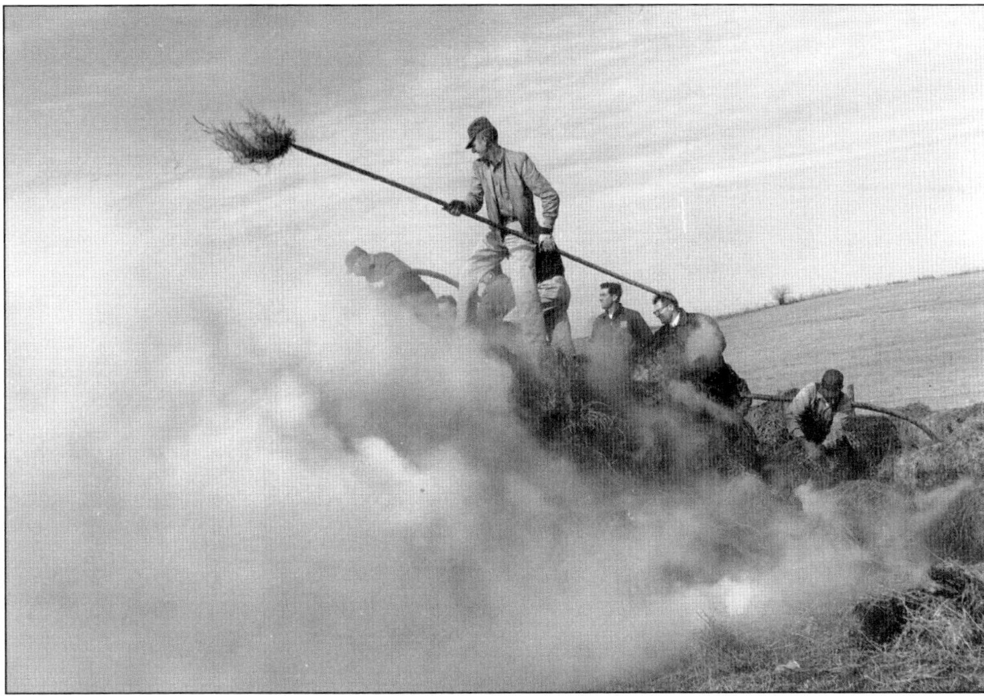

Don Stull of the Mount Ayr Volunteer Fire Department fights a hay fire west of Mount Ayr in the early 1960s. Don is using a pike pole to separate the bales. He is flanked by fellow firefighters Jack Hartman (to the right of Don) and Max Anderson (to the right of Jack). (Courtesy of Rick and Lora Stull.)

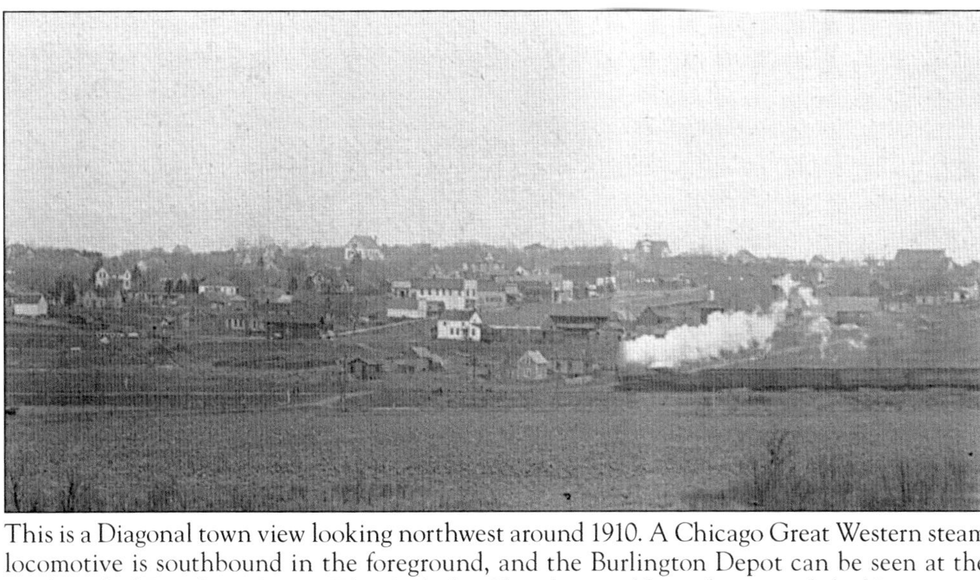

This is a Diagonal town view looking northwest around 1910. A Chicago Great Western steam locomotive is southbound in the foreground, and the Burlington Depot can be seen at the south end of Broadway Street. The Catholic Church is visible at the upper left. (Courtesy of Arlene Sobotka.)

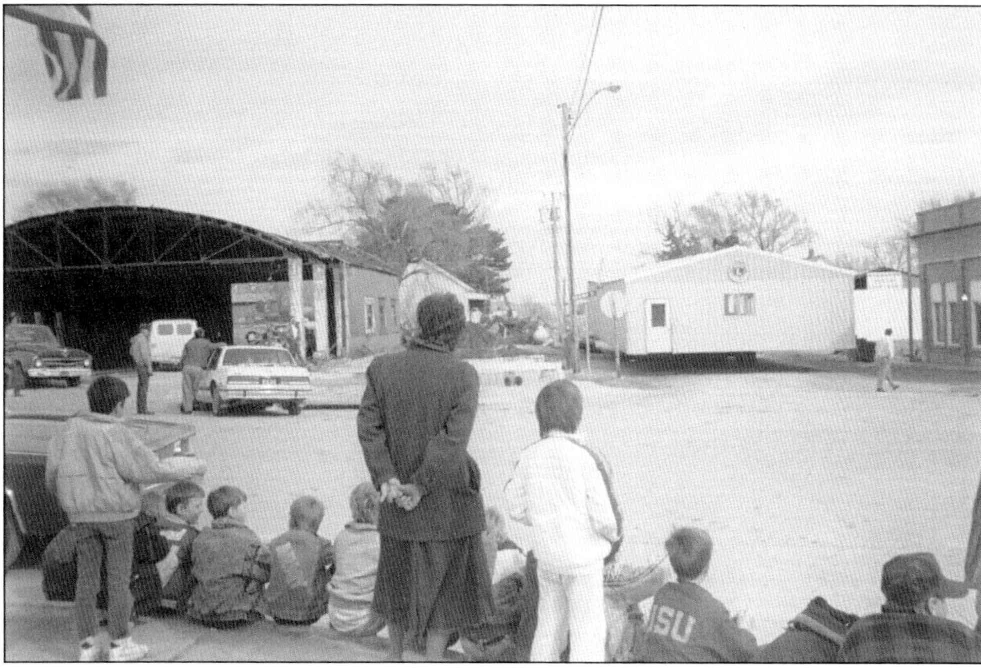

Sue Mobley's third-grade class looks on as the Diagonal Lions Building is moved one block east and one block south to become the new home of the Diagonal Volunteer Fire Department in March 1991. (Courtesy of Diagonal Printing Museum.)

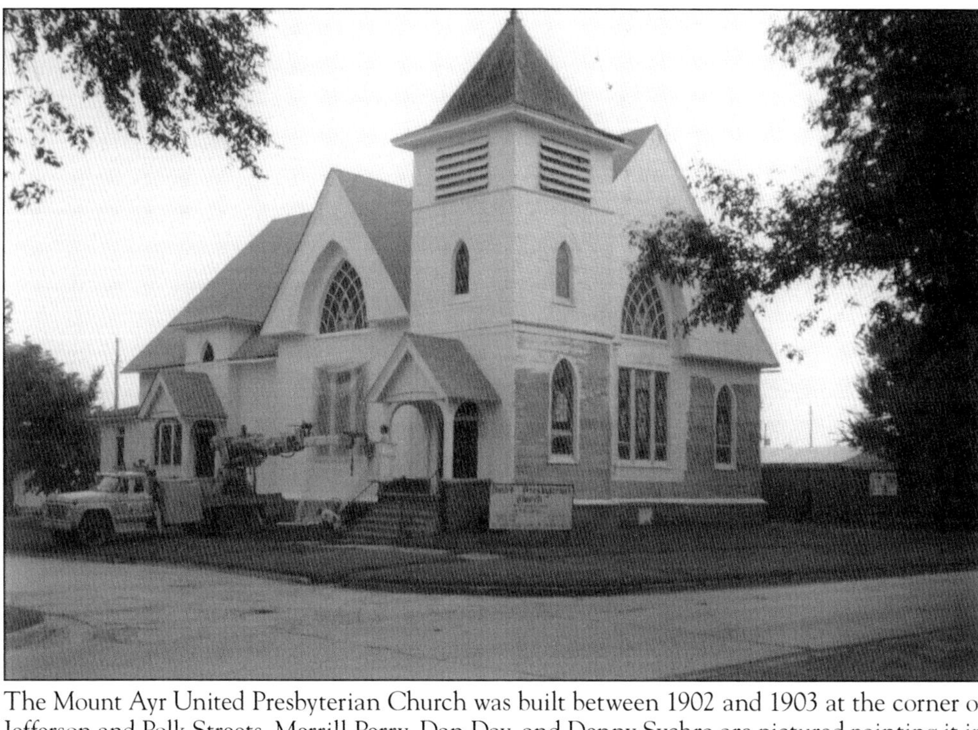

The Mount Ayr United Presbyterian Church was built between 1902 and 1903 at the corner of Jefferson and Polk Streets. Merrill Perry, Dan Day, and Denny Sychra are pictured painting it in 1982. The church was torn down in the winter of 2005–2006. (Courtesy of Mike Avitt.)

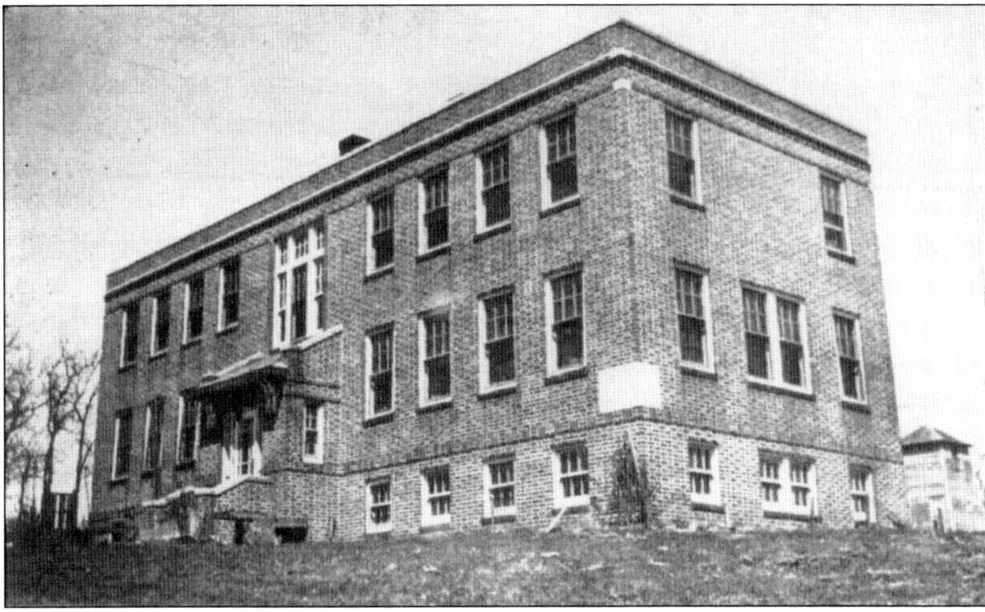

The Ringgold County Home was built in 1922 to replace a wooden structure that was condemned in 1919. Located about three miles north of Mount Ayr on Highway 169, the building measured 68 feet by 28 feet. It was built for $28,000 and came equipped with electricity and running water. (Courtesy of Mount Ayr Depot Museum.)

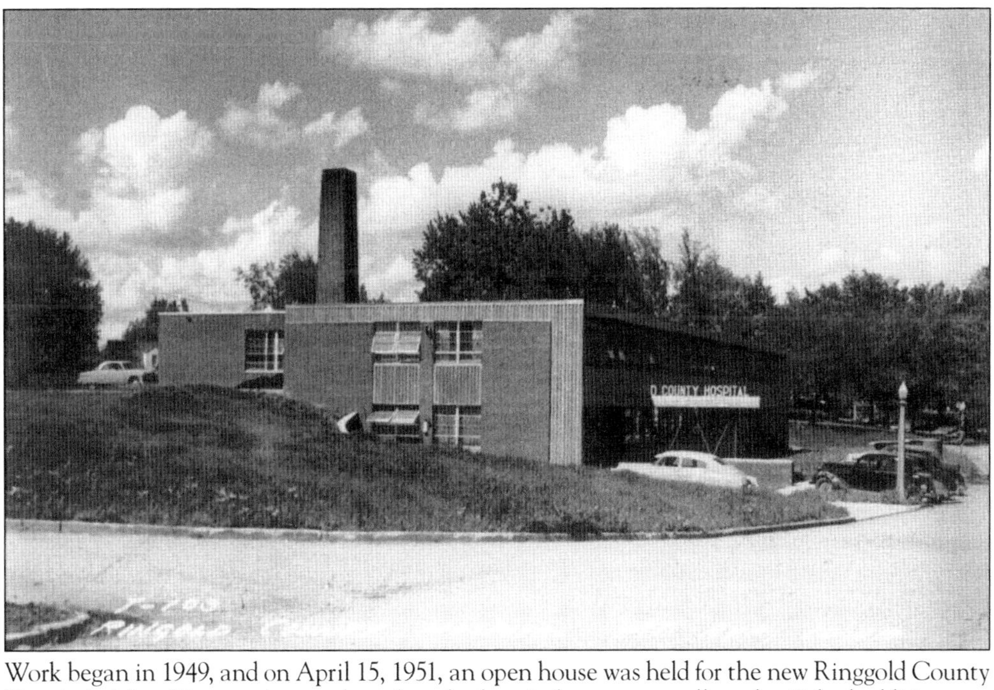

Work began in 1949, and on April 15, 1951, an open house was held for the new Ringgold County Hospital. After 20 years, it was clear that the hospital was too small, and a 16-bed addition was constructed in 1971. This facility ceased operation the third week of December 2009, as a new county hospital was built on Highway 169 in Mount Ayr. (Courtesy of Mount Ayr Depot Museum.)

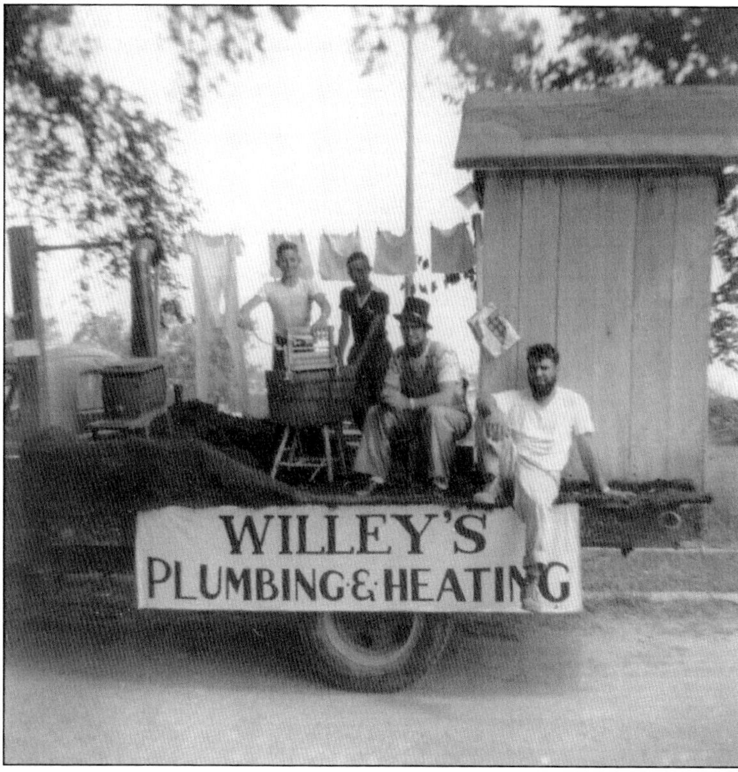

In preparation for the Ringgold County Centennial in 1955, Gerold Willey of Mount Ayr decided to design a float that reflected his business, Willey's Plumbing and Heating. He did not have to go far to obtain an outhouse; it is from his backyard. In this photograph are, from left to right, Ronnie Willey, unidentified, Barton Spencer, and Gerold Willey. (Courtesy of Mount Ayr Depot Museum.)

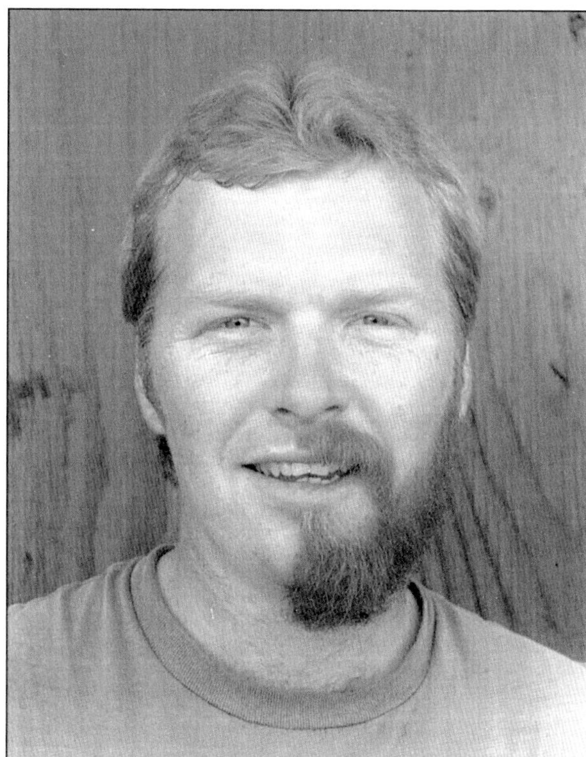

Most local men grow beards for their town's centennial, and Jim Newton of Diagonal did just that in 1988. Halfway through Diagonal's centennial celebration, Jim decided half the beard could go—the right half. (Courtesy of Arlene Sobotka.)

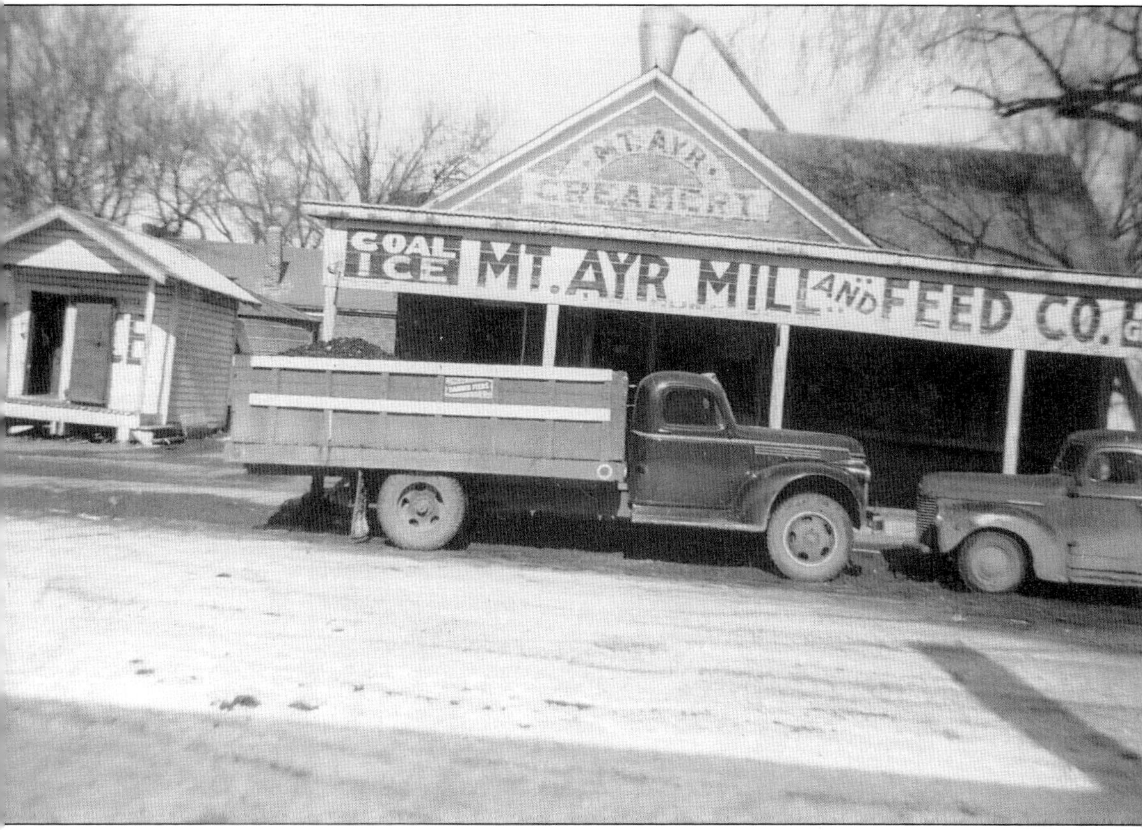

A load of coal is ready to be delivered and sits waiting at the Mount Ayr Mill and Feed in the late 1940s. Jesse Anderson and George Tennant bought the former Mount Ayr Creamery (the sign can still be seen on the front gable) in 1927. Anderson bought out his partner and constructed an icehouse in the mid-1930s. The mill also began to market its own private feed brand, MARCO Feeds. Jesse Anderson's son Max bought his dad's mill in the 1950s and continued the business until he retired in 1992, keeping it in the family for 65 years. At one time, the Mount Ayr Mill and Feed was the oldest Nutrena Feeds dealer in the United States. (Courtesy of Max and Maxine Anderson.)

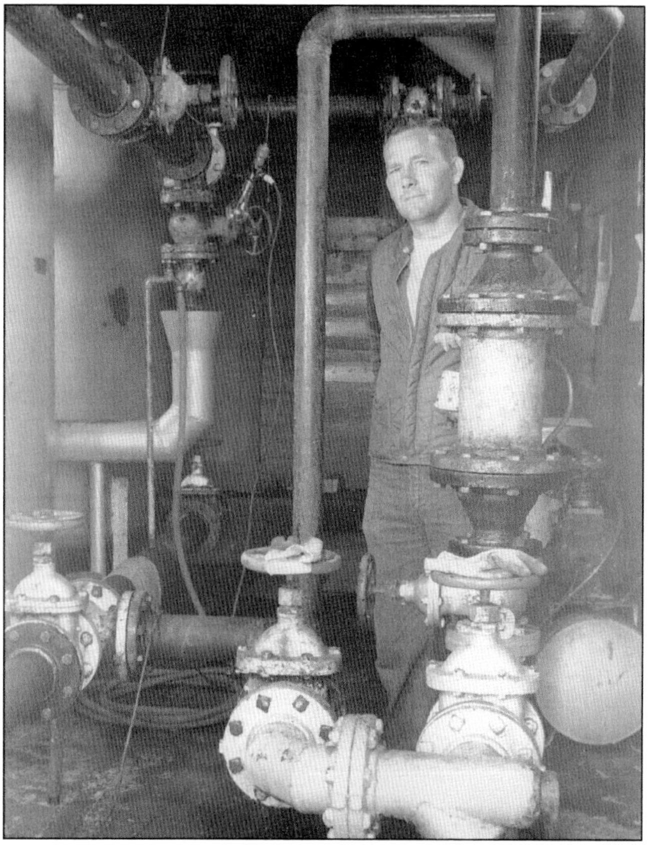

Richard Briner poses for Harold Turnbull at the Diagonal Water Works building. Harold was the editor and publisher of the *Diagonal Reporter*. (Courtesy of Liz Wiley.)

Fire broke out in the rear of Gambles Hardware Store in Mount Ayr on the afternoon of June 6, 1977. Due to a summer drought, water pressure was low, and fire departments from Lamoni, Creston, Diagonal, Tingley, and Kellerton were called. The store, owned by Melvin and Dorothy Wurster, was a complete loss, as was Lawhead Dental Clinic and McNeiley Drug Store. (Courtesy of Mount Ayr Depot Museum.)

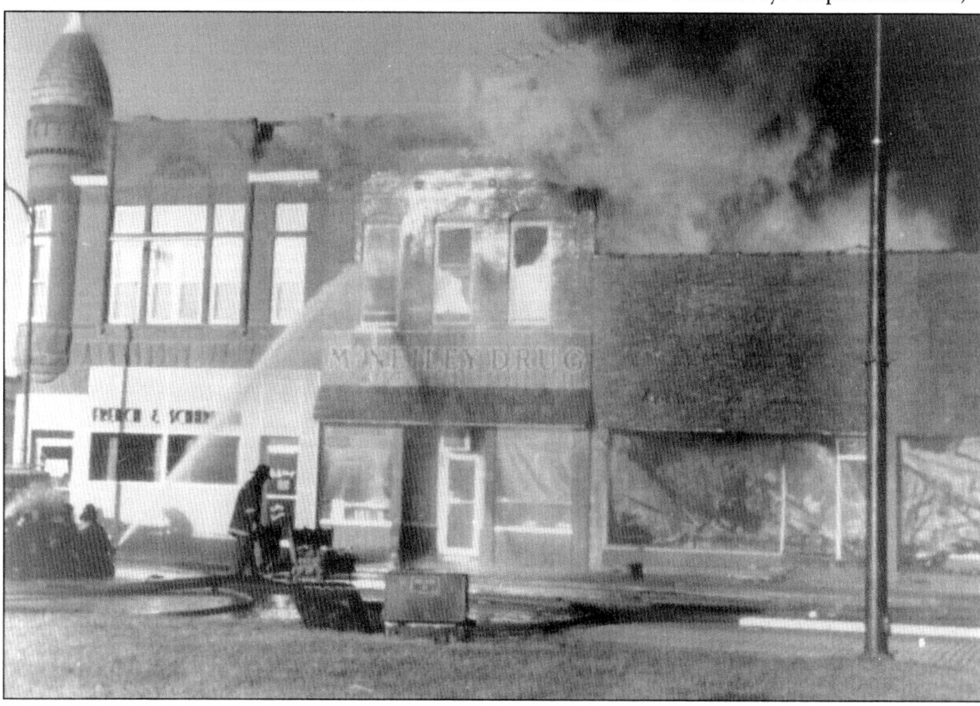

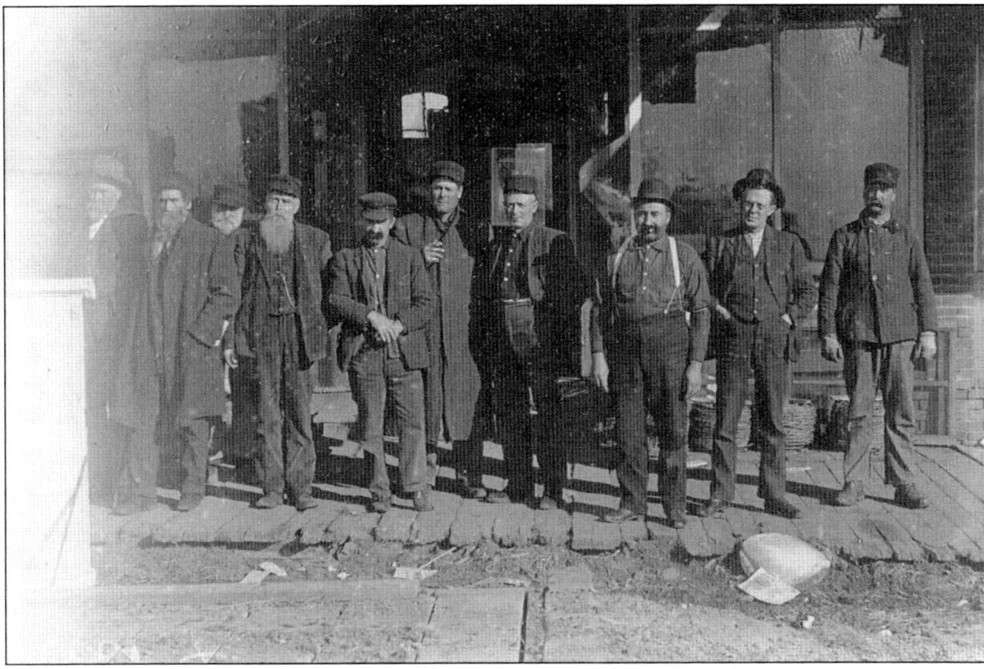

A crowd poses for a photograph in front of the Yaryan Store in Knowlton about 1910. Store owner Leander Elmer "Gan" Yaryan is pictured third from the right. Notice the scales to the lower left. (Courtesy of Diagonal Printing Museum.)

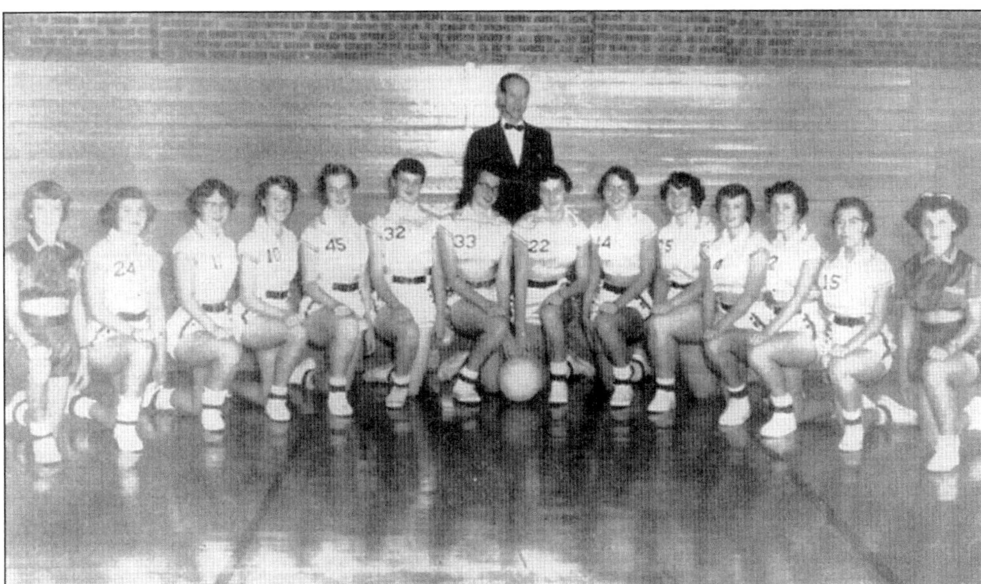

The Beaconsfield girls' basketball team made it all the way to the state tournament in 1956 despite a total high school enrollment of 19. However, in 1956, grade-school girls were allowed to play on varsity, so the team could be rounded out with seventh and eighth graders. (Courtesy of Eugene and Esther McAlexander.)

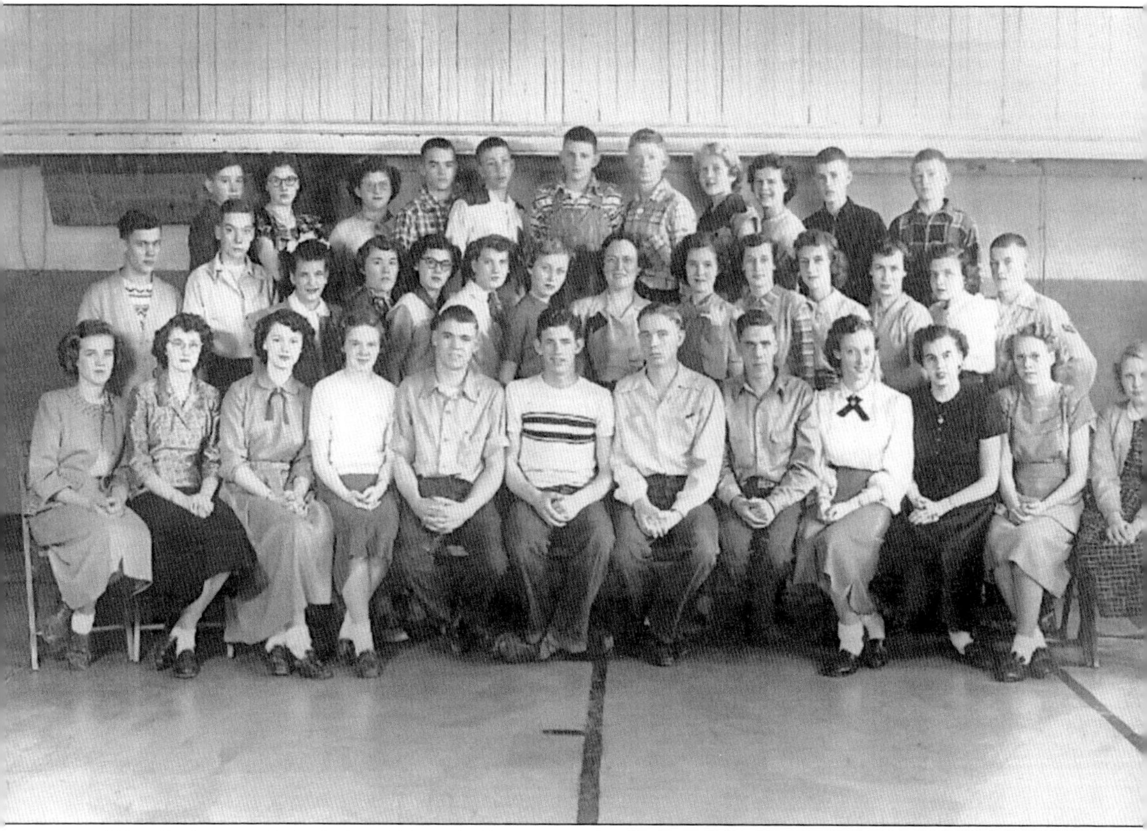

The Kellerton High School Mixed Chorus is pictured in 1951. This school merged with Grand River in 1959, creating Grand Valley Community School. The school closed in the mid-1990s. In this photograph are, from left to right, (first row) Donna Kaster, Phyllis Meadows, Janice Heggs, Janice Meadows, Robert Walker, John White, Arlen Hughes, Keith Sissel, Jo Ann Hanks, Janice Cox, Betty Wicker, and Carolyn Galbraith; (second row) Lyle Corll, Max Scott, Clara Mae Hogue, Louise Walker, Shirley Heggs, Betty Kaster, Reva Laird, director Mrs. Manning, Marilyn Epps, Norma Reed, Mary Hohneke, Nellie Gibson, Barbara Brimmer, and Marion Ethington; (third row) Marvin Corll, Evalyn O'Connell, Caryll Lou Higday, Marvin Lesan, Verlyn Hoff, Walter Lipe, Monte Ballou, Karen Laird, Ann Meadows, Jack Ethington, and Jim Meadows. (Courtesy of Mount Ayr Depot Museum.)

The Soldiers and Sailors Monument was dedicated on July 4, 1918, and stands on the northeast corner of the courtyard. The statue is a memorial to the men and women who have proudly served their country and expresses the gratitude for that service. Cecil Herrington took this photograph in December 1948. (Courtesy of Mount Ayr Depot Museum.)

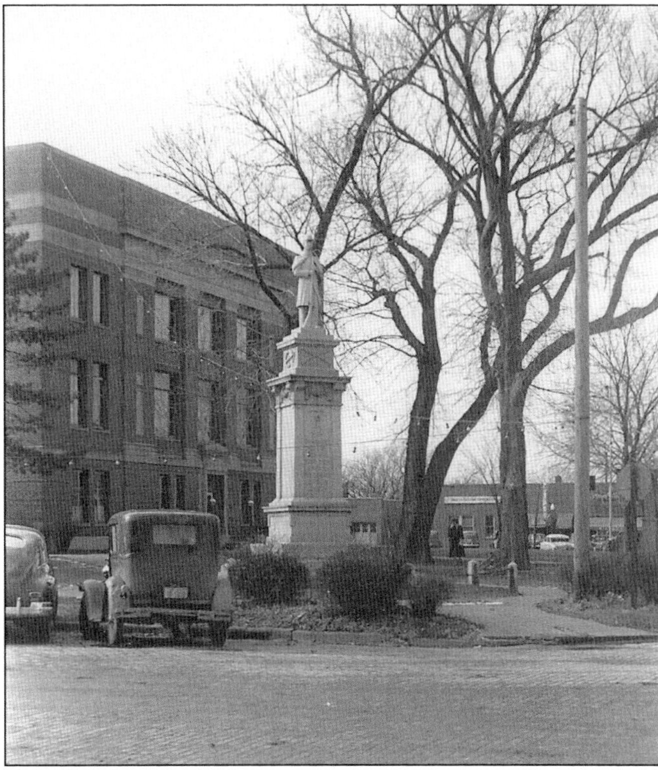

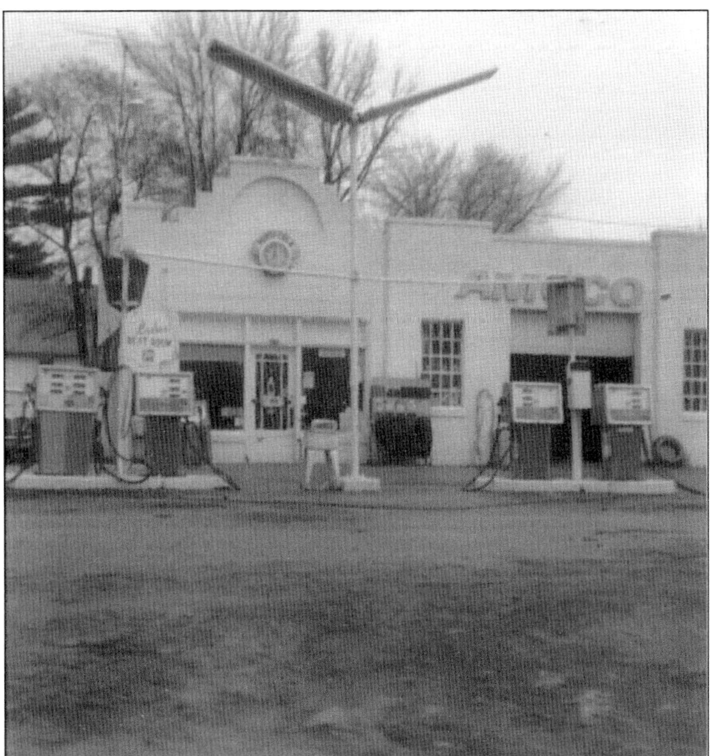

Day Shafer and his son-in-law John Denhart bought this service station in 1944, and it became Shafer's Service Station. Denhart eventually bought out his father-in-law and operated the station until November 1979, when it was sold to Carl Riggs. The station was located at South Taylor Street and Highway 2 and is pictured here in 1979. (Courtesy of Mike Avitt.)

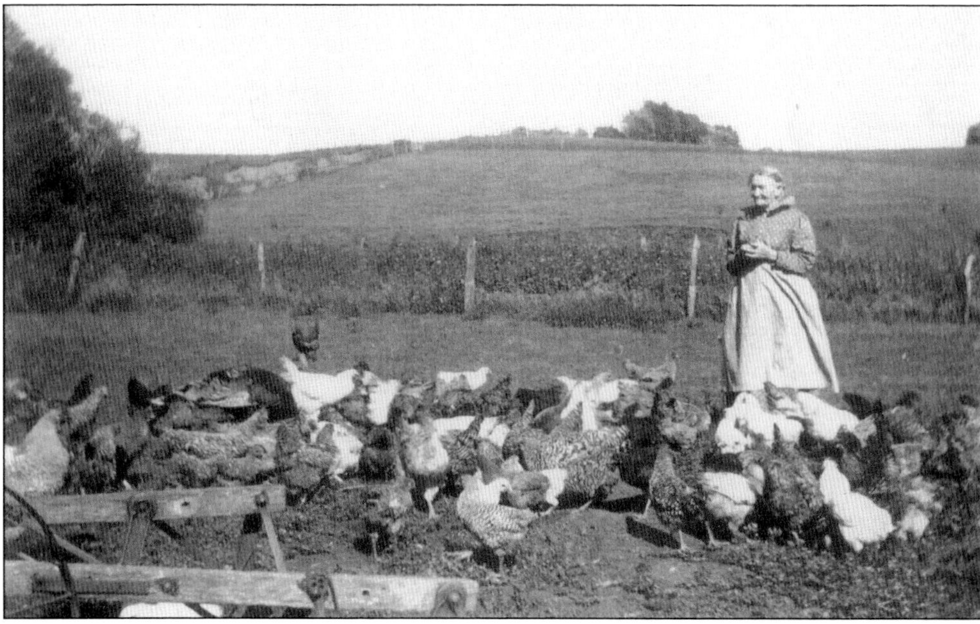

Catherine (Grogan) O'Grady tends to her chickens. "Grandma" O'Grady's farm was on the present-day site of Sun Valley Lake. (Courtesy of Rod and Deb Bastow.)

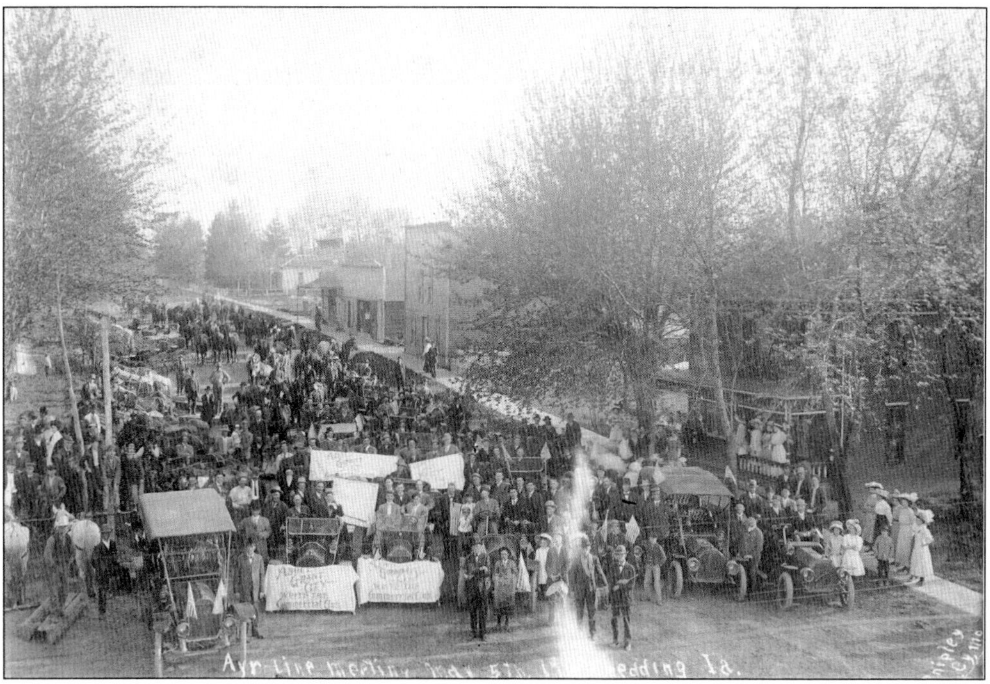

The Ayr Line Association was formed in 1911 with A.I. Smith as president and George Allyn as vice president. The purpose of the association was to build and maintain a permanent, direct highway between Des Moines, Iowa, and St. Joseph, Missouri. Rallies like this were sponsored by the association to promote attention of and donations to the project. Mount Ayr was the halfway point of the highway, hence the name Ayr Line Highway. This photograph depicts a rally on the west side of the Redding square. (Courtesy of Friends of Old Redding.)

Four

Little Ringgolders

Children are the greatest resource of any county. Little Ringgolders play, learn, and grow, sometimes growing up to be old Ringgolders. They might inherit the family farm or become teachers in the same school in which they were taught. Perhaps they grow to work in the same hospital in which they were born or pray in the same church as their grandparents. Sometimes the love of their home prevents them from leaving, and sometimes they take the love of their home to other lands.

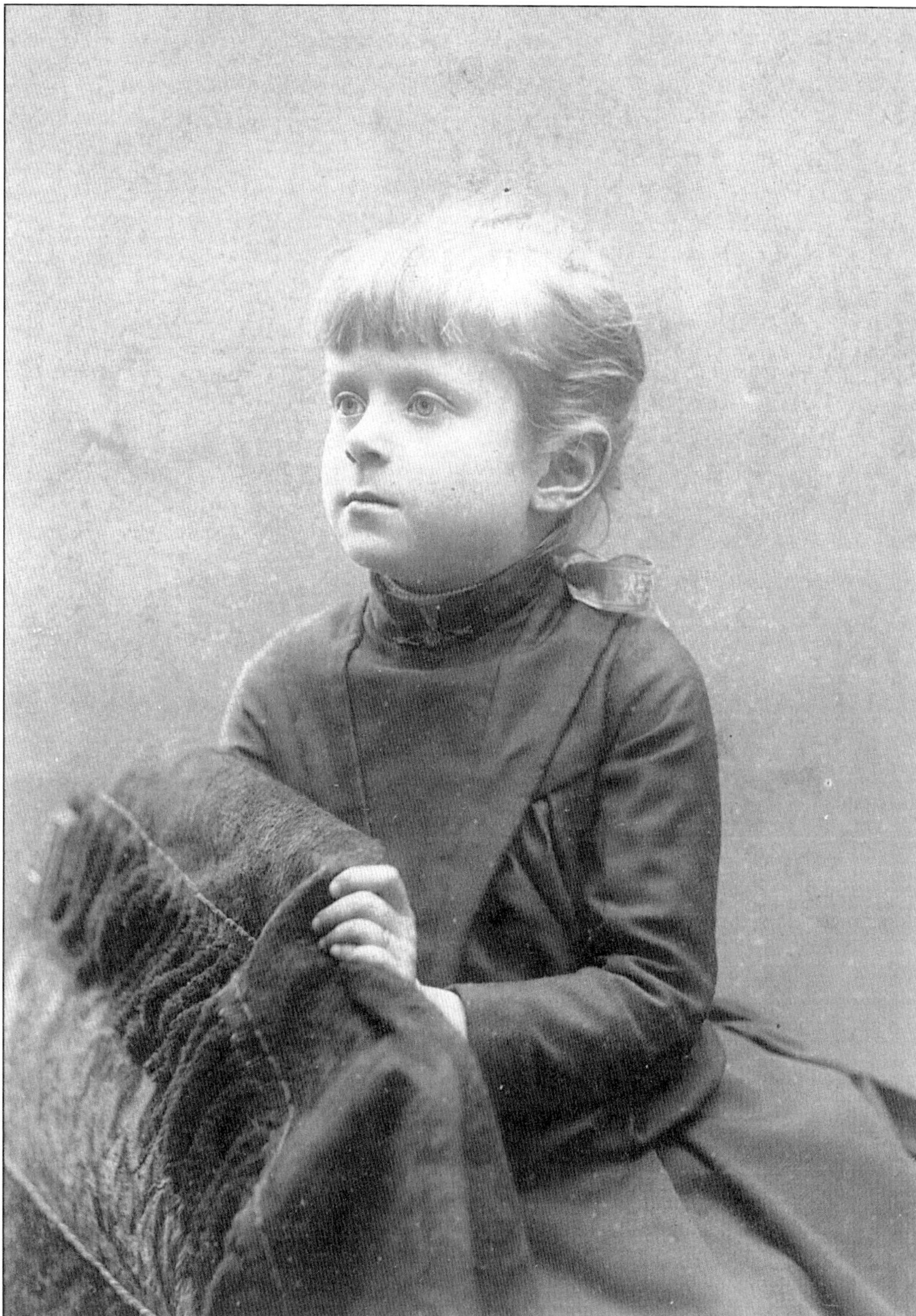

Nina Belle (Miller) Allyn was born on September 27, 1882, and was the daughter of John W. and Mary Ester (Critchfield) Miller. Nina married Earle Kinsell Allyn on October 27, 1908. Earle was the son of George S. Allyn, a state representative and leading citizen of Mount Ayr. (Courtesy of Mount Ayr Depot Museum.)

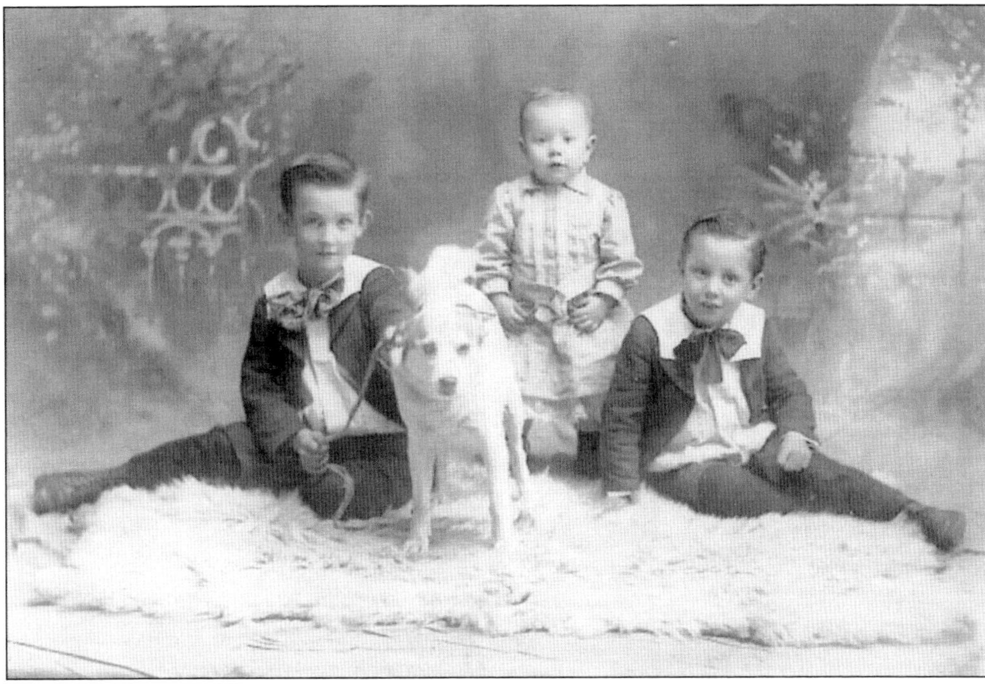

Pictured are, from left to right, Vern, Jocko, and Cleo Hacker with the family dog. Vern grew up to own and operate the Watterson Store with his wife, Vera Shields Hacker. (Courtesy of Phillina Smelser.)

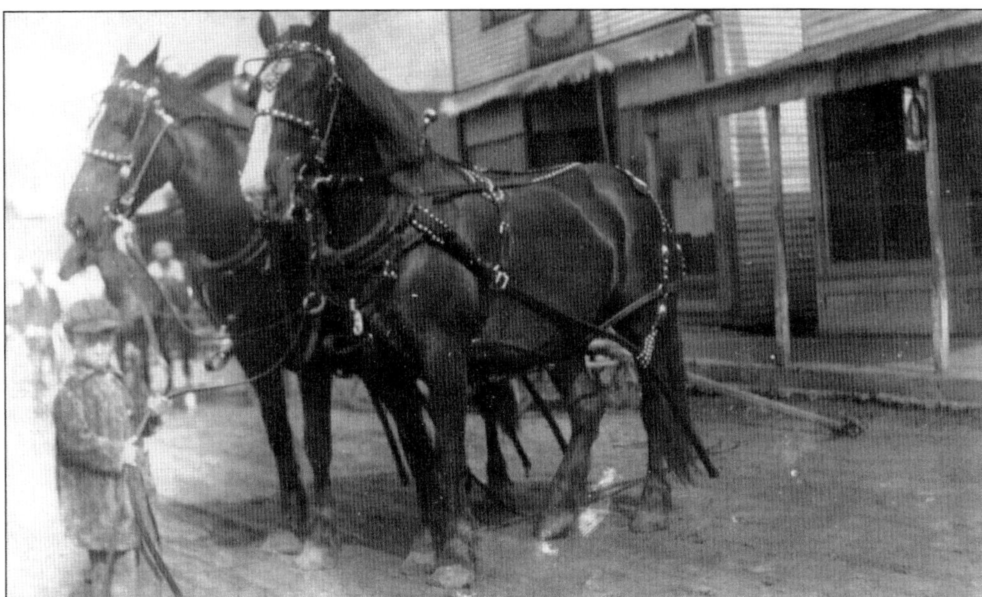

Raymond Johnston, pictured here at age four or five, poses with his grandfather's horses. At one time, Raymond's grandfather T.T. Johnston owned and operated the livery stable in Ellston. (Courtesy of Bill Adams.)

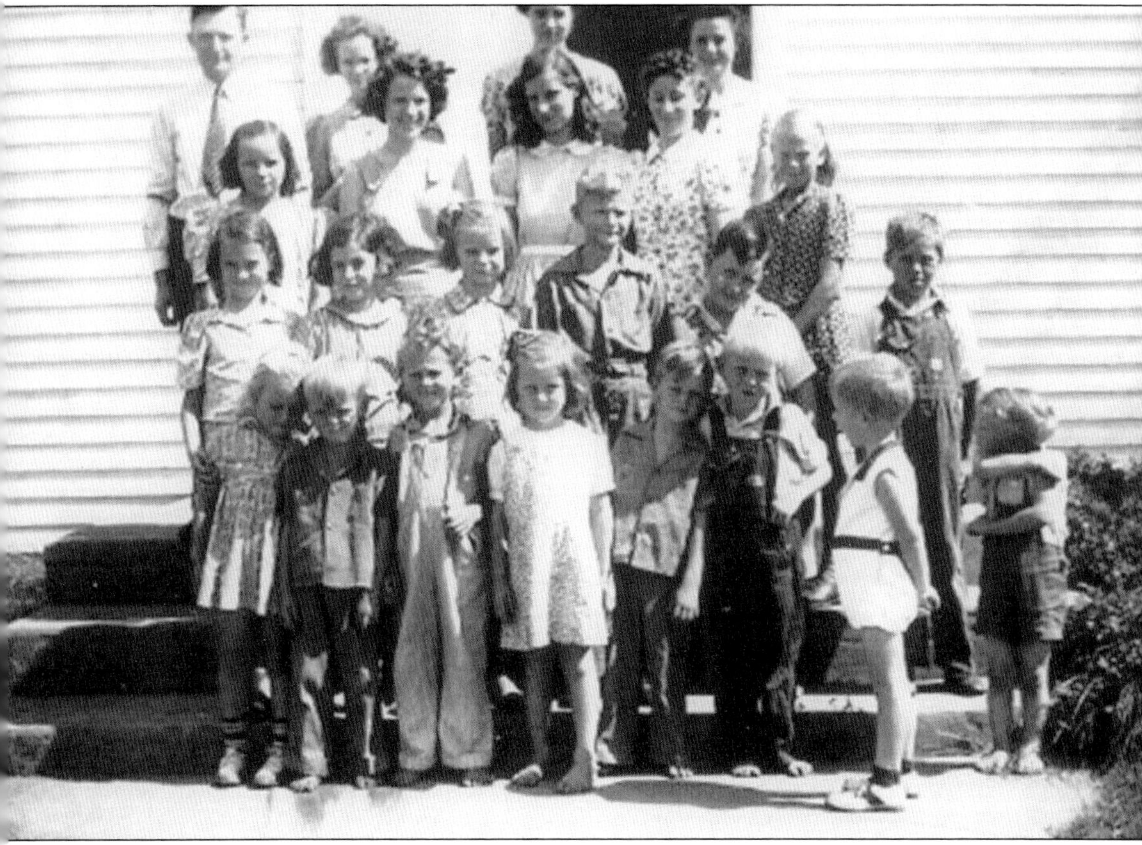

Bible school students and staff are pictured at the Middle Fork Methodist Church in 1941. Included are, from left to right (front row) Marjorie Ann Bagley, Johnny Sheumaker, Jackie Smith, Hazel Saville, Carroll Olney, Lowell Howie, David Waugh, and an Olney boy; (second row) Shirley Smith, Roberta Reynolds, Dorothy Saville, Tommy Sheumaker, Lloyd Cochran, and Leroy Howie; (third row) Delores Howie, Julia Sheumaker, Alice Deane Waugh, Ruth Saville, and Dorothy Smith; (fourth row) Reverend Stewart, Frances Sheumaker, Mary Waugh, and Ethel Saville. (Courtesy of Friends of Old Redding.)

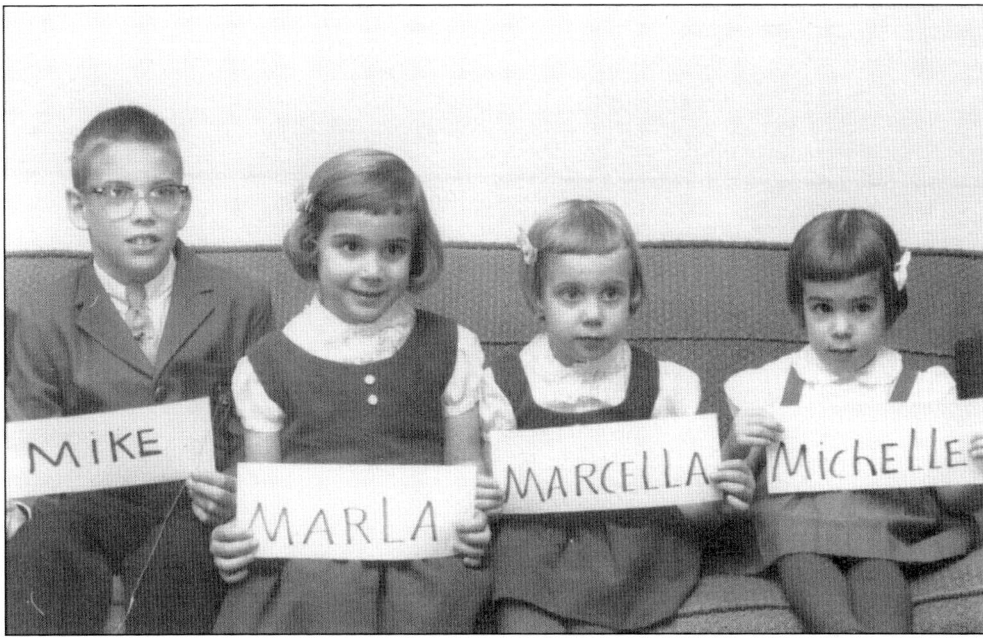

The children of the Reverend Merlin and Margaret Wilkins seem to be trying on the world's largest name tags. Their father was a teacher at the Mount Ayr Community High School for over 20 years. He was also pastor of the Kellerton Christian Church and Tingley Christian Church for several decades. (Courtesy of Mount Ayr Depot Museum.)

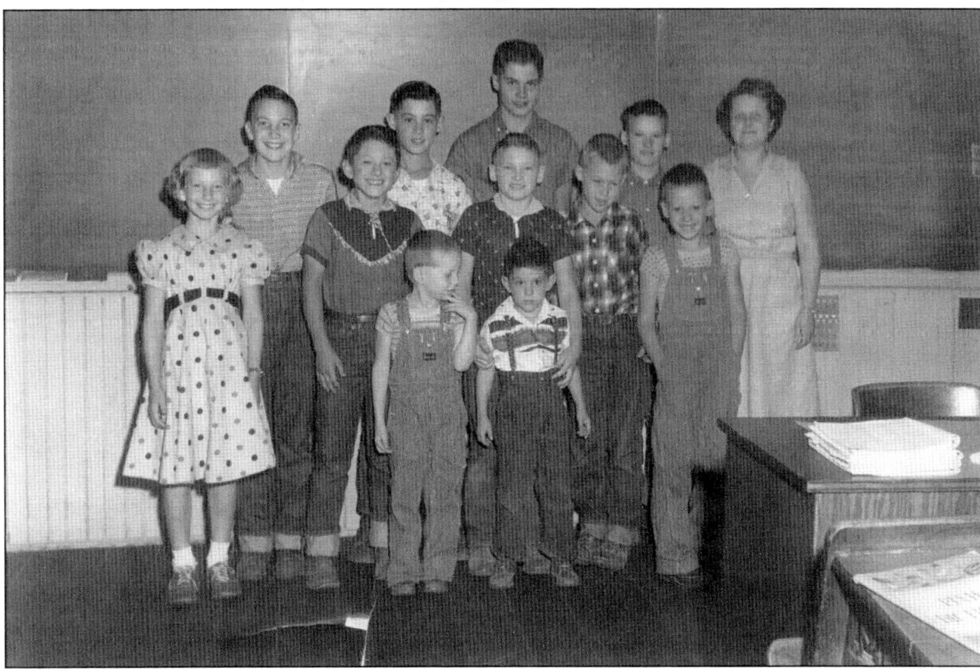

The last year the Caledonia School was in session was 1958. Included in this photograph are, from left to right, (first row) Gary Scott and Joe Shields; (second row) Beverly Deemer, Barton Shields, Jerry Shields, Jim Shaha, and Dean Scott; (third row) Dean Deemer, Derald Noble, Gerald Noble, Gary Shields, and teacher Evelyn Warrick. (Courtesy of Mabel Shields.)

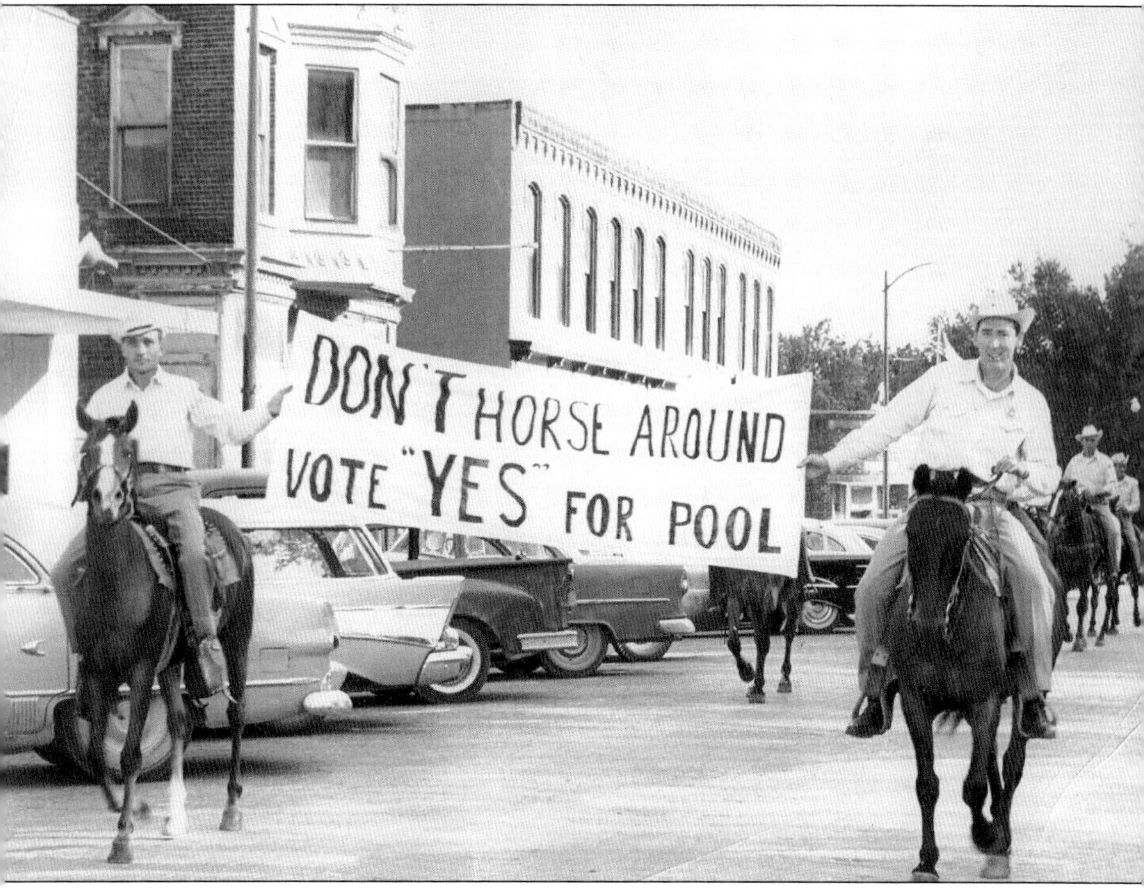

Marvin Reynolds (left) and Ringgold County sheriff Elbert Strange (right) encourage voters to vote "YES" on the upcoming swimming-pool bond issue. The bond passed later that summer (1962), and the new pool opened on June 26, 1963. The swimming pool, located at Judge Lewis Park in Mount Ayr, has been in continuous use ever since. Marvin and Elbert are seen here on the east side of the Mount Ayr square. (Courtesy of Doug Strange.)

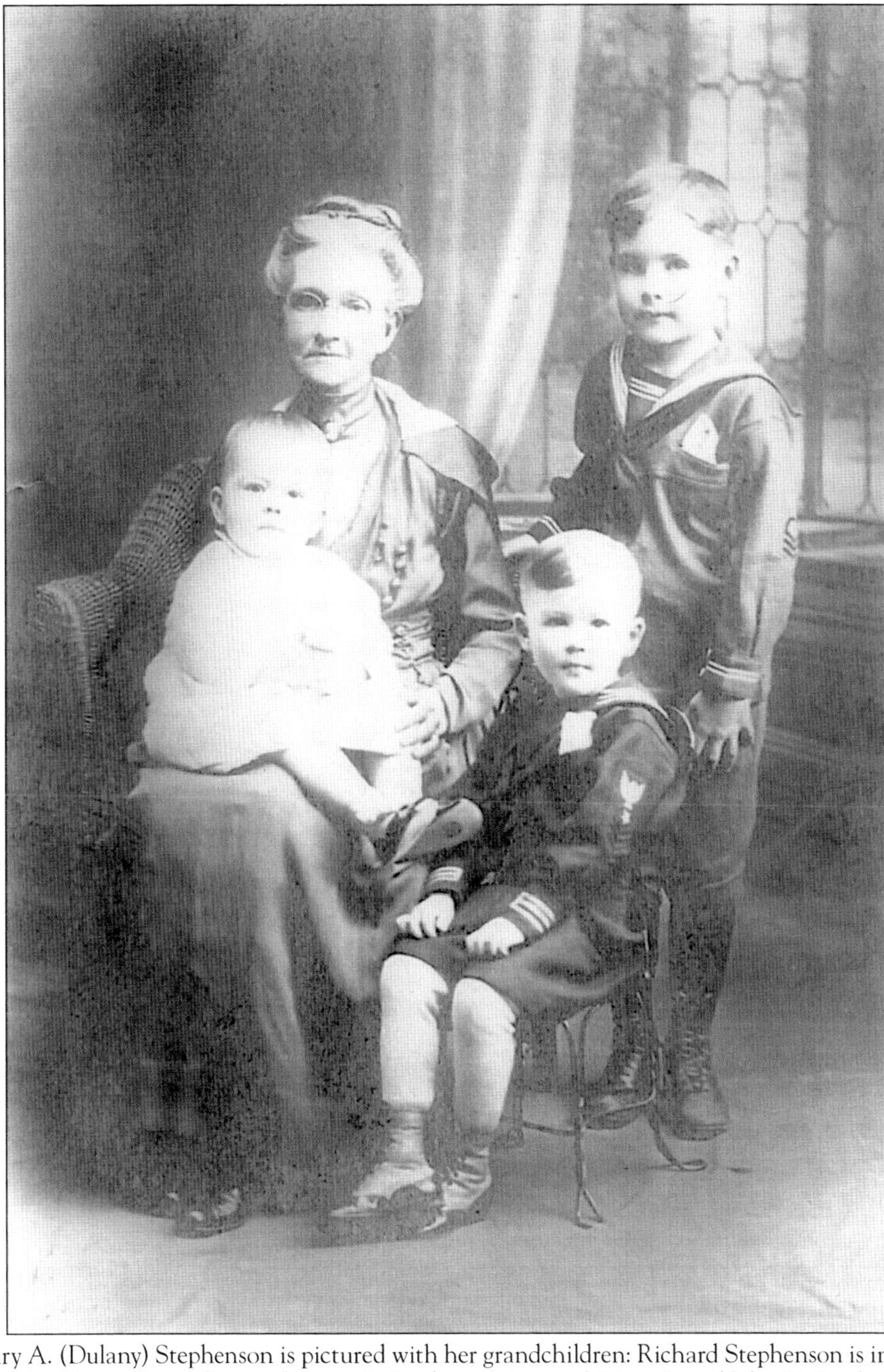

Mary A. (Dulany) Stephenson is pictured with her grandchildren: Richard Stephenson is in her lap, John Spence is standing, and James A. Stephenson is seated. Mary A. and John M. Stephenson farmed near Maloy. Richard and James were the sons of Vera M. (Merritt) and Perry Stephenson. John was the son of Ola (Stephenson) and Clarence Spence of Diagonal and grandson of Robert H. Spence of Mount Ayr. James A. Stephenson served as an Iowa representative from Ringgold County and was vice president of Mount Ayr State Bank. (Courtesy of Bill and Thelma Rusk.)

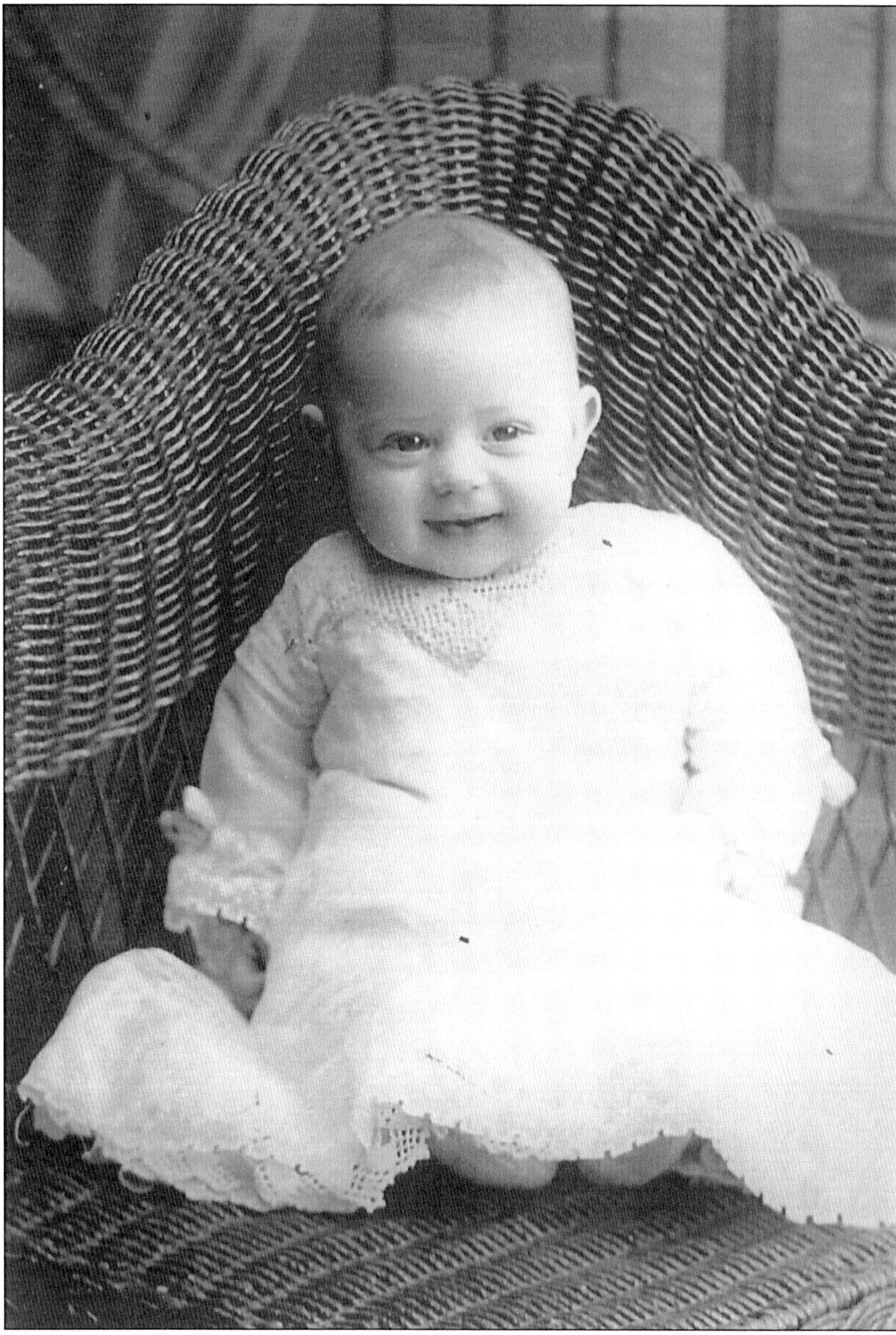

Many times a child's first portrait was printed as a postcard and mailed to relatives who lived far away. Here, Monefay Hanson of Tingley, at six months of age, poses for her postcard portrait. (Courtesy of Bill Adams.)

Five

Ringgold County Today

The cemetery at Ringgold City is older than the county itself. Evidence of the early days can still be seen throughout the county in the form of farms, railroad beds, pioneer cemeteries, and trails. Older structures, such as the Humeston & Shenandoah Depot at Tingley, the original Baptist church at Mount Ayr, and the Methodist church at Redding, still stand. Major undertakings, such as Sun Valley Lake near Ellston, have changed the face of Ringgold County, yet a great deal of the past remains. The past is celebrated with reunions and festivals. The Pioneer Center at Ellston and the Ramsey Farm at Lesanville were established as tributes to the settlers and farmers who shaped the county. Ringgold County's Amish community is a daily example of life before electricity, telephones, and running water.

Ringgold County continues to build and restore. In the recent past, a new hospital was built in Mount Ayr, Fogle Lake was constructed at Diagonal, and Kellerton has erected a new fire station/town hall. The restoration of old buildings is a constant and common occurrence, and many of the county's buildings are in the National Register of Historic Places. Not surprisingly, many of Ringgold County's residents are descendants of some of the earliest pioneers.

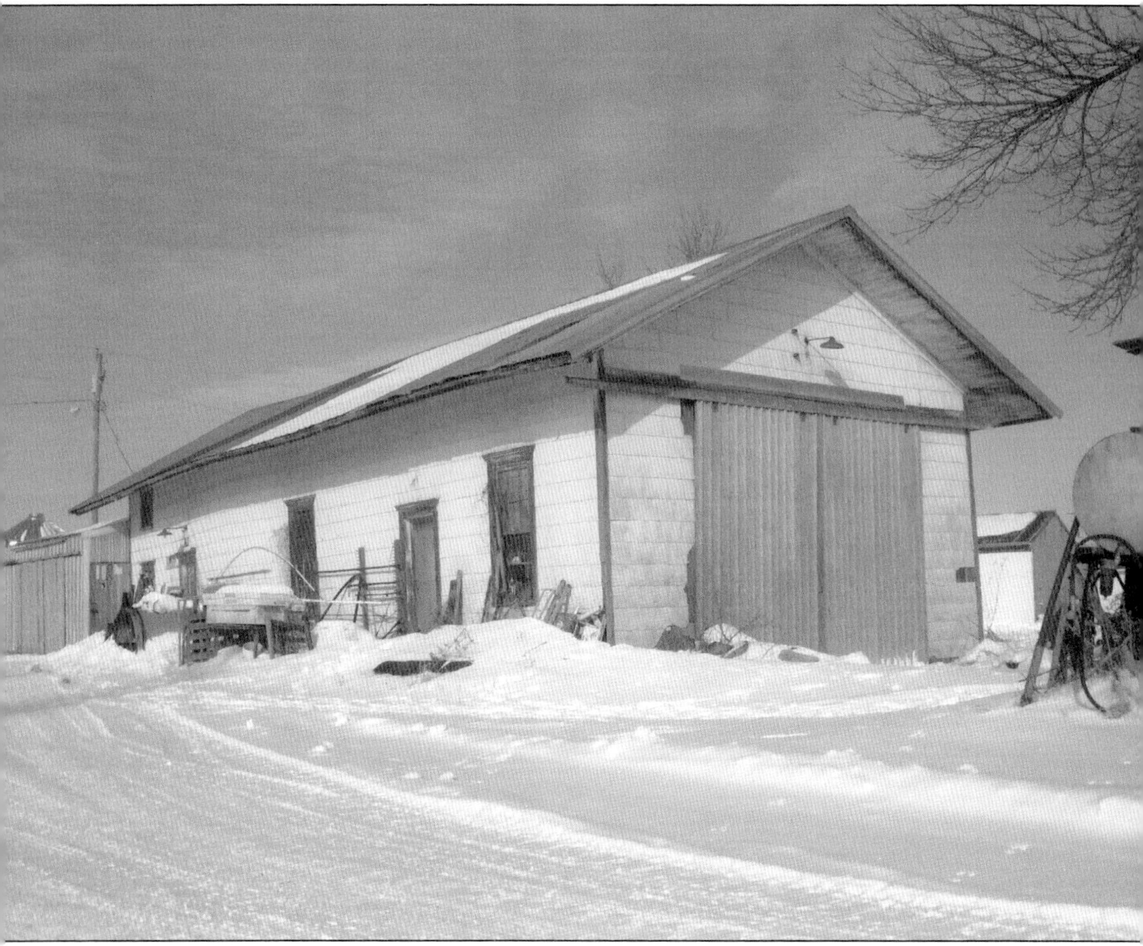

The Humeston & Shenandoah Depot in Tingley is still standing after 128 years. Built in 1882, the depot was on the H&S line of the K&W Railroad. Around 1895, the railroad was leased to the CB&Q, which took over as owner in 1901. This line was abandoned by the CB&Q in 1945. The depot served as a meeting place after its railroad days, and today it is a heavy machine shop. (Courtesy of Mike Avitt.)

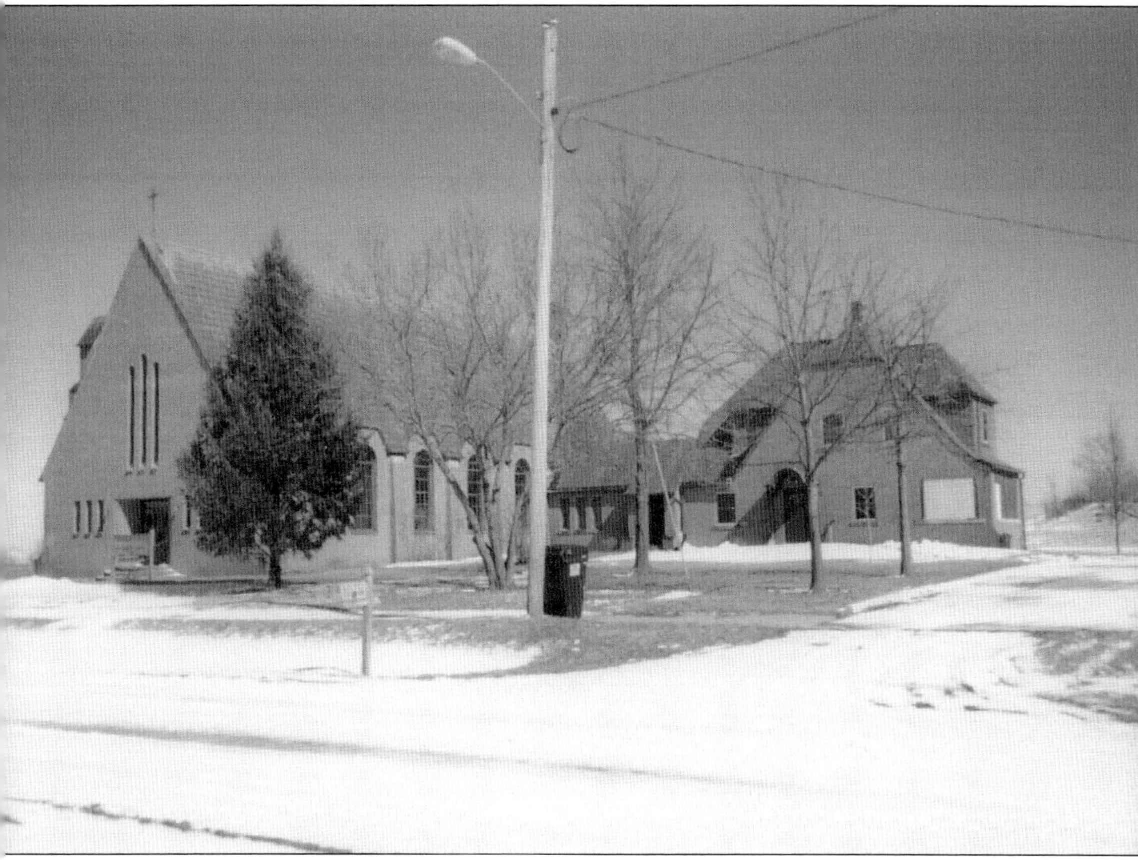

A fire swept through Maloy on June 17, 1931, that destroyed the Catholic church. Almost immediately, Fr. Maurice J. Culhane, an Irish immigrant and the parish's priest, organized the construction of a new brick church and rectory. The new church, Immaculate Conception Church, held Mass for the first time on August 18, 1932. Later that day, John D. Warin was married to Mary Shay, with Father Culhane officiating. On May 3, 2009, Mass was held for the last time, and the church was sold to a private individual. (Courtesy of Mike Avitt.)

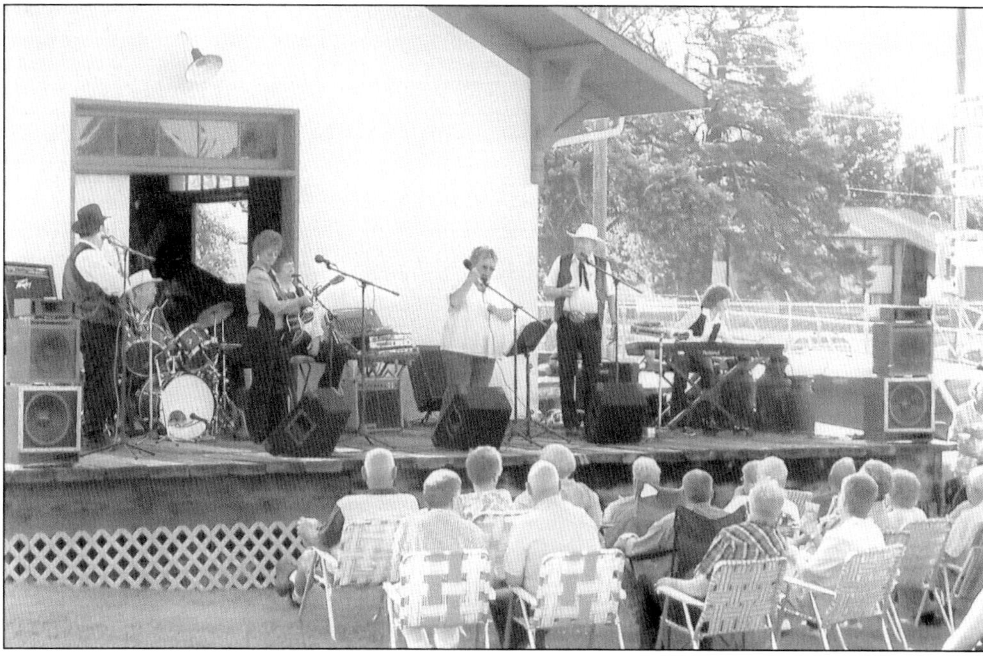

Butch (in the white hat) and Ina Chapin (keyboards) perform with their band, the Midwesterners, at the 2008 Mount Ayr Depot Hobo Supper. The Midwesterners played every week at the Midwest Country Music Theater in Redding. The Mount Ayr Depot was restored during the 1990s and opened as a museum on September 21, 2000. Many events have been held there, including the annual Hobo Supper. (Courtesy of Mike Avitt.)

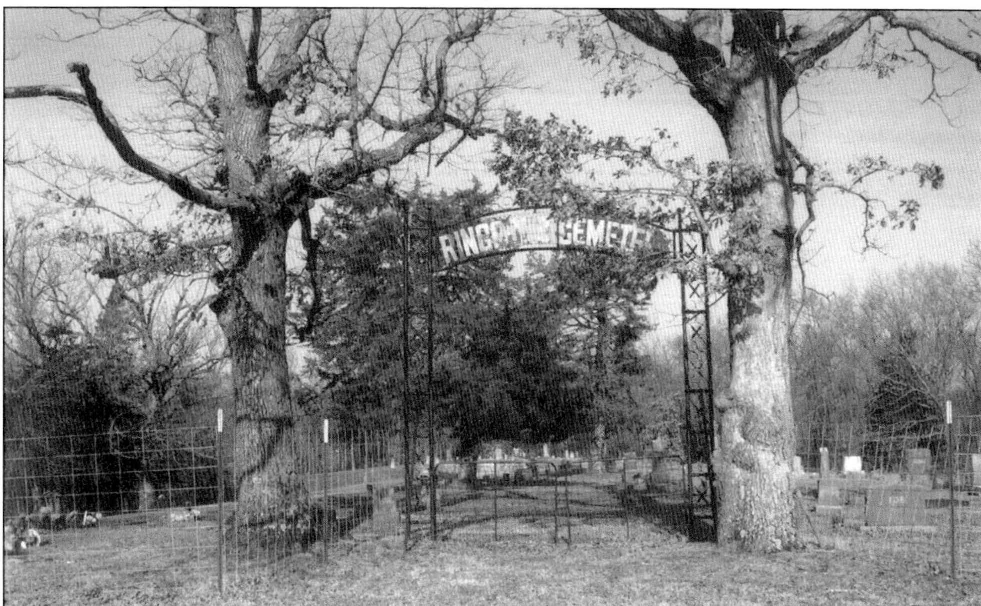

The Ringgold Cemetery is the oldest man-made site in Ringgold County. The first burial was in the late 1840s, when the county's first settler, Charles H. Schooler, laid his wife to rest. One of many pioneer cemeteries in Ringgold County, this graveyard is all that remains of Ringgold City, one of the county's first towns. (Courtesy of Mike Avitt.)

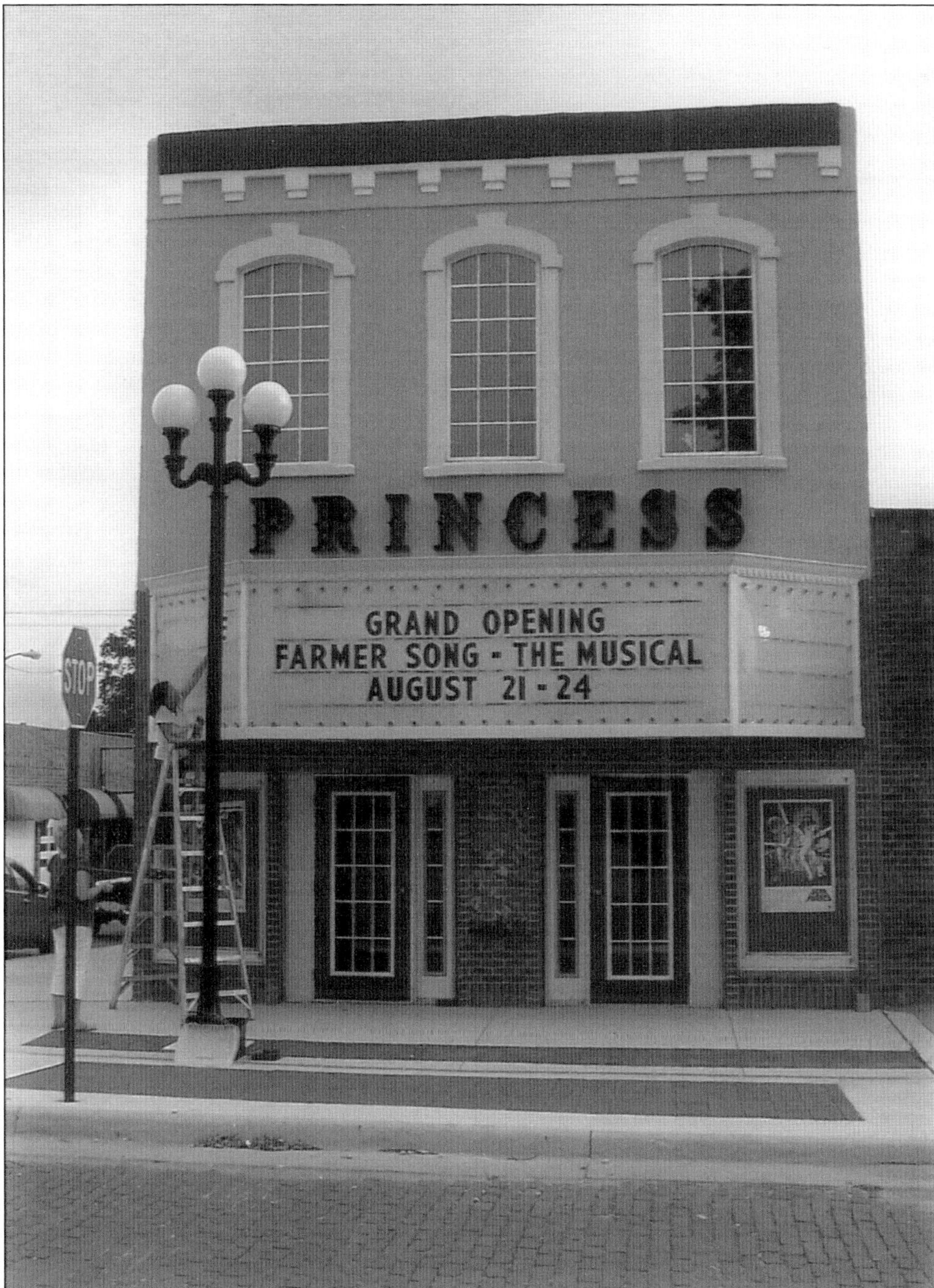

Pictured on July 25, 2008, Pam Poore and Michell Ricker are dressing the marquee at the Princess Theater in Mount Ayr. The theater opened in 1914 and operated until the 1980s, when it closed. It was used as a plumbing shop and bar before being purchased by Paul Ramsey. He donated the Princess to the local theater troupe, which restored it. Most of the work was done by Ron Landphair, and the Princess Theater again shows movies as well performances by the Princess Theater Troup. (Courtesy of Mike Avitt.)

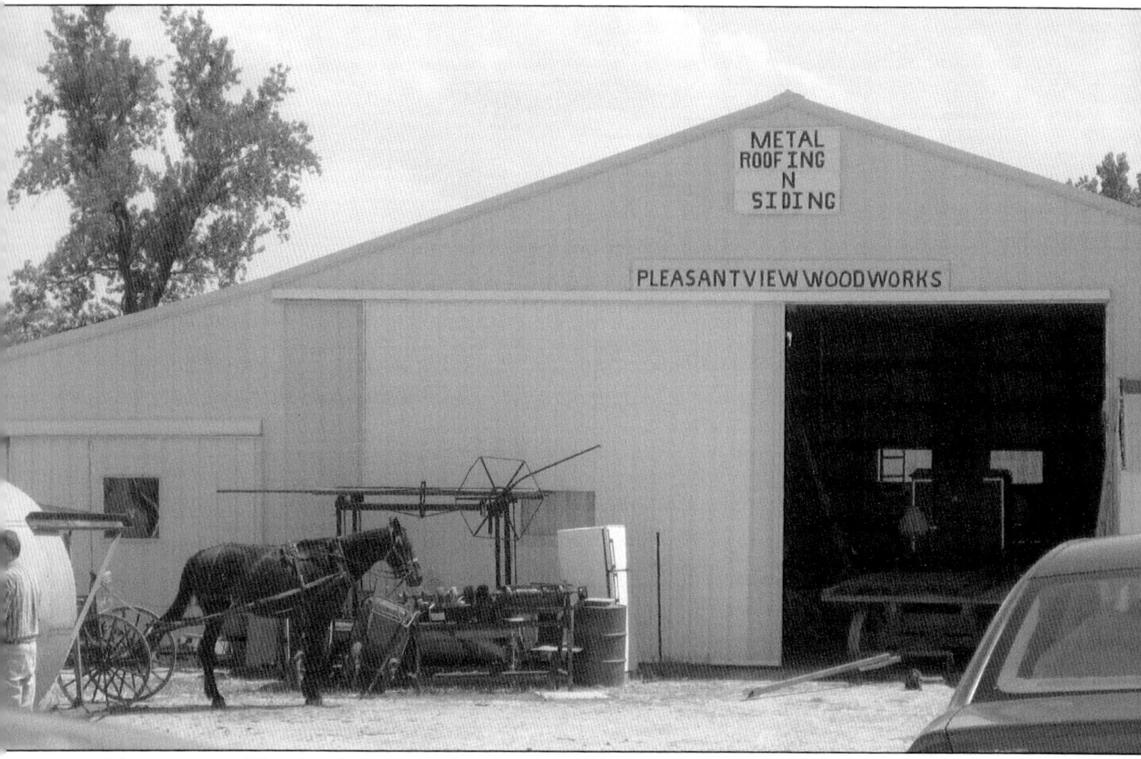

Pleasantview Woodworks is owned and operated by an Amish family and is located in the country east of Redding. Many Amish families have small enterprises on their farm. Greenhouses, sawmills, and furniture shops are common Amish businesses. (Courtesy of Sharon R. Becker.)

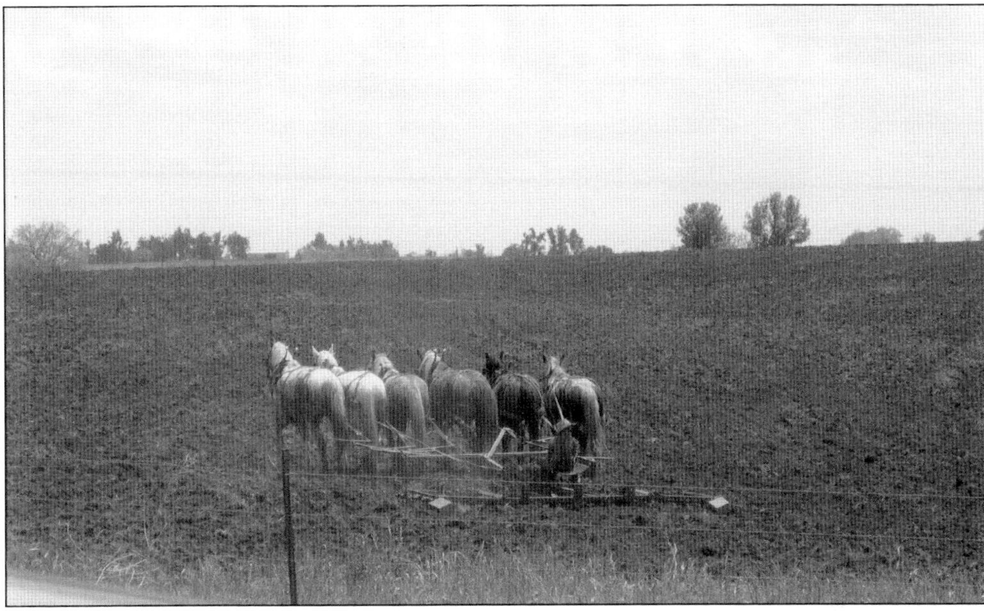

On his farm, located east of Redding, a young Amish boy harrows the field. Once again, the farmsteads are being worked with teams of horses, coming full circle back to Ringgold County's early days. (Courtesy of Sharon R. Becker.)

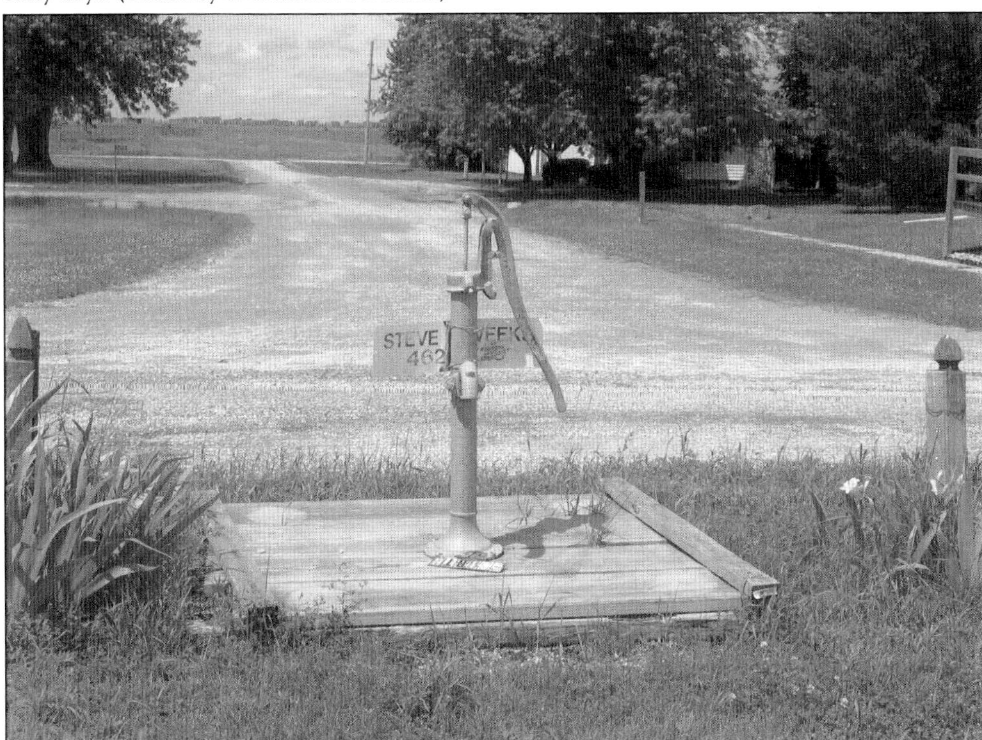

At one time, if there was no private well, residents obtained their water from the town pump. The town pumps of Beaconsfield and Tingley are still in place today. The pump pictured here is located in Beaconsfield. (Courtesy of Sharon R. Becker.)

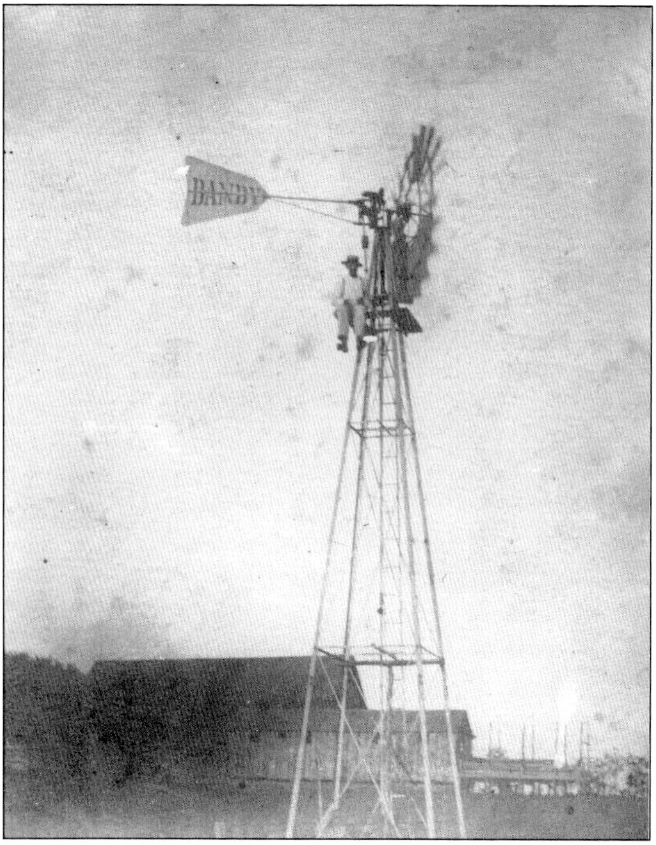

Windmills were once an important feature on what was considered a modern farm in the early 1900s up to the early 1960s. A farm windmill pumped in water for the livestock and the farm family. The farmer often did his own maintenance work on the windmill, as pictured here. Today, a farm windmill is a rare sight. (Courtesy of Norma G. [Foland] Becker.)

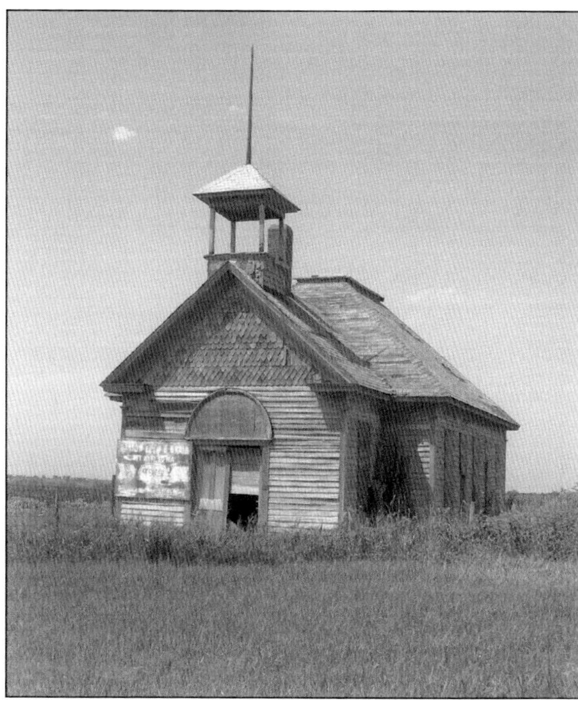

Eighme School's last day of classes in 1941 was January 20. Roger Morrison was the only student left after his classmates had moved away. The school is still a landmark, and the building is gracefully aging. (Courtesy of Sharon R. Becker.)

Redding's Opera House is the only remaining opera house in Ringgold County. Plays and basketball games were often held upstairs, while a business occupied the first floor. Redding had many disastrous fires throughout its history, but the Opera House escaped the flames and stands alone on the northwest corner of the square. (Courtesy of Sharon R. Becker.)

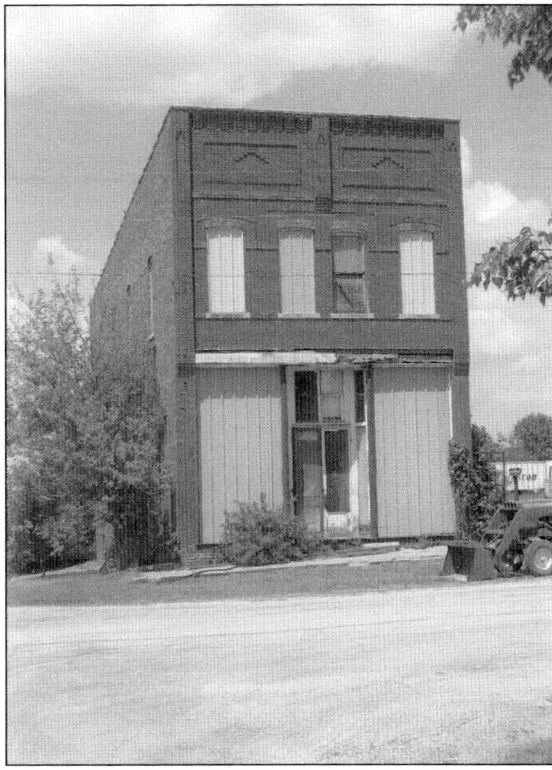

Benton's town jail survived a tornado in May 1981. It appears that it will be restored. (Courtesy of Sharon R. Becker.)

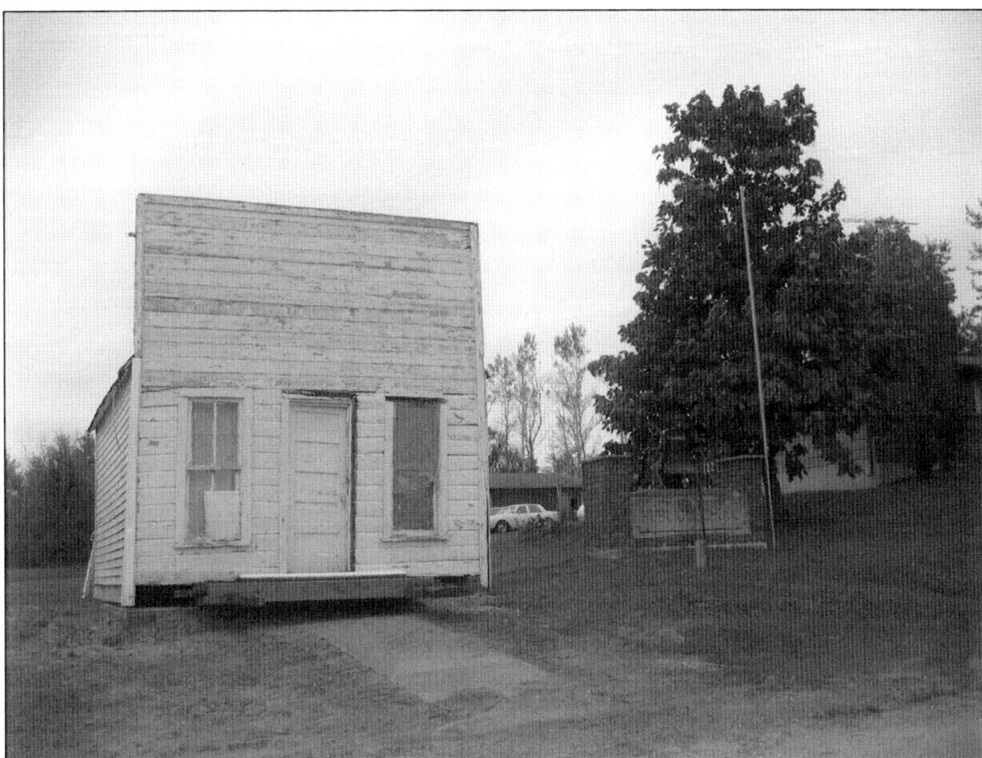

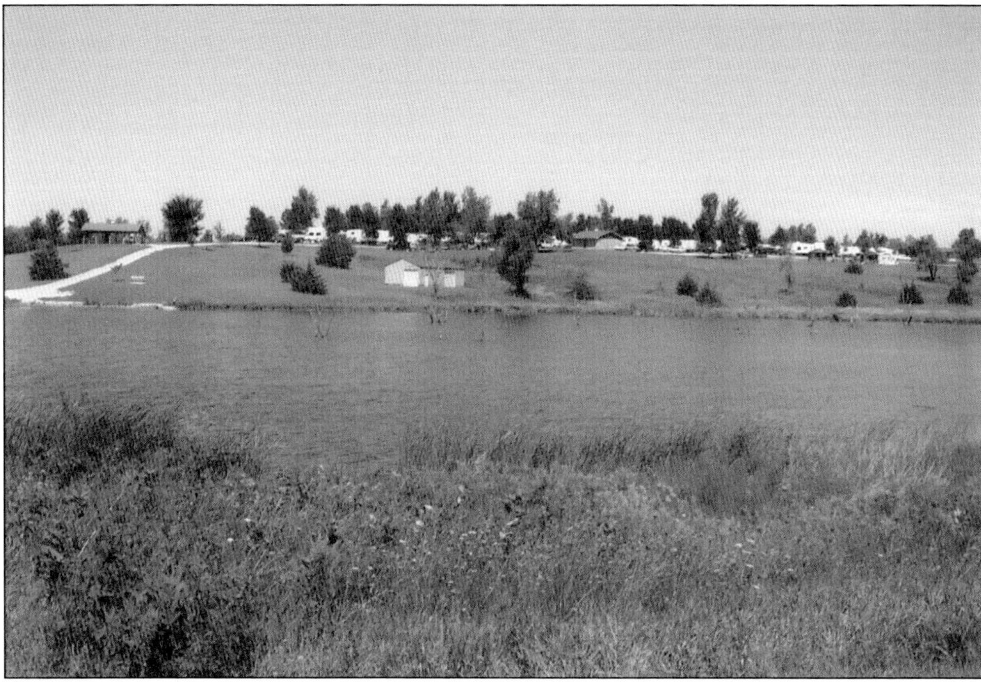

Fogle Lake is named after Marlin E. Fogle, who graduated from Diagonal High School in 1925 and went on to establish a very successful electronics business in New Jersey. Money from his estate helped build the 44-acre lake in the mid-1990s. It is located a quarter mile northwest of Diagonal and is active with fishing, camping, hiking, and archery. Cabins and a shower house complement the 350-acre Marlin E. Fogle Recreation Area. (Courtesy of Mike Avitt.)

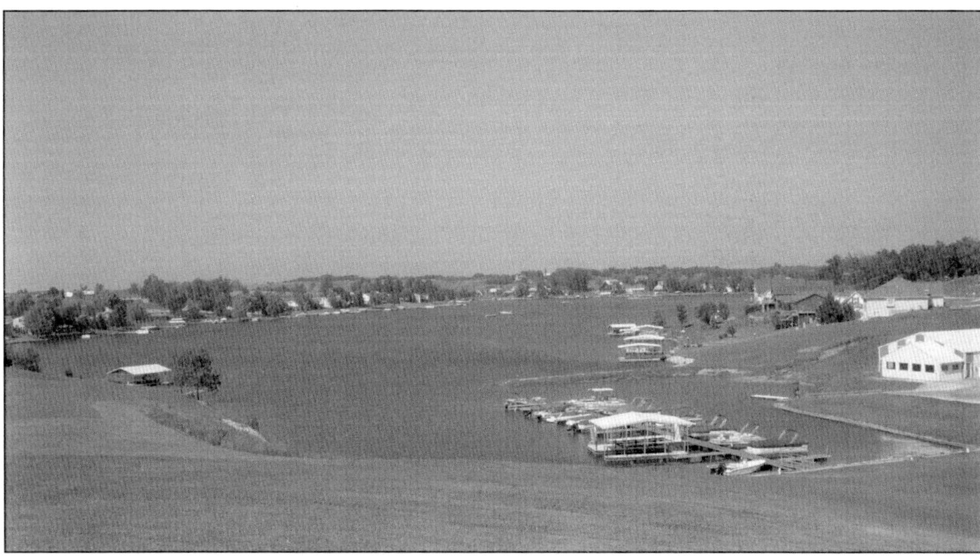

Quentin and Rita Anderson thought that the 1,500-acre tract of timbered hillsides would be an ideal recreational site. The area was abundant with natural springs, which now feed a 500-acre lake. Sun Valley, which opened in the early 1970s, provides activities year round, including ice-skating, ice fishing, boating, swimming, and other such pastimes. The facility has a golf course, and the lake is stocked with bass, walleye, catfish, and crappie. (Courtesy of Mike Avitt.)

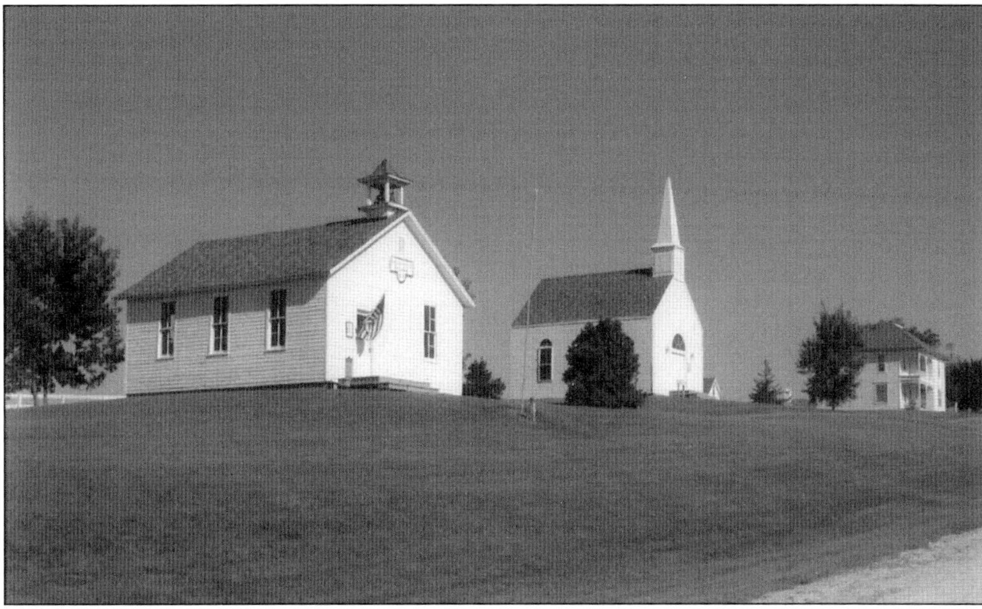

The Ramsey Farm at Lesanville reflects farm life in Iowa, especially from the 1930s. The village was developed by the Ramsey Farm Foundation, a nonprofit corporation established by Paul Ramsey and Phil Burmeister, in 2001. The schoolhouse here was originally the Mountain Brush School, located two miles north and half a mile east of Lesanville, which was once a flag stop on the old CB&Q railroad. (Courtesy of Mike Avitt.)

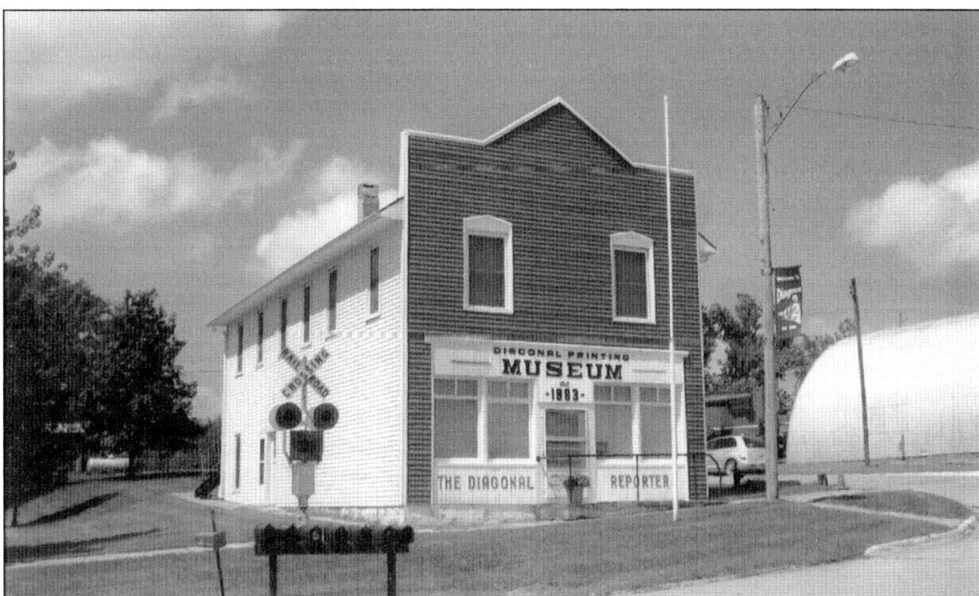

The *Diagonal Reporter* building was constructed in 1909 for Dr. A.E. Jessup. He and his family lived in an apartment upstairs, while the ground floor was used as a doctor's office and drugstore. In 1924, Thomas Waffle, owner of the *Diagonal Reporter*, moved his business here, and in 1934 Harold Turnbull, Waffle's only employee, took over the newspaper with the passing of his boss. Harold and his wife, Mildred, ran the business until 1972. The newspaper office became the Diagonal Printing Museum in 1983. (Courtesy of Mike Avitt.)

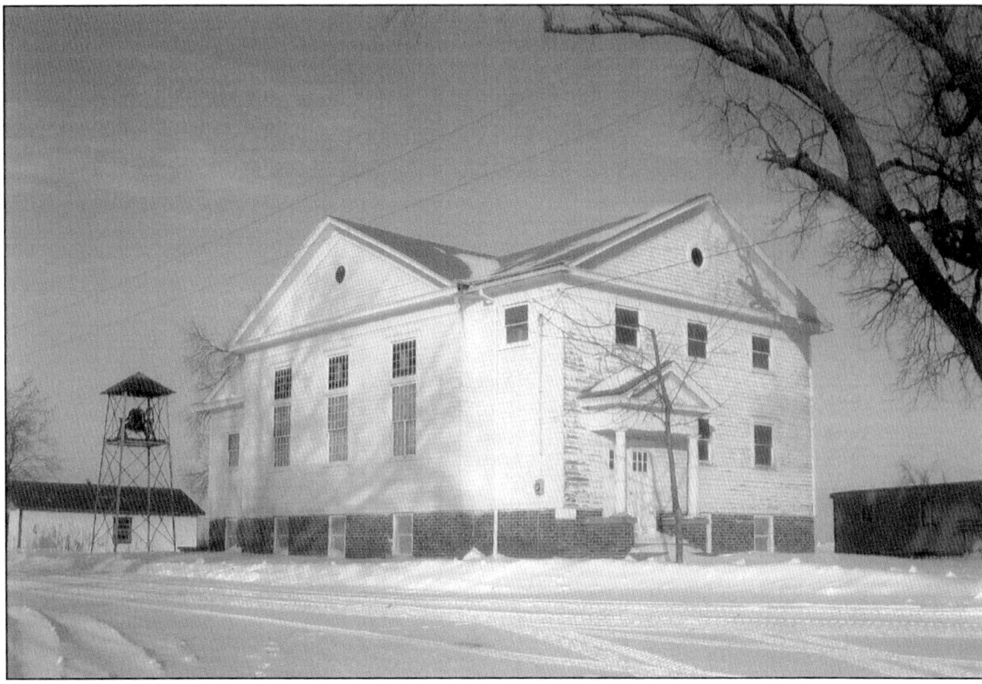

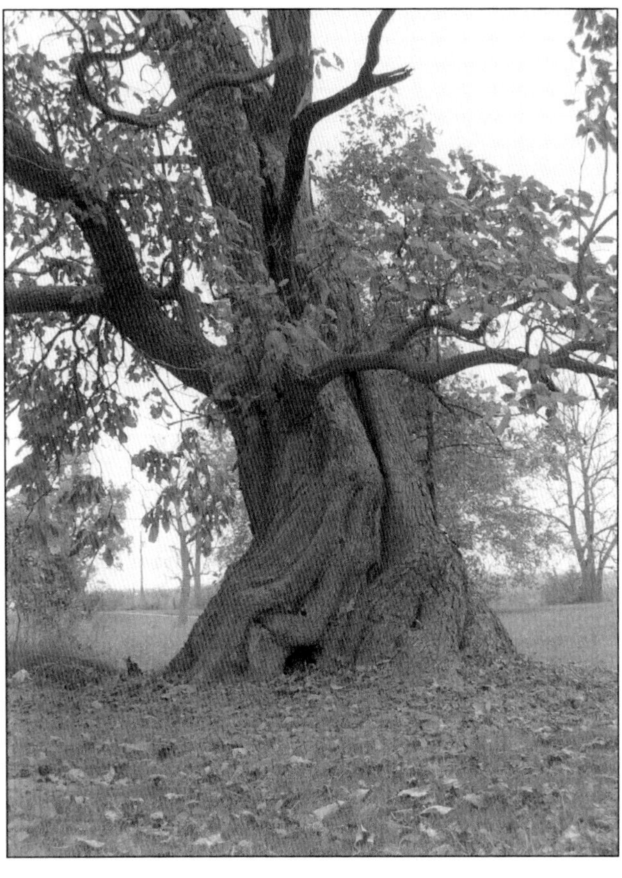

The First Baptist Church in Delphos was dedicated on May 14, 1922. The building was constructed from materials harvested from the Maloy Baptist Church. Maloy's church bell was hung in a bell tower behind the new building. Today, the church houses Delphos's museum. The last services were held in the summer of 2006, with Rev. Bob Pinkerton of Blockton in the pulpit. (Courtesy of Mike Avitt.)

Ringgold County native Myron Burdette wrote *The Diary of an Acorn*, which was copyrighted in 1974. The book tells of the life and times of early Ringgold County as seen from the viewpoint of an oak tree. Myron was a rock collector and a member of the Hawkeye Gem and Mineral Club of Southwest Iowa. He passed away in 1974. The tree is located in Tingley. (Courtesy of Sharon R. Becker.)

Bibliography

A Century of Memories: Ellston, Iowa, 1881–1981. Ellston, IA: Ellston Centennial Book Committee 1981.

Avitt, Mike. *Pages and Pictures from the Past . . . Ringgold County, Iowa: 1855–2005*. Mount Ayr, IA: Paragon Press, 2009.

Banner, Raymond V. *Ringgold City, Iowa 1844–2002: From First Settlement to Forgotten Community*. Mount Ayr, IA: J.V. Banner, 2002.

Biographical & Historical Record of Ringgold County, Iowa. Chicago: Lewis Publishing Company, 1887.

Diagonal, Iowa: Centennial History. Diagonal, IA: Diagonal Centennial Book Committee 1988.

Fetty, Jack. *Rings of Gold*. Iowa: Palindrome Publishing Co., 2007.

Kellerton, Iowa: A History to 1981. Kellerton, IA: Kellerton Book Committee, 1981.

Lesan, B.M. *Early History of Ringgold County: 1844–1937*. Lamoni, IA: Blair Publishing House, 1937.

Mount Ayr Record-News archives.

Ringgold County Honor Roll of Distinguished Citizens. 1976.

Ringgold Record archives.

Terry, Jack. *A Centennial History of Mount Ayr, Iowa 1875–1975*. Mount Ayr, IA: *Mount Ayr Record-News*, 1975.

Twice-A-Week News archives.

"Story of Knowlton." *Mount Ayr-Record News*. 1970.

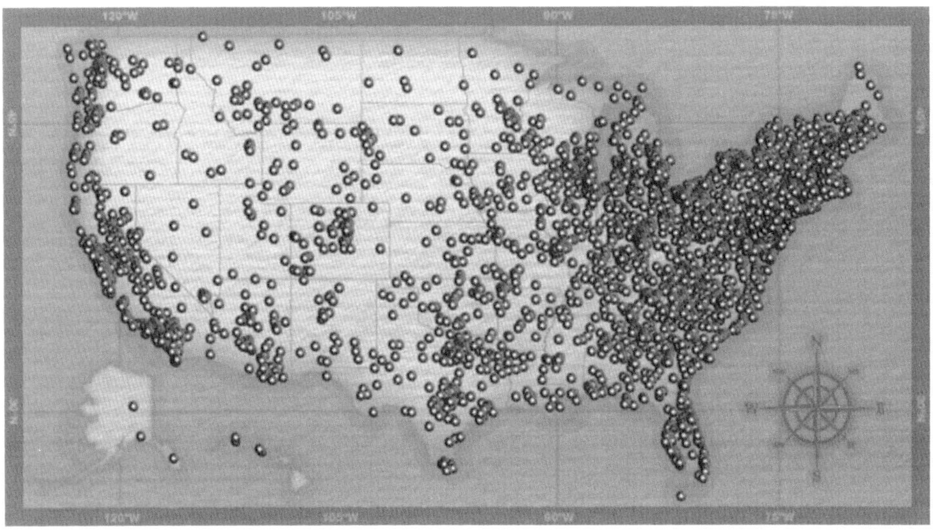

Consistent with our mission to preserve history on a local level, this book was printed in South Carolina on American-made paper and manufactured entirely in the United States. Products carrying the accredited Forest Stewardship Council (FSC) label are printed on 100 percent FSC-certified paper.

MADE IN THE USA